100 THINGS
SHARKS FANS
SHOULD KNOW & DO
BEFORE THEY DIE

100 THINGS SHARKS FANS SHOULD KNOW & DO BEFORE THEY DIE

Ross McKeon

TRIUMPH
BOOKS

Library of Congress Cataloging-in-Publication Data

Names: McKeon, Ross, 1959- author.
Title: 100 things Sharks fans should know & do before they die / Ross McKeon.
Other titles: One hundred things Sharks fans should know and do before they die
Description: Chicago, Illinois : Triumph Books LLC, [2016]
Identifiers: LCCN 2016003184 | ISBN 9781629371948
Subjects: LCSH: San Jose Sharks (Hockey team)—History. | San Jose Sharks (Hockey team)—Miscellanea.
Classification: LCC GV848.S26 M35 2016 | DDC 796.962/640979474—dc23 LC record available at http://lccn.loc.gov/2016003184

This book is available in quantity at special discounts for your group or organization. For further information, contact:

Triumph Books LLC
814 North Franklin Street
Chicago, Illinois 60610
(312) 337-0747
www.triumphbooks.com

Printed in U.S.A.
ISBN: 978-1-62937-194-8
Design by Nord Compo
Photos courtesy of AP Images unless otherwise indicated

Dedicated to my loving and supportive family

Contents

Foreword

In 1991, I knew I would not be returning to play hockey for the Chicago Blackhawks, and I was able to decide where my next NHL stop would be. One of those possible choices was the San Jose Sharks, an expansion franchise that had not even played its first game yet. I sensed something challenging and exciting about having the opportunity to be on the ground floor of a new team and to play a part in building something special.

It was one of the best decisions I ever made in my life.

I arrived in San Jose with my wife, Kathy, and four young children—who were ages seven, five, three, and one at the time.

But I also joined a new hockey family—with George Gund III as our patriarch—and we felt like a family of pioneers, bringing the game that we loved so much back to the Bay Area.

That first-year team was incredibly close and filled with quality people on and off the ice. Despite our struggles on the ice as an expansion franchise, it's stunning to look back and see how many players from that roster later moved into coaching or management in hockey, which is a testament to the group that George had assembled: Kelly Kisio, Dean Evason, Rob Zettler, Mike Sullivan, to name just a few. It's truly remarkable.

But the most incredible part was the way that the Bay Area fans accepted and welcomed our team. Usually, it takes years to create that kind of love and mutual respect between a sports franchise and its fan base but this feeling was instant. To this day, we still have over 800 original season ticket accounts, dating back to our days at the Cow Palace.

Throughout 25 years of Sharks hockey in San Jose, every player, staff member, coach, trainer, scout, and employee has had a hand in making this organization one of the most special in all of sports. They have helped foster this team and create an unbreakable bond with our extremely loyal and passionate fan base.

Part of that bond has been fostered through our dedication to our local communities. The Sharks have always strived to be a "good neighbor" and be an organization that gives back to those in need. The epicenter of that effort is the Sharks Foundation, which has donated more than $8 million via a variety of community and assistance platforms since its inception in 1994. It truly is at the heart of what the San Jose Sharks are about.

There have been so many memorable moments for this franchise over 25 years and most of them have been recalled here in grand detail by Ross, who has been there to witness most of them in person.

There have been many exciting highs and some painful lows along the way. We've even had our share of laughs. Heck, this is a franchise that once threw itself a parade after getting knocked out in the second round of the playoffs!

But through it all, everything we do has been for our fans. We would be nowhere without your support and the day will come when we bring the Stanley Cup to San Jose.

I would be remiss if I didn't specifically thank the wonderful owners we have had throughout 25 years in San Jose. It starts, of course, with George and Gordon Gund, who had the foresight to believe that the NHL could not only survive but thrive in San Jose. Today, that mantra continues, led by our majority owner Hasso Plattner, who gives our franchise all of the tools that we need to be successful and competitive in today's NHL.

I hope you enjoy this wonderful look back through Sharks history, and we look forward to adding new moments and chapters to this story in the years to come.

—Doug Wilson

1 Lose and Throw a Parade

Ray Whitney knows all about celebrations. That happens when you grow up in Edmonton—Alberta's city of champions—and you're a teenage stick boy for the Oilers during the mid-1980s. Paul Coffey and Wayne Gretzky were among Whitney's favorites. And not only because they were universal superstars, but both Coffey and Gretzky gave Whitney the time of day.

Fast forward to the Stanley Cup playoffs of 1994. The 21-year-old Whitney was starting to prove his NHL worth to the third-year San Jose Sharks. He and his teammates are devastated after losing Game 7 of a second-round playoff series against Toronto after the Sharks held a 3–2 edge.

Then imagine Whitney and his teammates' reaction when plans for a parade for the city's eliminated team were unveiled.

"I remember there being a parade for a reason. It's because they won the Stanley Cup," Whitney said. "I had never been part of a parade for coming close or having more success than you were ever supposed to have, I guess."

Yet that's exactly what happened. The city of San Jose threw the Sharks a parade.

Adoring South Bay fans wanted to show their appreciation for what the Sharks accomplished during that first season in San Jose. This after toiling for two well-documented losing campaigns at the Cow Palace while the team's sparkling new downtown arena was being constructed.

The fans wanted to say thank you for setting an NHL record with the greatest one-season turnaround to the next—a 58-point improvement in the standings. They wanted to shower a team that rallied from

1

an 0–8–1 start to not only qualify for the playoffs for the first time, but honor a scrappy Sharks team that managed to knock off top-seed Detroit in a dramatic seven-game first-round series.

So despite overcast, threatening skies and cold temperatures, more than 10,000 fans braved an unseasonably ugly mid-May day to end up at Guadalupe Park—just a slap shot from nearby San Jose Arena—for a raucous celebration.

"After we got there it was like, 'What the hell is this for?'" recalled Rob Gaudreau, a forward on the team. "I think we all just said, 'The hell with it, they've been great to us.'

"I think we were all proud, and the city was proud. It was a very interesting time because they really did adopt everybody, and it couldn't have been a nicer place to play," he added. "I don't think I've had a parade period other than that."

As much of a long shot as the upstart Sharks appeared, they really were hitting on all cylinders in late season, and were very close to taking down the Maple Leafs in Round 2. Forward Johan Garpenlov struck iron in overtime of Game 6 at Toronto with a drive that had series winner written all over it.

Creative defenseman Sandis Ozolinsh led an odd-man break in period two of sudden death, but inexplicably passed on a quality chance from the slot to feed an unsuspecting teammate in the corner. Either chance goes in, or victory instead of defeat two nights later in Game 7, and San Jose would have been in the conference finals against Vancouver, the West's No. 7 seed.

Instead, the Sharks were home for the offseason, yet part of a parade.

It was no secret rookie coach Kevin Constantine needed a little coaxing to get into the spirit. As fate would have it, there was Constantine long after the ceremony signing autographs for the team's loyal fans.

"There was disappointment. There really was," recalled Jeff Odgers, hard-nosed forward on the team. "In most other hockey cities, you'd come home and pick up the paper to find out what you did wrong or what you should have done to win the series being up three games to two. Instead it's a celebration and people acted like you just won the Stanley Cup."

2 Name the Team

The San Jose Blades.

If early franchise executives had gone with the most suggested nickname, that's what the National Hockey League's 22nd team would have been called.

Matt Levine was the yet-to-be-named Bay Area expansion hockey team's second employee. As a vice president in charge of business operations, Levine had the task of finding just the right name for the team. He had his own ideas, but wanted to hear from the public. A grand-prize trip to the 1991 NHL All-Star Weekend in Chicago would go to the sweepstakes' winner.

And, boy, did he hear suggestions.

"We ran one black-and-white newspaper ad of a hockey player in his equipment, but no uniform. It said, 'We have a team, now we need a name,'" Levine recalled. "We ran it one time, and these crazy names started coming in."

Without the Internet or social media to spread the word, Levine used his networking expertise to contact the *New York Times*, *Wall Street Journal*, *Business Week*, *USA Today*, and ESPN. All of the national news gathering sources were intrigued to the point of reporting on the Northern California hockey team that was creating excitement over selecting its name. Those stories carried the P.O. Box where entries could be submitted, including *USA Today*'s international edition.

"We received about 6,000 entries from every state in the union, from every province in Canada, and even two entries from Genoa, Italy," Levine remembered.

Approximately 2,100 different names were offered. Everything from sea creatures to fictional characters and computer components were submitted. Levine had done his homework beforehand, organizing 36 focus groups to descend throughout the Bay Area and research what might be most appropriate for the region.

The top 15 names submitted (in alphabetical order) were: Blades, Breakers, Breeze, Condors, Fog, Gold, Golden Gaters, Golden Skaters, Grizzlies, Icebreakers, Knights, Redwoods, Sea Lions, Sharks, and Waves.

Blades was the most popular suggestion with Sharks running second. Executives had concern because research gleaned from those focus groups determined *Blades* had more of a gang connotation in the Bay Area as opposed to an association with ice skating.

The team established a selection criteria to narrow the choices. The team name would have to be one no other pro team was using. It'd need to have a connection with the Bay Area and greater Northern California region. The name could not be one shortened in a newspaper headline. It needed to generate excitement with adults and children. And, finally, the name needed to translate into a broad range of graphic interpretations.

"When we started thinking about that, no, Blades did not hold up very well on a whole range of reasons," Levine said. "That's how we reinforced in our interest in Sharks."

Sharks, too, made sense in regional terms since the neighboring Pacific Ocean is home to seven different varieties of shark. Several area institutes channel time and funds to shark research, preservation, and education including the popular Monterey Bay Aquarium, Steinhart Aquarium in San Francisco, and Lawrence Hall of Science at UC-Berkeley.

In announcing their choice, Levine said, "Sharks are relentless, determined, swift, bright, and fearless. We plan to build an organization that has all those qualities."

A random drawing awarded the All-Star Weekend trip to San Jose attorney Allen Speare. Along with the grand prize. An additional 200 sweepstakes awards were presented to entrants.

3 George Gund III

George Gund wandered into Kevin Constantine's office looking for a stick of gum. The Sharks owner knew the reputed gum-smacking head coach had a stash. He'd been given a lifetime supply of Bazooka Bubble Gum, stored in canisters in a back room.

Constantine grabbed a handful from his ample supply and said to Mr. Gund, "Here, here, I've got a bunch. I'd rather get rid of them."

When the owner resisted the offer, Constantine was more persistent.

"He says, 'No, one piece will last me at least three weeks,'" Constantine said of Gund. "I couldn't resist asking, 'Three weeks! How?'"

Gund motioned to the breast pocket of his dress shirt and said, "I just put it in here. My wife doesn't like that very much."

"I'm sure he was serious," Constantine added.

Eccentric could only start to describe George Gund III, who, along with his brother Gordon Gund, owned the Sharks from inception until selling their majority stake in 2002. While Gordon remained in the background, George was very much the face of ownership—just not in a meddling sort of way.

Instead, George Gund preferred to dress as Santa Claus during the team's annual holiday family skate and hand out presents to the kids. He played in pick-up games of shinny hockey—or even skated alone—during afternoon hours in an empty arena before games. Then he'd ask for permission to use the private coach's shower.

"I always found it funny the owner of the team would ask," Constantine said.

And George Gund once arranged tee times at San Francisco's famed Olympic Club for then-players Doug Wilson and Brian Lawton. That is once he recalled he was actually a member.

"The first time I was introduced to him I thought it was a joke," Bernie Nicholls said. "George had on a pair of jeans, and he talked so friggin' quiet. I couldn't hear him. You had to get right up there. I just wanted to say, 'George, what are you saying? I can't hear you.'"

Then, when Nicholls was nursing a hernia injury and couldn't play, George Gund gave him a pair of tickets to attend the Oscars in person.

"He was just a nice guy," Nicholls said. "He wasn't around a lot, but you just knew when he was there. He enjoyed the game. And that's all you can ask from an owner. He's not in there telling you what to do. But he was always very positive, just a sweetheart of a man."

To say Gund was very soft-spoken is to say Wayne Gretzky set a lot of records during his career. A friend to stars of the silver screen, Gund was often ribbed by Robert Redford for his mumbling speaking style. Also striking was the incredible length of Gund's eyebrows. It was easy to get mesmerized looking at the bushes growing above his eyes while straining to listen to what Gund was saying.

The youngest of six siblings born in Cleveland, Ohio, George Gund III was bestowed a large inheritance from his father, George Gund II, who was a philanthropist and the head of Cleveland Trust when it was the largest bank in Ohio. Young George Gund dropped out of high school and joined the Marines at age 18 in a move that would lead to taking up residence in San Francisco.

Gund immersed himself in a number of unique lifelong passions including independent filmmaking, American Indian history, cowboy poetry, high art, and Japanese calligraphy, in addition to hockey. But Gund was never one to flaunt his wealth or social status.

"He was incredibly patient, and always respectful," Lawton said. "I've been around a lot of owners, and there are certainly a lot of great ones in the NHL right now. I was never around George and felt like this was a bottom-line business to him."

Perry Berezan distinctly recalls after the team's final home game of its inaugural season. The players gathered at a restaurant before ending the night at the home of Brian Mullen, the Sharks' second leading scorer in 1991–92.

"I think it was 1:30 or 2:00 in the morning, and we see the Sharkie van pull up with George Gund in his leather Sharks jacket driving," Berezan said. "He came in, sat at the kitchen table with a beer, and just listened to our stories.

"It was really cool. It was just one of those moments you think, *When does this ever happen?*"

In a lot of ways, Gund just wanted to be part of the team. He was routinely part of European scouting missions, not only to look at prospective talent but to help Sharks personnel gain entry into bordered areas that were otherwise a challenge to cross in the early '90s when the Cold War was still fresh on everyone's mind.

Gund always felt honored to be included in the annual team photo. The only problem was it couldn't be snapped until George arrived. Notorious for keeping his own schedule, Gund could keep the team waiting for hours.

There was the time Gund offered his yacht for the team to tour around Alcatraz, the infamous federal penitentiary located several miles from the shores of San Francisco.

"Everybody's like, 'Where the hell is George?'" Lawton recalled. "The whole team was on the boat except for him. Sure enough, we see this scooter come around the corner. And who do you think is riding it? George comes right up to the boat and jumps on. The guys are thinking, *No way.*"

Another time, with Sharks staff on a pre-draft scouting mission in Europe, Jack Ferreira was told to meet in the hotel lobby at 4:30 PM. The team's original general manager thought that was early for dinner, but didn't question Gund's suggestion. They went to dinner all right—after jumping on George's private jet, the group flew to Reykjavik, Iceland, and dined at one of Gund's favorite spots.

Constantine had a similar experience. He went with Gund & Co. on a scouting trip during the lockout of 1994–95. Besides watching hockey, the group detoured to the Country Western Art Museum, and made a stop later back in Cleveland to attend an event Gordon Gund was hosting.

"It was always those idiosyncrasies or eccentricities that made it fun to wonder what's next," Constantine said of Gund, who passed away in 2013 at age 75.

"He was just a real kind man," Lawton added. "The league was very, very lucky to have a guy like him as an owner. And I'm not surprised they gave him a team in San Jose."

4 Just Short of Hoisting Lord Stanley

It could have been the big red bow atop a silver anniversary present the Sharks were giving their fans during a season-long celebration of the team's 25 years in the NHL. Their first trip to a Stanley Cup Final didn't end the way they wanted—the Pittsburgh Penguins won in six games—but it was a positive experience for fans and the team nonetheless.

"The subtext of the 25-year journey, and all the people I've known over those 25 years, we're all very proud," general manager Doug Wilson said. "For the fans who come up to us and remember the journey, it just goes back to that emotion of pride."

The 2015–16 season started with a new coaching staff in place, led by 47-year-old Peter DeBoer, who was getting his third crack behind an NHL bench after previous stops in New Jersey and Florida. DeBoer was a finalist seven years prior when San Jose instead opted for Todd McLellan. In the meantime, DeBoer earned the kind of NHL coaching experience that convinced Wilson the timing was right to hire him now.

Wilson also made a number of key offseason acquisitions. He added free-agent defenseman Paul Martin to pair with the free-wheeling Brent Burns. Big-game veteran winger Joel Ward was plucked off the market. Wilson took a calculated gamble and traded a first-round draft pick, along with a prospect, to the Bruins for goalie Martin Jones within a week of the goalie getting moved from Los Angeles to Boston.

All three new pieces, in addition to a couple of in-season moves, blended perfectly into DeBoer's system and repaired a fractured locker room that was among the reasons why the Sharks fell short the previous year to snap a 10-year run of playoff appearances.

The Sharks broke from the gate with four straight wins—with Jones setting a franchise scoreless streak of 234:33 in the process—before early season adversity struck. Two-way star center Logan Couture suffered the first of two leg injuries that would cut his season short by nearly half.

San Jose was only 17–16–2 when Couture returned for good on December 30. That's when the Sharks took off, going 29–14–4 the rest of the way to land them in third place in the Pacific Division with 98 points, behind Anaheim (103) and Los Angeles (102).

With DeBoer's fresh message and a roster bolstered by late-season additions Roman Polak, James Reimer, and Nick Spaling, several Sharks enjoyed rejuvenated returns. Joe Thornton returned as a point-a-game player—82 points in 82 games—and Burns set franchise marks for goals (27) and points (75) by a defenseman, and in shots (353) for any skater.

"We made no secret of how much we enjoyed this group," DeBoer said. "They had great chemistry, they worked well together. We enjoyed being around them."

The uncertain feel for postseason expectations returned mostly because the Sharks matched up against their nemesis, the Los Angeles Kings, in the first round. Two years earlier, their California rivals made San Jose only the fourth NHL team to blow a 3–0 series lead.

San Jose was all over the Kings this time, winning three times in Staples Center to extend a trend as the NHL's best road team during the regular season, and eliminated Los Angeles in a tidy five games. San Jose next needed a seventh-game home win to bounce speedy Nashville, and the Sharks rewarded their loyal fans by winning the Western Conference crown over St. Louis at home in a Game 6.

Against the Penguins it was a different story. Pittsburgh flashed its speed with a 15–4 shot advantage in the opening period of Game 1 that provided a blueprint for how the series would play out. Pittsburgh won each of the first two games by one goal and widely outshot the Sharks 71–48. The Sharks won Game 3 in overtime thanks to rookie Joonas Donskoi's heroics, but Pittsburgh took command with a 3–1 road win in Game 4.

The Sharks were spoilers in Game 5 when an overflow crowd anticipated the first major pro sports title won in Pittsburgh since Bill Mazeroski's World Series homer in 1960. San Jose's 4–2 win sent the series back to the West Coast where the Penguins wrapped up their fourth Cup with a 3–1 win in Game 6.

"They started quicker in every game. I don't know how that crept in," DeBoer said. "We took pride in the first three rounds of being out of the gate quickly....We didn't change anything. Sometimes you have to tip your hat to them."

"We always had the belief in the locker room we could do what we did, but you always believe you can win," Couture added. "But, unfortunately, we weren't able to do that."

In all, when players and management stepped back, they could agree it was a special season.

"Our players played a lot of hockey this year, and in many cases they were fueled with heart," Wilson said. "The heart and character of this group is as good as I've ever seen."

5 The Shark Tank

The arena in San Jose has sported four sponsors throughout the years, but one unofficial moniker has stuck for more than a quarter of a century—the Shark Tank.

And regardless what fans call the building at the corner of N. Autumn and W. Santa Clara, it's synonymous with one word—noise.

"It's like a better old Chicago Stadium where they're right on top of you," Ray Whitney said. "You can feel the noise. You can feel the vibration on the bench. You can feel the excitement."

The arena, approved for construction by voters in June of 1988, wasn't done in time to house expansion San Jose for its first two years in the league. The Sharks played at the Cow Palace in Daly City while upgrades to original plans to meet NHL standards were made.

Shortly after the team moved into their new digs, the Sharks were made to feel right at home. After selling out 28 of 41 home dates in 1993-94, fans responded positively to the Sharks' surprising playoff appearance in Year 3 to fill the capacity of 17,190 seats for the next two seasons. Seven more seasons of playing between 98 and 100 percent capacity followed.

"I guess because I'm Canadian, and it's kind of our game, you just love to see fans come out and support your team," said Bernie Nicholls, a Shark from 1996–99. "And San Jose is as good as any of them."

Vincent Damphousse came to San Jose in 1999 after having played at hockey-mad venues in Toronto, Edmonton, and Montreal. He would have felt out of place if not playing in front of full houses. "It was one of the loudest buildings in the league and still is. When it was new every building had something that was special. Now the buildings are bigger and pretty much the same. I was surprised how many loyal fans there were."

Loyal, loud fans; the team skating out of a large shark mouth before the opening faceoff; good sight lines; and an entertaining game presentation have all been traits in San Jose. It helps, too, when the home team is competitive. All but four of San Jose's first 22 seasons at the Shark Tank have been included postseason games.

Playoffs or not, there have been numerous highlights. Here's a top five list of best moments at the Shark Tank:

1. With two goals late in the third period of the 1997 All-Star Game in San Jose, hometown favorite Owen Nolan pointed at Dominik Hasek and beat the East goalie to complete a hat trick;

2. Wayne Gretzky's second goal on March 20, 1994—a game-tying shot with 49 seconds left in the third period—was

No. 801, to tie Gordie Howe's NHL record the Great One would break three nights later;

3. Rookie defenseman Andrei Zyuzin scored 6:31 into overtime to break a scoreless tie and give San Jose a series-tying win in Game 4 of a 1998 first-round match-up against heavily-favored Dallas;

4. The Sharks killed a two-man advantage despite defenseman Scott Hannan and forward Mark Smith breaking their sticks midway through a 71-second kill—essentially making it a 5-on-1—during a 2-1 second-round playoff win over Edmonton in 2006;

5. At 38 years old, Jeremy Roenick scored two goals and added two assists to lead the Sharks to a 5–3 win over Calgary in Game 7 of an opening-round playoff series in 2008.

"You're not getting booed," Whitney said. "And it's not that they're with you only if you win. They're with you if you win, lose or tie."

Players who have played elsewhere also appreciate the relative solace they enjoyed away from the rink. While Sharks fans are supportive inside the building, they don't suffocate players away from it.

"I played in Calgary, which is like a fish bowl. I played in Chicago, which is a great sports town," said Gary Suter, a Shark from 1998–02. "In San Jose, the fans were awesome, but when you left the rink you were just another person."

6 Arturs Irbe

Arturs Irbe, the lovable, jovial, incorrigible Latvian-born goalie, might have been as well known for what he said as for what he did with the San Jose Sharks.

The entertainment value Irbe provided on the ice was matched only by his habit of saying the darnedest things with creative use and an innocent economy of the English language.

Irbe accomplished plenty during his relatively short time in San Jose (183 games spread over parts of five seasons). Irbe authored the first shutout in team history. He spearheaded the Cinderella upset of Detroit in the 1994 playoffs after setting records in the regular season. And he battled back from a career-threatening injury that also left deep personal and emotional scars.

"Tremendous work ethic; he spent so much time at his game," said Wayne Thomas, first a Sharks assistant coach and later part of management. "He was a perfectionist and such a competitor. He didn't like it when he didn't play."

Irbe thought he was doomed when the Kings beat the Sharks 11–4 on November 8, 1992, at the Cow Palace. Irbe was in for all 11 goals allowed—Jari Kurri, Luc Robitaille, and Mike Donnelly had hat tricks—as L.A. peppered San Jose's net with 49 shots.

"I was thinking, *Okay, I can pretty much pack my gear and go back to Kansas City, and just hope and pray I might get the call back,*" Irbe recalled.

Instead, he was summoned to general manager Dean Lombardi's office and told while it wasn't good enough, he'd get another chance in a couple games.

Nine nights later, with the Kings back in town, Irbe pitched a 39-save shutout, the first in franchise history.

"I'm glad I didn't fumble that one," Irbe said.

Twenty-five years since arriving from Latvia, Irbe is very Americanized and now has a solid grasp of the language. It wasn't always that way, and it led to some interesting moments.

While in the minors at Kansas City, during his first year in North America, Irbe had a unique ritual before games and at intermission. While teammates re-taped sticks, changed equipment, or mentally prepared, Irbe sat in his stall reading game notes and *USA Today*. Why? He would do anything he could to learn the language so he could someday communicate with his teammates.

"I'd ask the guy next to me, 'What is that word? What does it mean?'" Irbe recalled.

Irbe credits then Blades coach Kevin Constantine for support.

"I could have gotten crucified for that," Irbe said. "He just took me under his wing. He said, 'Guys, let him read, he's getting the job done, he's winning, we're No. 1 overall. When he learns and talks English he won't need a magazine, newspapers, or stats sheet to read. He will know it all.'"

Irbe learned to express himself well enough to come up with these ways to describe key moments in his career:

- **On 1993–94 run to the playoffs:** "There were crucial times when I messed up. I'm not going to deny it. We tend to remember the good things, but there were also not-so-great games. The team rallied around me and gave me special support."
- **Upset of Detroit in '94 playoffs:** "For our team, coming off its innocence and delivering—a love story between the city and the team—there was so much camaraderie and chemistry built from an unlikely group of players."
- **Fans chanting Ir-be, Ir-be:** "The name was kind of flashing on the small screens on the side of the arena. And the fans, you'd

have to ask them, who started it—chicken or egg?—but I was the beneficiary. I'm so grateful for those memories."

- **Earning nickname 'Like Wall':** "Somebody interviewing me said, 'You were standing on your head.' I asked what that meant. I was still learning. I kind of got it. It was good to hear. I said, 'In Latvia we would say, 'You were like wall.'"

- **On Kevin Constantine:** "Kevin's support was important to me because I was a different kid on the block. Teammates appreciated my skill and dedication, but the lack of communication, and my quirkiness—and goalies should be quirky—I always will be thankful he allowed me to do what I felt was crucial."

- **On injuries sustained by dog bite:** "Even if I might have been in trouble, I was going to show everybody that I was totally fine. That was my attitude. It wasn't easy. I had my internal battles—demons to fight—but I knew I had to show up strong, act strong and be positive."

The emotional accident in which Irbe's dog suddenly attacked him after getting nudged from a sound sleep resulted in the goalie needing surgery to repair nerve damage and a severed artery in addition to fracturing fingers on his left hand. His beloved Rambo—a mix of Newfoundland and Labrador—was subsequently put down.

It signaled the start of his downfall in San Jose. Following a subpar lockout season in 1994–95, Irbe appeared in only 22 games in '95–'96 before gaining his release.

Still, however, he remains a popular cult figure in San Jose.

"There are moments like winning my first game, the first shutout, beating Detroit," Irbe said. "And then you have your teammates embrace you without words, and it tells you how they appreciate what you do. That's what makes a player's career worthwhile."

Irbe Literally Breaks In His Pads

Brian Hayward saw a lot of strange things throughout his 11 seasons in the NHL. What Arturs Irbe requested in Hayward's final training camp, however, was a career first.

Irbe, a rookie netminder preparing for San Jose's inaugural season of 1991–92 along with the veteran Hayward, was in the process of breaking in new goalie pads.

"And Arturs said to me, 'Can I borrow your car?'" recalled Hayward, who was driving a 4-wheel drive Jeep at the time. "I asked why and he said, 'Because I want to break my pads in. I want you to drive your Cherokee over my pads. I want you to break some of the stitching on it.'"

Hayward must have done a good job, because Irbe wore those same pads for nearly his entire 13-year career. Originally white in color, the old-fashioned pads got so scuffed, stained, and puck-marked that teammates took to nicknaming Irbe the "Michelin Man."

7 Franchise-Altering Deal

Niko Dimitrakos and Jim Fahey were perched in the press level high above the ice at American Airlines Center in Dallas, watching as the Sharks took a pregame skate, a customary practice for healthy scratches on the road.

Then, they were gone.

Out of suits and ties, Dimitrakos and Fahey were in uniform and on the bench in time for the playing of the National Anthem. Teammates Brad Stuart, Marco Sturm, and Wayne Primeau, who all participated in the skate-around, were now scratched by game time.

Three sudden illnesses? Was this injury-related? Or were the three headed to coach Ron Wilson's doghouse in an attempt to end a nine-game losing streak? The answer came midway through the first period. Word spread the Sharks had swung a trade—a big, big trade. But who was coming in exchange for the three regulars was not yet known.

General manager Doug Wilson emerged from a private box at intermission and announced Joe Thornton was now, as of November 30, 2005, a San Jose Shark.

"He's a dominant player in the league, and we're excited to get him," Wilson said at the time. "Boston is getting three very good players, great people who have done wonderful things for this organization. All I can say is I thank the players who were here and I wish them all the best, and we're very happy Joe will be part of this organization."

Wow.

While the deal itself was a shocker, the fact the Sharks and Bruins hooked up on a swap made perfect sense. Less than two months into a new season, San Jose and Boston were in last place in divisions each had won the year before. Wilson and Boston's G.M., Mike O'Connell, coincidentally broke into the NHL on the same Chicago Blackhawks blue line as rookie defensemen in 1977. So there was a long-standing relationship and comfort level between the two.

Defenseman Kyle McLaren came to the Sharks via trade from the Bruins in January of 2003. He was selected by Boston in the first round of the 1995 draft (ninth overall), two years before the Bruins made Thornton the first overall selection in '97. McLaren knew first-hand what kind of player his Sharks teammates were getting.

"Joe is a dominant player," McLaren said at the time. "He's going to help our team tremendously offensively, defensively, and in the dressing room. He's a very skilled player, works his butt off, and he's very team-oriented. I was there when he was drafted and he's progressed into one of the top forwards in the league."

Despite producing 169 goals and 454 points in 532 games by the age of 26, including a team-high 33 points in 2005–06 at the time of the deal, Thornton ruffled feathers in Boston over contract negotiations that didn't go as smoothly or as privately as everyone had hoped. The two sides agreed on a three-year, $20 million deal after Thornton's camp was hoping for a five-year term.

The trade instantly made Thornton the top-paid Shark, but San Jose only took on approximately $1.34 million more when the contracts for Stuart, Sturm—two former first-round picks by San Jose—and Primeau, who came via trade, were taken off the books.

Criticism was swift and harsh in Beantown over the deal. O'Connell was lambasted in print because it was felt that the Sharks got the best player in the deal.

"Some of these deals general managers face, they take necessary courage to do them," O'Connell answered. "Some are going to work, some aren't going to work. If they work more often than they don't, you keep your job."

Thornton joined his new teammates in Buffalo the day after the trade was announced. A hasty, late-afternoon press conference was held in a conference room of the team hotel to introduce the newest Shark, sporting his trademark unruly blond locks and a 5 o'clock shadow.

"I thought I was going to be a Bruin for life," Thornton started. "I (felt like I) grew up in Boston; I was just 18 when I got there. But now it's exciting to play with some new faces, and get to know my cousin (Scott Thornton) better. I can't wait."

The native of London, Ontario, was joining the player taken just after him in the '97 draft at No. 2 overall—Patrick Marleau—and Thornton knew the Sharks would be looking for big things from him for years to come.

"I've always had a lot of pressure on me, playing in an Original Six city, so this isn't new," Thornton said. "I'm just going to play how Joe Thornton plays and see what happens."

Deal of the Decade

Regular-season stats for 11 years following the three-for-Joe Thornton trade between San Jose and Boston consummated on November 30, 2005. Dealt Sharks Brad Stuart, Marco Sturm, and Wayne Primeau went on to play for a combined 10 different teams:

Player	GP	G	A	Pts.	PIM	+/-	ATOI	Notes
Joe Thornton	835	208	679	887	488	174	19:43	'05-06 MVP, Art Ross
Brad Stuart	570	41	124	165	284	-27	21:52	Det, Cgy, Col, SJ*, LAK
**Marco Sturm	385	114	100	214	204	17	16:49	LAK, Wsh, Van, Fla
***Wayne Primeau	254	22	36	58	226	-34	12:59	Cgy, Tor

* Returned to Sharks as free agent for two seasons (2012-14)
** Retired after 2011-12 season
*** Retired after 2009-10 season

8 First Goal, First Win, and First Everything

Craig Coxe wasn't a big goal-scorer during his eight-year NHL career, collecting only 14. Bearing resemblance to actor and noted Boston Bruins superfan Denis Leary, Coxe was far better known for punching anyone who gave him the stink eye.

Coxe didn't back down either, earning 18 fighting majors alone in 1987–88 when he played for both Vancouver and Calgary. During his 48-fight career, Coxe tangled with Tim Hunter, Joey Kocur, John Kordic, Nick Futio, and Dave Brown. Coxe's pair of career bouts against Bob Probert were dubbed "two of the biggest toe-to-toe slugfests of all-time."

But on October 4, opening night for the 1991–92 season, Coxe used those otherwise rugged hands for a more productive result. He scored a most historic goal—an even-strength marker at 4:09 of the third period inside the Pacific Coliseum at Vancouver—that put the expansion San Jose Sharks on the scoreboard for the first time in their debut game. Assists went to former U.S. Olympian Mark Pavelich and defenseman Neil Wilkinson.

Maybe it was only fitting goal No. 1 came off the stick of Coxe, a California native who was born in Chula Vista and spent many of his formative years living in Laguna Beach. That's where he learned to skate, both on ice and on pavement wearing inline skates. Coxe even played two seasons of Roller Hockey International after he was done with professional ice hockey.

Tall at 6'4" and a lanky 220 pounds, Coxe raised eyebrows when he denied the Hockey Hall of Fame's request for the historic first-goal puck. He insisted on giving it to his father, who was the recipient of all of Coxe's mementos because, as the son said, "It's no disrespect to the Hall of Fame, but if it wasn't for my father I wouldn't be here, and he helped me out a lot with getting to where I was."

While Coxe's goal ignited a three-goal rally, that first Sharks win would have to wait. Trevor Linden broke a 3–3 tie with just 19 seconds remaining and the Canucks won 4–3 a night before Vancouver also spoiled San Jose's first home game 5–2.

That first win came on a Tuesday night when the second of 53 straight sellout crowds at the Cow Palace was delighted to witness the Sharks beat Calgary 4–3. Kelly Kisio scored a power-play goal with 3:15 left to break a tie, and veteran goalie Brian Hayward made 36 saves. Never mind the expansion team would lose its next 13 games.

The first win on the road came on November 30, 1991, again against the Flames, who finished 35 points ahead of the Sharks in the Smythe Division. San Jose escaped the Saddledome with a 2–1 win on the strength of goals from Steve Bozek and David Bruce. Goalie Jeff Hackett's bid for the team's initial shutout was denied at 18:31 of the final period when future Shark Gary Suter scored.

Doug Wilson was the first and lone representative for the 1992 NHL All-Star Game as the veteran defenseman suited up for the Clarence Campbell Conference in Philadelphia. It marked Wilson's seventh All-Star Game appearance.

The inaugural season even featured the first work stoppage in league history, a 10-day strike by the NHL Players Association late in the season that delayed San Jose's final three games of the regular season.

The 23-year-old Hackett, one of five goalies who faced a lot of rubber during that first season, was selected as the inaugural team's most valuable player. Claimed by San Jose from the New York Islanders during the expansion draft, Hackett was 11–27–1 in 42 games with a 3.84 goals-against average.

"The way the Bay Area fans took to the team and supported us even when times were tough really impressed me," Hackett said at the time. "We also had a great bunch of guys that I enjoyed being around."

One week after participating in their second draft, original general manager Jack Ferreira was a surprise casualty of the first season. His void was filled by a three-headed management team consisting of vice president Dean Lombardi, director of player personnel Chuck Grillo and head coach George Kingston.

9 Those Cow Palace Years

It was from humble beginnings the Sharks franchise grew. Frankly, after their first two seasons in the league, San Jose had only one direction it could go.

The first-year roster of 1991–92 was cobbled together through three drafts—a dispersal draft with the Minnesota North Stars, an expansion draft with the league's other 20 teams minus Minnesota, and participation in the '91 entry draft. Free agents were signed and eventual team captain Doug Wilson came via trade from Chicago on the eve of the Sharks' first training camp.

"It was neat to be part of an inaugural experience like that, and you're in with everybody trying to feel their way through," said Kelly Kisio, who was 32 at the time. "As a veteran, and one of the captains, we had growing pains and all that. We had young kids coming in with very little experience and there was Doug Wilson with 1,000 games in the league."

Led by George Kingston, an astute, patient, polite man getting his first chance as an NHL head coach at age 52, the expansion Sharks went 17–58–5 to finish with the fewest points (39), fewest goals (219), and most goals-against (359). San Jose's revolving-door roster featured 45 different skaters in addition to five goaltenders.

"We knew what we were: a pretty rag-tag bunch," said Brian Hayward, an ex-goalie. "Those of us who had been in the league awhile—and there were a bunch of guys who hadn't been in the league for a while—most knew after the expansion draft, and when the team didn't pick up any high-priced players, the writing was on the wall."

After Hayward backstopped the team's first win during the team's third game, the Sharks went on to lose their next 13 and were 1–15–0 one month into the season. San Jose didn't win on the road until it lost its first 13 on foreign ice. The Sharks allowed 10 or more goals three times, including 11 versus Detroit during a 10-goal loss in February.

"You're very naive at that part of your career, and you think you can do things maybe you can't do as a team because you just don't have the horses," Hayward said. "But at that moment, we thought we were going to win a lot more than we did."

Individually, the franchise's first entry draft pick—Pat Falloon—led in goals (25), assists (34), and points (59) while playing in all but one game. Enforcer Link Gaetz had a cult-like following as he rolled up 326 penalty minutes in just 48 games. Goalie Jeff Hackett was voted team MVP in spite of these numbers—11–27–1, 3.84 goals-against, and an .892 save percentage.

As grim as all this sounds, Bay Area hockey fans fell in love with the team—selling out the intimate Cow Palace that first season—and teammates bonded more than one might expect.

"To come together as misfit toys, we were all parts that no one wanted," said Perry Berezan, a journeyman forward. "Somehow it just all came together. If you really thought you had an ego when you left your previous team, there weren't many big egos with the Sharks most of that year."

Then, just when you thought it couldn't get worse, it did.

A three-headed management team which wasn't always on the same page replaced fired general manager Jack Ferreira. The revolving-door roster started all over again with 46 skaters dressed in teal, including 20 who did not play in Year 1. And it was the same goalies minus one as the over-matched Jarmo Myllys returned to Finland to finish his pro career.

The Sharks won only 11 of 84 games, set an NHL record with their 71 losses—including a record-tying stretch of 17 in a row—yet still managed to finish behind expansion Ottawa based on having one more win, thus missing out on the 1993 first overall pick. San Jose's 218 goals were 23rd out of 24 and its 414 allowed were dead last.

"George Kingston, Murdoch, and Drew Remenda. They had to be magicians every single day to try to keep everyone positive," Berezan said. "Looking back, and I've told George this, he did a tremendous job trying to keep us away from the pain, agony, and stress that comes with losing."

There were positives. Goalie Arturs Irbe authored the franchise's first shutout with 39 saves against visiting Los Angeles on November 17, 1992. Rookie forward Rob Gaudreau notched the first hat trick a few weeks later on December 3 in a loss to Hartford. And he collected another three-goal game on December 12, in a home loss to Quebec.

And the fans were still loyal. The Sharks' sellout streak at the outset of the franchise stretched to 52 games before ending. But San Jose played to only eight non-capacity crowds that second and final year at the Cow Palace. The players will never forget those supportive followers.

"Sometimes fans don't realize even one of them can make a difference," Berezan said. "I remember to this day, as we're walking besides the stands back toward the dressing room, someone yelling, 'Way to go Sharks, we love you guys!' after a shellacking. I can remember actually turning, looking at the person and thinking to myself, *Wow, these guys are unbelievable.*"

Just the same, it was high time to move on, literally and figuratively.

10 SoCal Rivals

When the NHL expanded to San Jose and Anaheim, joining the established Los Angeles Kings in California, the league hoped natural rivalries would form.

They did, and it didn't take long.

Usually it takes an encounter in the playoffs to get a good hate going between two rival cities. The Sharks and Kings found common ground early on, and the Mighty Ducks of Anaheim weren't far behind.

Goalie Arturs Irbe recorded the first shutout in franchise history during San Jose's second season, and the Kings were the victims on November 17, 1992. Offensive threats Luc Robitaille, Jari Kurri, Paul Coffey, and Rob Blake dotted the L.A. roster, but none of the team's 39 shots eluded Irbe during a 6–0 Sharks victory.

"From that point forward, Irbe was unbelievably tough for us, and every game was a challenge," said Kelly Hrudey, who was in goal for the Kings that night. "That changed the landscape, and now the Sharks were a team we had to contend with. And every single game was an absolute battle."

When the Sharks clinched their first playoff berth a year later, they did it on the Kings' Forum ice on April 5, 1994. That was expansion Anaheim's first year in the league, and the Sharks claimed the final Western Conference playoff spot by 11 points over the Ducks, who lost all six regular-season meetings to San Jose.

Two rivalries born in two seasons.

"If you talk to people about who is the biggest rivalry, L.A. probably gets mentioned first," Sharks radio voice Dan Rusanowsky said. "But I've always felt it has see-sawed between the two depending what the stakes were."

Wayne Gretzky scored his 801st career goal when the Kings visited the Sharks on March 20, 1994. Owen Nolan scored four goals against Anaheim on December 19, 1995, a team record that stood for nearly 18 years before Tomas Hertl matched it in 2013. When Jonathan Cheechoo scored a franchise-high 56 goals to win the 2005–06 Maurice "Rocket" Richard Trophy, he notched three of his league-leading five hat tricks against Anaheim.

There's more.

Anaheim traded fan favorite Teemu Selanne to San Jose in early March of 2001. A dozen games later, during his first meeting against his former team, Selanne recorded a hat trick—as did his former running mate Paul Kariya for the Ducks in the same game—but the Sharks won 7–4. And the Kings beat the Sharks 2–1 during a 2014 outdoor game in Santa Clara that boasted the largest attendance for an NHL game in California.

But clearly, the best moments of SoCal–NorCal rivalries have occurred in the Stanley Cup playoffs.

Topping the list is the Kings' epic comeback from a 3–0 deficit in games to stun and eliminate the Sharks during the first round of 2014. It was a rematch of a second-round meeting the previous season when Los Angeles edged San Jose in a seven-game series that featured the home team winning every game.

The two times San Jose beat Los Angeles in the postseason were in 2011, when the No. 2 seed in the West knocked off the No. 7 Kings in six games, and in 2016, when Los Angeles and San Jose were Nos. 2-3 in the Pacific and the Sharks won in five.

"As players, you love playing in rivalries, you love playing against them," Bernie Nicholls said. "If you ask anybody on the Sharks or Kings, 'Who you like beating?' If you had one team you wanted to beat, you know who it would be. I'm sure it's the same with the Kings."

The only playoff meeting between the Sharks and Ducks turned out to be a significant upset. The Sharks were Presidents' Trophy winners in 2008–09, but lost in six games against No. 8 Anaheim.

"It's just a reflection of the natural rivalry between the two areas, and different lifestyles," Rusanowsky said. "Each side is very proud of what they have, so they're naturally contentious. It's very evident."

Nicholls is one of a number of high-profile stars to have played for both Los Angeles and San Jose. He's joined on the list by Tony Granato, Rob Blake, Marty McSorley, and Brad Stuart. Selanne leads a similar list of name players to have dressed for San Jose and Anaheim. Sandis Ozolinsh, Andrei Nazarov and Kent Huskins did, too.

"When I changed from L.A. to San Jose, of course I wanted to beat my old team as desperately as any other guy would," Hrudey said.

There's been cross-pollination behind the bench and in upper management, too. Al Sims served as Ron Wilson's assistant coach for three years before the Sharks plucked him from Anaheim in 1996 to be their fourth head coach. Two coaches later, Wilson was behind San Jose's bench. Sandwiched between the two was Darryl Sutter, who later coached the Kings to a pair of Stanley Cups. And who was L.A.'s general manager? None other than Dean Lombardi, a top San Jose exec for seven seasons.

"It's a great experience in California to watch those three teams battle it out," Hrudey said.

Sharks Playoffs vs. SoCal Rivals

San Jose played a combined five playoff series against its Southern California rivals through 2016. The Sharks and Kings split four series while San Jose lost its only postseason match-up against Anaheim.

2008–09: No. 8 seed Anaheim upset No. 1 San Jose, the Presidents' Trophy winners during the regular season, 4–2 during a first-round match-up;

2010–11: No. 2 San Jose beat No. 7 Los Angeles 4–2 in the opening round;

2012–13: No. 5 Los Angeles beat No. 6 San Jose 4–3 during a second-round series that featured the home team winning every game;

2013–14: No. 6 Los Angeles was the fourth team in NHL history to advance after losing the first three games against No. 4 San Jose in what was a first-round series.

2015–16: No. 3 San Jose in the Pacific beat No. 2 Los Angeles 4–1 during a first-round series that saw the Sharks win three games on the road.

11 Owen Nolan

When a 23-year-old Owen Nolan came to the Sharks in a trade from Colorado, San Jose knew it was getting a gritty, determined, skilled power forward who possessed leadership characteristics and a great nickname for any hockey player: "Buster."

Dean Lombardi was San Jose's general manager who swung the late October trade in 1995, a deal that signaled the start of a rebuild. And while Lombardi agreed with what everyone projected for the former No. 1 overall draft pick, he had probably the most accurate way to describe Nolan's play: "He's a bull in a china shop."

"Everyone knew how tough he was, how hard he played the game," said former teammate Mike Ricci, who built a close friendship with Nolan that continues today. "But he had great hands. He had great finesse and skills to go with that as well."

Nolan played 18 years in the NHL with six different teams, but he enjoyed his most productive and impactful seasons during the eight spent in San Jose between 1995–2003. While a Shark, Nolan produced 206 of his career 422 goals, 245 of his 463 assists, 451 of his 885 points, 934 of his 1,793 penalty minutes, and 568 of his 1,200 games. When Nolan left the Sharks, he was the franchise leader in goals, assists, points, power-play goals, short-handed goals, game-winners, shots, and hat tricks, and was second all-time in penalty minutes and games played.

It wasn't always easy for Nolan in San Jose, however. He joined a team destined to finish in last place in 1995–96 while leaving behind a Colorado squad that would go on to win the Stanley Cup. Nolan was the centerpiece of a grand rebuild in San Jose where Lombardi assembled a number of seasoned vets including Bernie Nicholls, Tony Granato, Kelly Hrudey, and Marty McSorely to

Owen Nolan raised his arms in celebration of a goal 206 times during his eight seasons with the Sharks. He scored 15 more during 40 playoff games with San Jose, which he made his home after retiring from the game.

surround and mentor the likes of Nolan and other young Sharks embarking on their NHL careers.

The arrival of Darryl Sutter as head coach heading into Nolan's third season would ultimately catapult San Jose's young star to a new level. A gritty player in his own right before injury cut Sutter's career short with the Chicago Blackhawks, the new coach demanded Nolan lead the group and insisted he pay as much attention to the defensive side of the puck as the offensive side.

"I definitely owe a lot to Darryl," Nolan said. "I think before he came along, I was a one-dimensional player who scored goals and didn't play defense.

"I remember going through a slump when Darryl grabbed me into his office and told me, 'I don't care if you don't score another goal the rest of the season. But you will not allow another goal while you're on the ice,'" Nolan recalled. "That part really sunk into me with the way he put it."

Nolan's game evolved along with his leadership as he was named Sharks captain in October of 1998. A year later Nolan would enjoy his best season by scoring 44 goals and 84 points to finish fifth in the league's MVP race.

"He said things in the room that needed to be said, and that rubbed off," Patrick Marleau said. "He could walk the walk. There was a lot of leadership with that group, but he showed it on the ice every night."

The native of Belfast, Northern Ireland—one of only six players in league history to be born in Ireland—Nolan had come a long way considering he didn't begin skating until age 9 in Thorold, Ontario, where he grew up after his family relocated from the United Kingdom to Canada when Nolan was a toddler.

Now everyone in the hockey world was taking notice. Nolan landed on the cover of the most popular hockey video game, and was one of the first eight Canadians selected for the 2002 Winter

Olympics, which ended in Salt Lake City with a gold medal going to Team Canada.

"I remember Mario Lemieux sitting beside me, and you look across the locker room and there's Steve Yzerman," Nolan recalled. "You're playing with the greatest players in the world, against the greatest players in the world and you beat them. It was just a great experience."

A great experience soon turned to a great disappointment. Nolan was dealt at the 2005 trade deadline to Toronto when it became apparent the Sharks' run of five straight postseason appearances would end.

"I did not want to leave here," Nolan recalled. "I understand it's a business, I did not have a very good year and when your team doesn't make the playoffs, moves are going to happen."

Regardless, Nolan had given the Sharks an identity, and led them from a doormat franchise to a perennial playoff threat. He was mean, nasty, and ornery toward opponents, yet supportive, productive, and accepting as a teammate.

"He does deserve an awful lot of credit for where this franchise got over hurdles and achieved the next level," said Doug Wilson, who succeeded Lombardi as the team's G.M.

"I'm certainly not going to take credit for it," responded Nolan, who invested in two restaurants and makes his post-career home in the San Jose area. "I played a certain way and if younger players learned something from it, that was my goal. I know every player is different in his own way, but I tried to compete every night, give it the best I had and I hated to lose."

12 Patrick Marleau

Kelly Hrudey had an idea as training camp in 1997 progressed. Embarking on the last season of his 15-year NHL career, the veteran goalie wanted to give something back. He watched as a 17-year-old, baby-faced, soft-spoken roster hopeful skated circles around the ice and had a thought.

Hrudey received the blessing of management and invited Patrick Marleau to live with his family for the season instead of having to venture out on his own. The offer wasn't extended until Marleau met Hrudey, his wife, and their three elementary school-aged children for dinner, and gained overwhelming approval from all.

"Patrick was a really quiet guy, but what stood out to me was he was a great listener," Hrudey said. "He was a fantastic person to share our living space with, and I've had a soft spot for Patrick ever since."

A native of tiny Aneroid, Saskatchewan, Marleau found a comfortable first-year landing spot inside the Hrudey abode, and has made San Jose his home for a long and illustrious playing career. And there wasn't a question of whether the No. 2 overall draft pick just months prior was ready to leap from junior hockey into the NHL.

"I just remember a kid coming in with so much speed and so much skill," Tony Granato said. "He was quiet, but very, very mature, and I think it was out of respect for everybody. He just wanted to come in under the radar."

Simply put, Patrick Denis Marleau spoke softly and carried a big stick.

"We were between drills and Tony Granato says to me, 'I can't believe how powerful his stride is, and he makes it look effortless. I'm doing everything I possibly can to even try to keep close to him,'" Hrudey said.

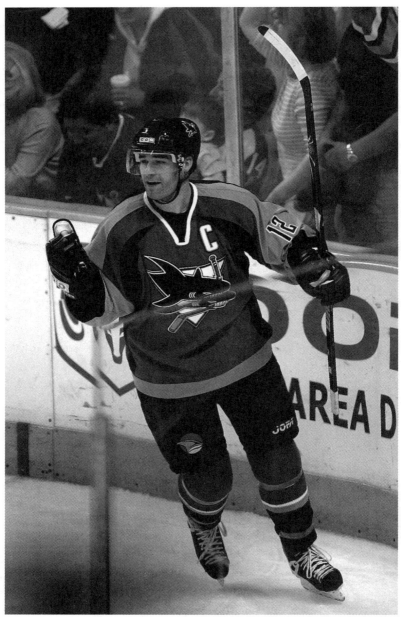

Patrick Marleau holds virtually all of the franchise records for offensive production in addition to captaining the team from 2004–09.

Marleau caught scouts' eyes with his blazing speed and offensive skill that translated to 51 goals and 125 points during his final year of junior hockey with the Seattle Thunderbirds of the Western Hockey League. Chosen behind only current teammate Joe Thornton (picked No. 1 by Boston), Marleau suited up for 74 of San Jose's 82 games in 1997–98, the first with taskmaster Darryl Sutter behind the bench. Sutter showed patience with Marleau, who didn't even turn 18 until just before the start of the regular season.

"We'd have some talks that would reveal his confidence, but he would never let anyone else know it," Mike Ricci recalled of Marleau. "That's how Joey Sakic was. I'd ask him, 'Do you know how good you are?' He knew how good he was, but he didn't feel the need to tell anybody."

"Patrick was way too good to go back to junior," Hrudey added of the three-time All-Star. "He proved to the veterans all year that he was going to have a phenomenal career, and that's proven to be true. Very few players have the ability to shoot that hard with that release."

Granato remembers rooming with Marleau on a preseason trip to San Diego when the rookie scored against the Kings. Granato recalls that raised eyebrows for himself along with his recent ex-Kings teammates Jimmy Carson and Luc Robitaille on the opposite bench.

"I was excited to have him as a teammate, and knew how great he would be for the organization," Granato said. "You don't see a kid showing you that much very often."

Marleau's production, durability, and loyalty with San Jose are unsurpassed.

In the span of a couple weeks in 2006–07—only Marleau's ninth season—he was already setting franchise marks for goals, assists, and points. By the end of 18 seasons after 2015–16, Marleau owned the vast majority of all the club's offensive records for both the regular season and postseason.

"I just love playing, and it's still fun," said Marleau, who won Olympic gold for Team Canada in 2010 and '14. "I grew up in the middle of nowhere in Saskatchewan. This is my dream, just being able to come to the rink and play."

Like the phonetic pronunciation of the surname he shares with the wine, Marleau, too, has gotten better with age. From age 18 to 24 Marleau averaged 0.59 points per game by scoring 153 goals and 327 points in 558 games. He jumped to .090 points per game from ages 26–29—often reserved for the prime of a player's career—with 123 goals and 283 points in 313 games. Then, while appearing in all 458 possible games between ages 30–35, Marleau scored 180 goals and 378 points (0.83).

"I was lucky to play with a guy who has done so much in the game," Granato said. "He's as selfless of a player and person I could have played with."

Marleau was the youngest player in league history to reach 1,000 regular-season games played with one franchise. He was the youngest, regardless of whom he played for, to reach 1,300 and 1,400 and games played. Imagine if he didn't lose out on another possible 150 games due to three lockouts early in his career.

"He's a machine," Ricci said. "He can go as long as he wants, I think."

Marleau has been a fitness freak throughout his career, filling out a 6'2" frame to a solid 220 pounds. In addition, he's picked up some pointers along the way. Classy veteran center Vincent Damphousse spent five years with the Sharks, formative years 3–7 for Marleau.

"I had a good relationship with Patrick, he was willing to learn," Damphousse said. "I showed him how to protect the puck by using your body. He's very durable. When you're aware of your surroundings you can stay away from injury."

Twice Marleau passed on the opportunity to test the lucrative free-agent waters. He signed a four-year, $27.6 million deal following 2010 (age 30) and agreed to a three-year, $20 million extension in January of 2014 that kicked in at age 35.

"I'm glad he's stayed with one organization, it's pretty special," Granato said. "That's an unbelievable compliment to the player. I smile every time I see him."

Years later, Hrudey holds a fond Christmas Eve recollection of Marleau.

"He helped Donna and I put together the Barbie motor home and a basketball hoop we had out in the driveway to surprise the kids with in the morning," Hrudey said. "I have just really fond memories of a kid who was raised really well by his parents."

Writing the Record Book

It helps to play 19 years with one team to set franchise records. And it helps even more when that player possesses the skills of Patrick Marleau, who was 17 years old in training camp one month before starting his NHL career in 1997-98. Categories he's tops in club history follow:

Total goals, even-strength, power-play, & shorthanded goals, regular season

Total goals, even-strength, power-play, & shorthanded goals, postseason

Most overtime & game-winning goals, postseason

Most game-winning goals, regular season

Most points, regular season & postseason

Most shots, regular season & postseason

Games played, regular season & postseason

Most seasons with 10+, 20+, and 30+ goals as a Shark

Youngest Shark to reach 1,000, 1,100, 1,200, 1,300, & 1,400 regular-season games*

*Youngest player in NHL history to reach 1,000 regular-season games with one team, and youngest player in league annals to achieve 1,300 and 1,400 games regardless of number of teams.

13 Color Me Teal

Look at the San Jose Sharks today and you wonder how the team could wear anything but teal. Back in 1990, when the team was deciding on colors a year before their expansion season, they were basically told, "What do you mean, *teal?*"

Matt Levine, the team's vice president of business operations, received a letter from CCM's Howard Zunenshine, president of the Canadian-based hockey equipment and apparel company that outfitted the NHL. Zunenshine suggested the Sharks pick a more traditional hue, advising a blue worn by the New York Rangers, St. Louis Blues, or Toronto Maple Leafs. He reiterated if San Jose insisted on the untested teal color, CCM would have to create a brand-new yarn.

"I wrote back, and also called him," Levine recalled. "'Howard, I appreciate your position, but I'm not changing and we're moving forward. And one day you will thank me.'"

That day probably fell right around the release of NHL merchandise sales following the Sharks' first season. Their $150 million in sales accounted for 27 percent of the league's total. Individually, the Sharks ranked second among North American league sales behind only the National Basketball Association champion Chicago Bulls.

"I knew we were going to be successful," Levine recalled. "I could never have dreamed the magnitude of the success we received."

The marketing guru wasn't taking a shot in the dark; his decision was a result of homework. Levine contacted reps with L.L. Bean, Neiman Marcus, Bloomingdales, J. Crew, and Starter with one question: What shade of blue will have legs for five to 10 years?

Independently, the answer all five times was teal.

The Sharks also had to convince NHL Commissioner John Ziegler, who demanded to see what teal looked like on television before signing off. An employee at Madison Square Garden donned a teal jersey and skated onto the ice surface with the cameras rolling before a Rangers game, which was enough to satisfy Ziegler.

Levine organized an elaborate press conference to unveil the look. He invited retired hockey great Gordie Howe to join team owner George Gund—one wearing the Sharks' road teal and the other donning the team's home white jersey—to skate on a local rink with makeshift bleacher seating on the ice. Crews from national networks including CNN, ESPN, and CBS, along with a host of local newscasts, had cameras rolling as 300 invited guests, who had all suggested "Sharks" during the name-the-team contest, filled the bleachers.

While wearing teal was unique and eye-catching, the team's well-planned logo—or family of logos as Levine puts it—contributed greatly to the appeal, popularity and success of San Jose's initial look. Levine rubber-stamped artist Terry Smith's design of a three-finned Shark biting down on a hockey stick with one modification.

"Initially, we had blood coming out of the Shark's mouth," Levine said. "We decided against that because we knew the parents wouldn't let the kids buy it."

Taking note at a trade show how fashion designers were drawn to the Chicago Blackhawks' under-displayed secondary logo—two crossed Tomahawks over the letter *C*.

Levine opted also for a circular shark-fin shoulder patch in addition to the team's primary shark crest. Graphic designer Mike Blatt contributed pro sports' first three-dimensional logo made of an entire alphabet in the form of a "gothic triangle" font to round out the Sharks' variety of looks.

Levine reached out to Dr. John E. McCosker, a nearby scientist who was an expert in ichthyology (think fish). McCosker educated

Levine that his Sharks resided near the Red Triangle, a 200-mile stretch of Pacific Ocean waters that was a breeding ground for seven different species of sharks.

Perfect, Levine thought.

A triangle would not only pay homage to the shark-infested Red Triangle, but also represent the three major Bay Area cities— San Francisco, Oakland, and San Jose—to promote the Sharks as more of a regional team. The triangle provided a background for the shark-biting-stick, and the look was complete.

A number of teams change their look after a number of years. Would that happen in San Jose?

"Never," Sharks radio broadcaster Dan Rusanowsky suggests. "They slightly darkened it about five or six years in, but it really hasn't changed that much. They're never going to change from teal."

14 Odd Night with a Legendary Guest

One of the strangest nights in team lore occurred on January 4, 1992, when the Sharks hosted Montreal halfway through San Jose's inaugural campaign.

The Sharks certainly wanted to put on a good show with the NHL's most fabled, successful, and respected organization in town. It just didn't turn out that way.

It started when after the pregame skate, as the teams retreated to their dressing rooms before the final 20 minutes to puck drop, Zamboni driver Ken Yackel Jr. accidentally dragged a Marsh Peg around the ice, cutting a groove into the Cow Palace's playing surface that caused a 55-minute delay to repair.

"Everybody was always concerned about his habit of leaving the peg in, but Ken said he'd never had a mistake. Ever," franchise-long radio play-by-play man Dan Rusanowsky recalled. "And I was on the air the whole time."

If the name Yackel looks familiar that's because his father was a member of the 1952 U.S. Men's Olympic team that lost in the gold medal game to Canada at Oslo, Norway.

"I loved it," said Perry Berezan, a Sharks forward at the time. "We're all just sitting around—what else are you going to do?—talking about how pissed off the Canadiens must be. They see this stupid rink, and they're so used to getting pampered that we all started laughing."

Two things occurred during the delay not revealed until two decades later.

Berezan managed to get a picture he had of young Montreal superstar goalie Patrick Roy signed that still hangs to this day in the hockey player turned financial planner's basement.

Also, a batch of pretzels were delivered to the Sharks' dressing room during the second intermission.

"By the third period they hadn't eaten anything for hours because it started so late," said Drew Remenda, an assistant coach for the first two seasons. "I'm not sure whose idea it was. But I know a couple guys went out for the third period with mustard on their jersey."

The first intermission wasn't without intrigue either. It featured a wedding on the ice between a pair of Sharks season ticket holders.

"I remember when they were about to say, 'Do you take so-and-so' there were people screaming, 'Don't do it. It's a trap. Don't do it!'" Rusanowsky described. "And the minister was trying to get everybody settled down. 'Please, this is a respectful ceremony.'"

On many nights, including this one, fans in the higher seats were treated to the sight of a few trapped birds flying around the rafters. Good thing it wasn't raining, too, because the Cow Palace roof would leak in one corner during downpours.

As for the game?

It was a goaltenders' duel all the way. Eventual Sharks MVP Jeff Hackett matching Roy save for save through a scoreless regulation. Finally, Canadiens captain Guy Carbonneau scored on a pass from Mike Keane exactly one minute into sudden death for a 1–0 final.

Hackett finished with 32 saves, Roy with 25 and one of his 66 career shutouts. The game's referee, Don Koharski, was early in a long career that spanned three decades and included almost 2,000 games officiated.

"And, if I can remember, we almost got a win," Berezan said. "I say almost got a win because if it was within a goal or two it was like a win back then."

15 Hometowns

Let a player glimpse an opposing team roster and the first column he'll look at is "birthplace." Everyone seems to want to know from where everyone hails. Even with an influx of European talent over the last 25 years, the NHL's world remains a small one. Players satisfy their curiosity and find commonality based on geography.

Then there's the case of Patrick Marleau and his hometown of Aneroid, Saskatchewan.

Veteran forward Murray Craven came to San Jose in a trade with the Chicago Blackhawks in time to see Marleau break into the NHL following his No. 2 overall selection by the Sharks in the 1997 entry draft. A native of Medicine Hat, Alberta—with its 60,000 population and located approximately 150 miles southeast of Calgary—Craven drew a blank at Marleau's hometown.

"My dad's lived in Medicine Hat all of his life and even he's never heard of Aneroid," Craven said. "I don't think you'll ever see me there unless I'm lost."

Throughout the years, at least half of those to play for the Sharks came from Canada whether it was a western-most city such as Brentwood Bay, British Columbia (Matt Irwin), or Fermeuse, Newfoundland, and Labrador (Ryane Clowe) to the east. They hail from large cities, small towns, and from places very few have ever heard of, too.

A 2006 census count of Aneroid residents totaled 45 inhabitants. That figure represents a 19.6 percent drop since 2001 because two families moved. Aneroid was incorporated as a village until it was classified as a special service area by 2009. A large, black-iron sign marks the town's entrance: "Aneroid Home of Patrick Marleau." It's displayed along with an oversized lefty, puck-handling, silhouetted figure.

The out-of-the-way farming community of Aneroid may be small, but it's got something on Bernie Nicholls' hometown. At least Aneroid is on the map.

An 18-year NHL vet, Nicholls finished with the Sharks from 1996 to 1999. Despite being listed as a native of Haliburton, Ontario (population 1,800), Nicholls is quick to remind he grew up 10 miles northwest of the Canadian city in a town called West Guilford. A detailed map of the area that fails to recognize West Guilford triggers a reaction from Nicholls.

"Hey, if Eagle Lake is on this map, West Guilford should be, too," Nicholls said. "They're no bigger than us!"

The rise from literal obscurity to the bright lights of the NHL with San Jose for native Canadians has played out in so many of the tiny communities that dot the Great White North's landscape. But as far away as their professional careers take them, players such as Marleau and Nicholls never forget where it all started.

"West Guilford has one garage, one store, one laundromat, one restaurant that everyone in town has owned at one time, including myself," Nicholls started, "and that's it. You're surrounded by lakes and trees. It's beautiful. There are a lot of dirt roads. And it's quiet.

"West Guilford is the kind of town that when someone drives by your house at 11 at night you know who than person is. You can't find anyone who is more backward than me."

The Marleau family didn't see many cars at 11:00 PM, not surprising since unmarked dirt roads lead to the home.

"Aneroid is as small as you can imagine," Marleau said. "There's not a lot going on there."

Like Marleau, Jeff Friesen was a speed-burning, skilled forward selected in the first round by San Jose. Chosen 11th overall in 1994, Friesen also came from a small town in Saskatchewan—Meadow Lake. And while the farming community had more than 5,000 people living inside its borders, Friesen knew there was much more out there waiting for him.

"When I grew up I always wanted to get to a big city and play in the NHL," Friesen said. "And I knew it wasn't going to be in Meadow Lake."

Craven, Marleau, Nicholls, and Friesen all played for coach Darryl Sutter, who, along with five brothers who also played in the NHL, put the small town of Viking, Alberta, on the map. Ron Sutter was the last of the six to retire. He was a Shark from 1996 to 2000 before playing a final year in Calgary in 2000–01.

"There's a main street, although it ends after about three blocks," Sutter said of the town located an hour's drive from Edmonton. "It's a typical small town. Everyone knows everybody's business no matter how private you try to be. Nothing's really changed over the years. Good people. Everyone cares about each other."

It would be easy for the Sutters to say they come from nearby Edmonton, or Lethbridge, because that was the Alberta city where each enjoyed junior hockey success. But to all of the Sutters, they are proud of their Viking roots despite living without electricity and indoor plumbing for much of their early years.

"We don't look at ourselves as anything special," Ron Sutter said. "There is a lot of mutual respect between us and the people there.

"If somebody asked me if I could change it growing up, I wouldn't."

16 Sharkie Gets Stuck

S.J. Sharkie navigated the catwalk in the rafters of the Shark Tank—not fit for those with a fear of heights—and attached a rig of rope to begin a gradual descent from high over the ice.

The mascot's intent of rapelling to the surface during pregame was to rile San Jose's fans into a feeding frenzy right before a big game.

This time, however, Sharkie got stuck.

When the Sharks played host to Detroit on March 12, 1999, the start of the game was delayed 12 minutes before Sharkie was rescued after hanging perilously halfway between the roof and his target below, just in front of the Red Wings net.

"I remember Scotty Bowman thinking it was a tactical ploy on our part to slow down the start and neutralize Detroit's power," Tony Granato said of the Wings' legendary coach. "You try to explain it to people, and, 'Oh my God, he's stuck up there. How are they going to rescue him?' I was thinking, *I don't know.*"

Gravity prevented Sharkie from fixing what had gone terribly wrong. The Fearless Finned One was secure; he just couldn't go up or down. A wave of anxiety swept through the sold-out arena, however, when gymnastic-style thin mats were stacked on the ice under where Sharkie might land if he fell.

"I'm thinking if he hits that it's not going to make any difference," recalled Sharks radio play-by-play man Dan Rusanowsky. "He's still going to splatter all over the ice."

The teams emerged minutes before the opening faceoff and took a couple of twirls on the ice. The National Anthem was sung with the starters lined up on their respective blue lines. The entire time, Sharkie dangled over the ice.

"I remember Darryl (Sutter) was calm, but once it started to go on and on, Darryl looked over and said, 'Just cut him down, let's go,'" Mike Ricci recalled. "I was saying, 'Well, maybe not.' But I think I was saying it, too, after 10 minutes."

Sharkie tied a rescue rope, dropped from above, around his torso and held on as he was lifted back from where he came. But there was one last problem: Sharkie's head wouldn't fit through a small opening to return to the safety of the catwalk.

"They were telling him to take it off," Rusanowsky said. "And, as a character, knowing kids were present, Sharkie absolutely refused to take off the head."

The Sharks shut out the Wings as Patrick Marleau and Joe Murphy scored the only two goals, and goalie Steve Shields made 26 saves. As for Sharkie, his pregame disaster wasn't about to deter him from trying the same bit when San Jose hosted Ottawa the very next night.

"It's right back in the saddle," Sharkie told the *San Francisco Examiner* at the time.

How did Sharkie come to be, you ask? While having a mascot was in the plans, the Sharks weren't ready to debut theirs until it literally fell right into their hands.

Marketing director Matt Levine was working late one night midway through the team's inaugural season when he was summoned around 10:00 PM. "'Come down, look at this, and you're not going to like it,'" was the message for Levine, who wasn't planning a mascot until Year 2.

Levine found Philadelphia native Dean Schoenewald entertaining his staff in the lobby while wearing a Sharks costume he'd spent $25,000 to make. Months before, Schoenwalt was told to stop practicing a similar stunt as an unofficial mascot of the Philadelphia Eagles. So he researched who might want a mascot, chose the Sharks and drove cross-country with his girlfriend in a van custompainted to resemble a land shark.

All Schoenewald wanted was a chance, no money, no promises. He saw the Sharks were scheduled to host his hometown Flyers on a Friday night with the Montreal Canadiens in town one night later.

Levine agreed to allow one game with the following stipulations: don't interfere with play, don't do anything untoward to women or children, the Sharks will not recognize your presence, and, lastly, he reserved the right to give Schoenwald the hook at any time.

"His first bit, he finds someone in the visitors' jersey," Levine started. "He buys out one of the vendor's boxes of popcorn, dumps it all over the fan and everybody went crazy. I let him come back."

Schoenewald performed throughout January before signing a deal with the Sharks over Super Bowl weekend. By 1992–93, however, Schoenewald was gone and the Sharkie costume has been filled with different performers throughout the years.

17 Oh, That Expansion Draft

The Sharks built their initial roster and began to stock their minor-league system with free agents and through three drafts—dispersal, expansion, and the NHL entry draft of 1991.

Seeing how San Jose struggled early to be competitive, it didn't take the NHL long to realize the Sharks got the short end of the stick. As the league added eight more franchises over a decade, rules were modified to give expansion teams more of a fighting chance.

"In retrospect, because it was the first one, at that time organizations were really concerned with losing their talent," Brian Lawton said. "They didn't really get the purpose of it. The purpose from the league was to enlarge the footprint of the sport—to grow the sport."

The dispersal draft was unique. Denied a request to relocate, owners George and Gordon Gund compromised with the league to receive a Bay Area expansion franchise for $50 million in return for sale of their Minnesota North Stars. A condition included the Gunds' new team—the Sharks—would have the right to draft players from Minnesota's depth chart.

The North Stars were allowed to protect 14 skaters and two goalies who had played at least 50 NHL games by the end of 1989-90. San Jose was allowed to select 14 skaters and two goalies from Minnesota (excluding 1990 draft picks) before the two teams alternately chose from a pool of unclaimed players until the Sharks' roster reached 30 names.

In the expansion draft that followed, the 20 other NHL teams protected 16 skaters and two goalies each. Then the Sharks and North Stars took turns selecting 10 players each—20 players total—and no more than one from each franchise.

Finally, the Sharks participated in the 1991 entry draft where their first three picks—Pat Falloon, Ray Whitney, and Sandis Ozolinsh—enjoyed future success in the league. San Jose was allowed to pick first in every round except Round 1 since it was agreed that the previous season's last-place finisher—Quebec—would have an opportunity to select The Next One—i.e., Eric Lindros.

Ozolinsh spent the most time as a Shark of the three. He played into his fourth NHL season with San Jose before being dealt to

Colorado for Owen Nolan. A defenseman with an offensive flair, Ozolinsh scored 46 goals in 212 games as a Shark. He returned to San Jose for the final 39 games of his career at age 35 after playing for five other teams.

Falloon scored 76 goals and 162 points during 258 games spread over five years with the Sharks. Having failed to live up to his draft hype, Falloon wound up playing for four more teams over four seasons.

Whitney was the hidden jewel, but didn't blossom until leaving. The first 200 games over six seasons were spent in San Jose of an eventual 1,330-game NHL career that saw Whitney rank among the league's all-time top 65 scorers.

Six of the players selected in the expansion draft saw time with the Sharks. Goalie Jeff Hackett, chosen from the New York Islanders, was the team's MVP in its inaugural season of 1991-92. And defenseman Jayson More (from Montreal) logged the most career games (287) and years of service (five) in San Jose.

Latvian goalie Arturs Irbe made the biggest impact of any player selected from the North Stars during the dispersal draft. Despite a sub-.500 record (57–91–26), Irbe led San Jose to its first playoff appearance and a first-round upset of Detroit in 1993–94. Fourteen other players from the draft appeared for San Jose—ranging from forward Peter Lappin's one game to 225 for defenseman Tom Pederson.

"We're talking about probably a $400 to $500 million business back then. And, I mean as a league, compared to what it is now," Lawton said of the more than $3 billion industry. "I think the league just went cautiously, especially with the Sharks."

18 Kelly Kisio

It seemed like just another late-season morning skate until Kelly Kisio glanced into the stands at old Chicago Stadium. That's when he noticed members of the Blackhawks coaching staff—Mike Keenan, Darryl Sutter, and Rich Preston—intent on his actions.

"I'm thinking, *What the hell are they doing looking at me?*" Kisio recalled.

The skate ended and the Sharks returned to their hotel and had a pregame meal. Kisio retired to his room for a mid-day nap to prep for that evening's game.

Then the phone rang.

Just 20 minutes before the NHL trade deadline, San Jose coach George Kingston called to inform Kisio he had been dealt to Chicago. Five minutes later Kisio received a call from Sutter, the Blackhawks' associate coach, telling him to come to the rink early and they'd decide if he'd play against his sudden ex-teammates.

Kisio broke the news to his wife, told his roommate, and prepared to leave the room when Sutter called again 30 minutes after the mid-day deadline passed to say, "Kiss, there's been a problem—fax machine, and it didn't go through. Just come down tonight and we'll get this straightened out."

With his equipment already moved to Chicago's locker room where now a red Blackhawks sweater hung with his name on the back, Kisio walked into Keenan's office to spot the head coach on the phone with the league. Because a flood of deals were made at the deadline, documentation of the 'Hawks–Sharks swap did not spit out of the league's fax machine in time. Keenan told Kisio the league would have to vote whether to allow the deal, but that wasn't going to happen that night.

Told to catch a flight home and wait, Kisio went to the airport, saw he had hours before a Bay Area-bound departure, and settled into a lounge to watch the San Jose–Chicago game. Coincidentally, Kisio ran into hockey executive Brian Burke, working for the Vancouver Canucks at the time, and shared his wild story. Overhearing the conversation, the bartender glanced at the TV and asked Kisio which team did he play for? "Both. Neither. I don't know," Kisio said.

Three days passed and Kisio heard from no one.

"Chicago phoned me the fourth day saying the trade didn't go through. You're not traded, and now you're back on San Jose," Kisio said. "I got a call from San Jose next saying, 'We're having a team picture in 45 minutes and can you make it?'"

In his typical show of professionalism, Kisio not only made the team picture, but scored the game-tying goal during an eventual win against New Jersey in his first game back with the Sharks, too.

"You had to let go with a lot of issues the way the team was run, the players who went way off—the Link Gaetz craziness—and the revolving-door in and out of the lineup," said Perry Berezan, a teammate and longtime friend of Kisio. "You had to be a really patient guy and let it go. Kelly fit that mold perfectly."

"I remember his patience, his professionalism, and he approached every day whether we lost 10 in a row or won, he was just very professional approach to the game," ex-Sharks forward Rob Gaudreau added. "You certainly took note of it."

Kisio was 32 years old, had 572 career NHL games between Detroit and New York, and had been the Rangers' captain for 3½ seasons before getting traded from Minnesota to San Jose (The North Stars chose him in the expansion draft from New York). With 178 career goals and 502 points during his first nine NHL seasons, Kisio instantly became expansion San Jose's first-line center.

Kisio responded with a modest total of 11 goals and 37 points in 1991–92 before breaking through with a career year in '92–93. He matched career highs in goals (26) and points (78) in 78 games with a dreadful Sharks team that managed only 11 wins in 84 games. At age 33, the Peace River, Alberta, native was rewarded with his first All-Star Game appearance after replacing the injured Pat Falloon.

"He was a much better hockey player in person that I ever thought, and not that I didn't think he was a good hockey player," ex-Shark Ray Whitney said. "He had a quietness about his game. He wasn't a rah-rah guy, he just came and did his work.

"He treated everyone with respect. He wasn't a guy who said, 'Hey, rookies, go to the back of the bus.' He was always very cordial. One of the reasons he was there was to build that culture, and he did a great job," Whitney added.

Kisio departed through free agency before San Jose's turn-around 1993–94 season. A solid Calgary team signed the veteran after noting his production and leadership with the Sharks.

"The couple of years there were beneficial to him," Gaudreau said. "I think he saw it for what it was—an opportunity to teach some guys, and an opportunity to get an extraordinary amount of ice time."

"Oh yes, I loved San Jose," Kisio admitted more than two decades later. "I was treated very well. Mr. Gund treated us great. You like to think you laid a good foundation there for the young guys coming in."

19 Thornton's Amazing Season

He drew the opening faceoff to a teammate, got the puck back, streaked over the blue line along the left boards, wound up, and let go with a slap shot that rang off the a goal post nine seconds into his first game with the Sharks.

Welcome to San Jose, Joe Thornton.

Thornton contributed two assists during his Sharks debut, a 5–0 win at Buffalo that snapped a 10-game losing streak two nights after San Jose acquired the star center from the Boston Bruins in a blockbuster, headline-grabbing, three-for-one trade. Oh, and the Sharks were a lifetime 0–11 at Buffalo, too. But that was B.T.— Before Thornton.

His two assists—both passes onto the tape of Jonathan Cheechoo's stick—served as an appetizer for what would come during the final 58 games of the 2005–06 season for Thornton, who produced nine goals and 24 assists during his first 23 games for Boston.

"I just felt real comfortable," Thornton said reflecting on his new organization, teammates, and surroundings. "I'm just in a new place playing the same game I always played."

He was playing the same game he always played with one significant difference: Thornton had never played it this well in his life.

Starting with that memorable December 2 game in Western New York, Thornton lifted a last-place San Jose team into fifth place in the competitive Western Conference. The playoff-bound Sharks went 36–15–7 after Thornton's arrival while the 26-year-old Canadian native of London, Ontario, went on an absolute offensive tear.

Thornton scored 20 goals and assisted on 72 others in 58 games with San Jose to give him a season total of 29 goals, 96 assists, and 125 points—the latter two figures led the league. He did wonders for his new linemate Cheechoo, a 25-year-old right wing who, in his third full season possessed a dangerous shot that wasn't getting used to its full potential while he toiled on a third line. Before Thornton's arrival, Cheechoo had 15 points (seven goals, eight assists) in 24 games. With Thornton, Cheechoo scored 78 points, including finding the back of the net 49 times.

Thornton won the Hart Trophy as league most valuable player. The Art Ross Trophy came automatically since it goes to the league's top point producer. And Cheechoo, Thornton's literal right-hand man, won the Maurice "Rocket" Richard Trophy for leading the league with 56 goals.

Broken down, Thornton's streak nearly redefined the term offensive consistency. And there was a direct correlation between Thornton's point spurts and the Sharks enjoying an upward move in the standings. Thornton collected either a goal or an assist in nearly 80 percent of San Jose's games (46 of 58), and produced at least two points 30 times. He had four four-point games, 10 of three points and 16 two-point outings.

Thornton managed multi-point games during each of his first six games with the Sharks, and went nine games before finally failing to land on the score sheet. San Jose won seven of those first eight with Thornton, including each of the first six.

Thereafter, and until the end of the season, Thornton's streaks went like this:

- Scoreless in two followed by scoring in five straight (three goals, 10 points);
- Scoreless in one, then scored in another five straight (two goals, seven points);
- Scoreless in two, then scored in four straight (one goal, six points);

- Scoreless in one, then scored in six straight (five goals, 14 points);
- Scoreless in one, then scored in eight straight (two goals, 14 points);
- Scoreless in one, then scored in two straight (no goals, six points);
- Scoreless in three, scored in another eight straight (four goals, 19 points);
- Scoreless in the season finale.

The Sharks went 34–12 in games in which Thornton collected at least one point, and won just twice out of the 12 in which he didn't manage to dent the score sheet.

Thornton's 96 assists alone represented more points by the 2003–04 league leading scorer (Martin St. Louis of Tampa Bay with 94). Thornton's assist total was the highest since Adam Oates collected 97 helpers with Boston in 1992–93.

And it goes on.

Jumbo is the only player in league history to win the Hart Trophy while playing for two different teams during the same season. He set an NHL record for the most points by a player traded during a season, and became the only player to win the scoring title while playing for two different teams.

Thornton, who edged Jaromir Jagr (54 goals, 123 points for the Rangers), tried to put his season into perspective after receiving the Hart Trophy from ex-NHL great Mark Messier during the league's annual postseason awards ceremony.

"I was a big hockey fan so I would always watch these awards. Wayne [Gretzky] would always take it home, and obviously Mario [Lemieux] and Mark [Messier]," Thornton said. "It's just very humbling just knowing I'm going to be on the same page as these guys."

Scoring Consistency

Joe Thornton was either first or second in team scoring during his first nine seasons in San Jose:

2005–06: Jonathan Cheechoo 93, Thornton 92

2006–07: Thornton 114, Patrick Marleau 78

2007–08: Thornton 96, Milan Michalek 55

2008–09: Thornton 86, Marleau 71

2009–10: Thornton 89, Marleau 83

2010–11: Marleau 73, Thornton 70

2011–12: Thornton 77, Logan Couture 65

*2012–13: Thornton 40, Couture 37

2013–14: Joe Pavelski 79, Thornton 76

* 48-game season

20 The Gunds & Golden Seals

Before owners George and Gordon Gund were granted NHL expansion rights on May 9, 1990, to what would become the San Jose Sharks, the wealthy brother duo nearly saved the Bay Area's first venture into the NHL 14 years earlier with the California Golden Seals playing in nearby Oakland.

In the 1975–76 season, the Gunds became minor investors in the Seals' ownership group that had designs to move the eight-year-old franchise into a new arena planned for San Francisco. When the arena project got scrapped following a mayoral election, the league dropped its previous rejection for relocation and the franchise moved to the Gunds' hometown of Cleveland.

In short, the Seals became the Cleveland Barons, who, after two failed seasons at the box office morphed into another struggling franchise—the Minnesota North Stars. The Gunds, now majority owners, wanted to return to the Bay Area with the North Stars, but the league didn't want to abandon Minnesota. The Gunds sold their rights to the North Stars in exchange for an expansion team.

So how exactly did the Gunds know the Bay Area was ready to support the NHL when it didn't work before, and when a litany of minor pro teams flamed out after enjoying initial success in the area?

One person with a good inkling things could work was Len Shapiro, the Seals' last public relations director, who helped promote a handful of NHL exhibitions in the Bay Area when hockey wasn't even on the radar. Shapiro had an eye on Gund during that final Seals season. Gund attended Seals games, sat with the general manager, and displayed an obvious passion for the game.

"I don't know if he was active in terms of business decisions, but he was certainly there at the games," Shapiro said. "He tried to be a player's owner, he had the guys come up to Sun Valley (Idaho) in the offseason, play up there, he'd skate with them. He was quite active in that department."

The sport all but disappeared for a five-year period during the late 1970s and into the early '80s. The Seals booster club, which surprisingly still exists today and meets typically on the last Friday 11 months out of the year, was 800 strong at one point and even traveled to out-of-the-area NHL games even when the Seals had moved. That was the only way for Bay Area residents to see the NHL, which wasn't on television locally during the early part of the '80s.

After a proposal to John Ziegler for the Bay Area to host several regular-season games was shot down, San Francisco businessman Eric Clarke was satisfied when the NHL commissioner said he'd endorse and help to put on exhibition games in an area the league wanted to test again for interest. In reality, the success of those preseason contests helped convince the Gunds and the league that the time was right.

"The first year we sold out the Cow Palace, and the game was a rousing success," Shapiro said. "It was like a big homecoming party. There were signs, enthusiastic fans, all kinds of support. It was pretty amazing."

Waiting to stage the annual games close to the regular season so teams would have more recognizable names on the roster, Clarke and Shapiro got an unexpected but huge break before Los Angeles and Detroit were set to square off during the fall of 1988.

"The game sold out in 90 minutes because during the summer Wayne Gretzky got dropped in our lap. He had been traded to L.A.," Shapiro said. "So the first time he appeared in California as a King was at the Oakland Coliseum."

Not only did fans gobble up the Kings-Wings tickets, they bought another 9,000 for Detroit-Winnipeg two nights later to make it 22,000 tickets sold in very short order.

"I think that was a key for the NHL to say, 'Hey, George Gund, let's bring hockey back to the Bay Area, it's time,'" Shapiro said.

21 Venerable Old Cow Palace

The stairs.

Oh, those stairs.

Players who skated for the Sharks during their first two seasons inside the venerable Cow Palace have a lot of memories, but the one unanimous recollection is the long flight of narrow, wooden stairs that led from ice level to the undersized and amenity-free home locker room.

The venerable old Cow Palace—the Sharks' cozy and antiquated home for their first two seasons—played to a full capacity house of 10,888 all 40 times in 1991–91, a sellout streak the hit 52 in a row before ending 12 games into the club's second season.

"I remember walking up those stairs, especially after a long fight," ex-Sharks tough guy Jeff Odgers said. "I had to stop at the bottom to muster enough energy, then stop at the top to catch my breath again because I was exhausted."

"The stairs to the room, all made by 2-by-4s and plywood," Perry Berezan added. "Ha."

"Mine was the stairs," Kelly Kisio chimed in. "Especially after a long game or a long practice. They weren't very wide. You had to be very careful going up those stairs or you'd go down either backward or forward."

Yep, the stairs have it, hands down.

The same building in Daly City that played host to the Beatles, Republican national conventions, Liberace, Frank Sinatra, and the Grand National Rodeo since 1941 was the expansion team's barn—literally and figuratively—from 1991 to 1993 while the Sharks' brand new permanent home was being built 44 miles to the south in San Jose.

"I don't think I ever called it a dump, yet it was a dump when you consider it was an NHL building," Berezan said. "But it was home."

Then there's Rob Gaudreau's perspective.

"It seemed like the Taj Mahal to me as it was my first NHL rink," he said.

The Cow Palace's 50-year anniversary coincided with the Sharks' inaugural season of 1991–92, and fans flocked there to fill the 10,888 seats for all 40 of San Jose's home dates. As much as the Sharks struggled, they managed to go 14–23–3 in front of their hockey-starved following, the fans still filled the joint.

"The angle of the seating was so far from the surface. And that one corner, if it rained, the water was coming in where the people were sitting," Odgers said. "You talk about a character arena, you can tell your kids or grandkids, 'I played NHL hockey in here.'"

The ice was smaller than most regulation 200-by-85-foot surfaces. Space was taken out of the neutral zone, and the corners were tighter that most rinks in the league. The single-deck seats ascended gradually from the glass making sight lines less than appealing. Luxury boxes? You jest. Those first-year prices weren't all that bad, however, ranging from a corner seat starting at $12 to a $55 "club" seat.

The neighborhood leading to the Cow Palace could be sketchy, too.

"I remember skid row and that liquor store with the same four to five guys in front with their little paper bags," Berezan said. "And as our bus was either coming in or leaving they would wave to us at exactly the same time."

While everyone agreed the building once dubbed as a "palace for cows" by a newspaper columnist certainly had a certain charm, it posed difficult challenges in which to play.

"As a goaltender who liked to handle the puck, I hated it because the boards were terrible," Brian Hayward recalled. "You got some absolutely brutal bounces. I can't count how many times I got caught out of the net where a puck was being rimmed around the boards, it ended up in front of the goal crease, and someone tapped it in."

The second and final season at the Cow Palace was a test of patience for the fans. The Sharks managed to win only eight of 42 games there where the capacity had increased to 11,089. The two-year sellout streak reached 52 in a row before ending during the Sharks' 13th home game—a visit by the Hartford Whalers in early December of '92—when capacity fell 190 fans short on a Thursday night Gaudreau scored the franchise's first hat trick.

And, of course, if the team didn't stink the building sure emitted an ever-present, all-too-familiar scent. Housing cattle and rodeos on an annual basis will do that to an old barn.

"Obviously the smell, you always remember that," Whitney said.

"It had a smell to it," Gaudreau concurred. "But I grew up around rinks that all had smells to them, and that lent to the charm of it."

"I guess little shacks have a personality of their own. There was something very intimate about that," Berezan said.

22 Whitney Douses Flames

One year after upsetting the mighty Red Wings in their first post-season, the Sharks found themselves right back in a similar position for the 1995 Stanley Cup playoffs.

San Jose managed to qualify despite another sub-.500 regular season (19–25–4) during a lockout-shortened 48-game campaign. This time the Sharks were a seventh seed in the West, and facing a formidable first-round obstacle versus Pacific Division champion Calgary.

The Flames featured such stars as Theoren Fleury, Joe Nieuwendyk, and Phil Housley while the fourth-year Sharks were still transitioning as Ulf Dahlen, Jeff Friesen, and Ray Whitney represented the season's top scoring threats.

San Jose's thought was stop the Flames first and see where the series goes from there.

"We needed to do a job on Nieuwendyk," Kevin Constantine recalled of his coaching strategy. "The guys who got that assignment were key. It went one step further than shadowing him or even putting out a checking line. We just put someone on that guy."

San Jose caught a break when Nieuwendyk didn't play the first two games—a pair of surprising 5–4 wins by the Sharks at Calgary—but he returned to score two goals during a 9–2 route in Game 3 at San Jose. The Flames won the next two on the road, too—6–4 and 5–0—to take a seemingly commanding 3–2 lead back to the Saddledome.

Wade Flaherty replaced Arturs Irbe in goal for Game 6, and the Sharks rallied behind Craig Janney's two goals for a 5–3 win. It marked the third time in six games that Flames starting goalie Trevor Kidd had surrendered five goals.

"I remember telling my assistants if they change goalies we've got a chance," Constantine said. "If you're struggling enough to have to change goalies in the middle of a series you're destroying confidence."

Veteran Rick Tabaracci replaced Kidd for a spell early in the series. And while the goaltending move worked for San Jose—Flaherty stood on his head with 56 saves in Game 7—a shaken Kidd would indeed surrender five goals in the decider for a fourth time in the series.

With the score tied 4–4 early in a second overtime in front of 20,230 red-clad Flames fans, the moment came—Whitney, with his stick positioned low and just outside the crease, redirected a pass by Sergei Makarov from the far edge of the right circle past Kidd to end the drama a total of 21:54 into sudden death.

"First of all I remember Wade Flaherty," Whitney recalled. "That game should have been long over. He was just unconscious that entire game and overtime. I think they had out-chanced us 2- or 3-to-1, at least."

On the game-winning sequence, Igor Larionov drove the Calgary zone with defenseman Sandis Ozolinsh on a 2-on-2 rush. Larionov broke free to the slot on his backhand, but did not shoot. He instead curled near the goal line and sent a forehand toward the net that was blocked out to Makarov, who circled on the outside and feathered a forehand toward Whitney.

"I tipped it just enough that it kind of froze Trevor Kidd into thinking, *Did it really move that much?*" Whitney recalled. "When it slid by him I thought, *Holy shit, we did it again.*

"Right after that I thought, *Okay, now we've got Detroit, and they weren't doing what they did the year before,*" he added.

Dead set on revenge, the Red Wings swept the Sharks in round 2 by scores of 6–0, 6–2, 6–2, 6–2.

"We obviously paid the price beating Detroit the year before," Constantine said. "They paid us back quite nicely with those big tennis scores."

Sharks All-Time Game Sevens

San Jose is 6–4 all-time in deciding seventh games of playoff series. That includes a 3–1 record at home and a breakeven 3–3 mark on the road.

1994 West quarterfinals: Sharks 3, Red Wings 2 at Detroit

1994 West semifinals: Maple Leafs 4, Sharks 2 at Toronto

1995 West quarterfinals: Sharks 5, Flames 4 (2OT) at Calgary

2000 West quarterfinals: Sharks 3, Blues 1 at St. Louis

2002 West semifinals: Avalanche 1, Sharks 0 at Colorado

2008 West quarterfinals: Sharks 5, Flames 3 at San Jose

2011 West semifinals: Sharks 3, Red Wings 2 at San Jose

2013 West semifinals: Kings 2, Sharks 1 at Los Angeles

2014 West quarterfinals: Kings 5, Sharks 1 at San Jose

2016 West semifinals: Sharks 5, Predators 0 at San Jose

23 The Linkster

His time as a Shark was short—48 games, to be exact. His legend? People still wonder just what Link Gaetz could have done if he stayed clean and sober in San Jose.

"We still tell stories about Link," Kelly Kisio said more than two decades later. "He was an interesting cat, that's for sure."

No player in the history of the team received more attention for doing less. Gaetz scored six goals, 12 points, and marched to the penalty box to serve a team-leading 326 minutes in 1991–92, San Jose's inaugural season in the NHL. Yet, he filled reporters' notebooks on a daily basis, had opponents looking over their shoulders and teammates wondering what he was going to do next.

Gaetz possessed a rare blend of raw strength, charisma, and talent to bring Sharks executive Dean Lombardi to say, "He could be as popular here as Joe Montana."

And he was right.

"Link had the body of Adonis, was good-looking like a movie star, had all the skill in the world, and was as tough as anybody on the ice," said Drew Remenda, an assistant coach at the time. "Today he would be a $5-6 million hockey player."

Today, he is lucky to be alive.

Gaetz came via a dispersal draft with Minnesota that supplied the Sharks with their first 24 players. Chuck Grillo was San Jose's director of player personnel. Of Gaetz's selection he said, "He's one of the meanest kids playing hockey. In fact, I think he's one of the meanest kids living."

When the North Stars drafted Gaetz in 1988, general manager Lou Nanne said, "In the first round we drafted Mike Modano to protect the franchise. In the second round we drafted Link to protect Mike. In the third we should've drafted a lawyer to protect Link."

Fittingly, Gaetz showed up to that draft with two black eyes, the result of a bar fight the night before.

"He was very unpredictable, which—for a short period of time—made him very effective," said Perry Berezan, a Shark from 1991-93. "But then, with that type of personality, everything starts to implode and his life became a train wreck on and off the ice."

It wasn't a train wreck, but rather a car accident that nearly ended Gaetz's life. Riding as a passenger with a friend in early April 1992—as the NHL season paused during a 10-day players' strike—Gaetz sustained a bruised brain stem and was left semi-comatose for eight days after getting thrown from the speeding car on a South San Francisco off-ramp in mid-morning. Gaetz's mother, summoned from the family home in Vancouver, B.C., sat vigil in the hospital by her ailing son's side.

Gaetz pulled through, partially paralyzed on his left side and with no recollection of the accident. His friend and the driver, Patrick Bell, was charged with driving under the influence. Months later Gaetz confounded doctors by regaining movement and speech through therapy. He returned to the ice and skated twice a week by late summer.

The Sharks were set to give Gaetz another chance until he was arrested and convicted for drunk driving in the fall. San Jose gave up and traded the 23-year-old to Edmonton for a 10th-round draft choice. "I'm just throwing my hands up in the air," Lombardi said at the time.

Rewind months earlier, and Gaetz was the talk of early season.

"In camp, we're talking and talking and talking, and finally (G.M.) Jack (Ferreira) says, 'You know what? I guarantee you, we will talk about Link more than anyone on our team,'" Remenda recalled. "And we spent more time and more effort talking about how we could help Link than we did with any of our other players. We all thought that the payoff could have been tremendous."

The team's newspaper beat writers fell into a similar trap. Tired of Gaetz dominating conversations, they instituted a fine system whereby $1 was collected every time one of the writers mentioned Link's first or last name. The self-policing worked for only so long. Eventually the writers got around the fine system by referring to Gaetz as "23"—his uniform number.

Gaetz became an instant cult hero as the team's rabid new fans gravitated to the most intimidating young player in the game. Gaetz scored goals here and there, but what brought patrons out of their seats were his fights. Gaetz dropped the gloves 14 times, none more hyped and anticipated than an early-season bout with Bob Probert, who was regarded as the league's reigning heavyweight champ. Gaetz and Probert waged a brutal battle that ended in a draw, both players exhausted but still on their feet, just like the fans inside the Cow Palace.

"Link was the only guy I played with who I was actually scared for guys on the other team," said Jeff Odgers, a tough customer in his own right. "When he went over the edge he didn't care if he speared you or took your eye out. As a teammate you didn't know what he was going to do."

Odgers experienced that uncertainty first-hand opposite Gaetz during a scrimmage. Odgers stepped in for a teammate that Gaetz had been giving it to, and then came the moment of truth.

"We were face-to-face, and that was the closest we'd ever been to going," Odgers recalled. "He just kind of looked at me. There's a fine line between crazy and stupid. I was hedging on stupid. I'm not going to lie, I'm glad it didn't happen."

Even if Gaetz wasn't in the mood to fight, teammates always had to be on the lookout. Primarily a defenseman who sometimes skated at forward, Gaetz didn't like getting beat in practice.

"Depending what day it was—you had to read him—if you made a move and went by him, he might swing his stick and you'd hear it go right by your ear," said Kelly Kisio, an alternate captain. "Next time you'd go down the other side because he was on a twist that day."

"If he was into it, he wouldn't get beat," Odgers added. "Forwards start on the goal line, defense skates backward from the hash marks. They blow the whistle and you go. When he wanted to, we didn't have a guy on the team who could beat him."

Gaetz's unpredictable behavior was not restricted to practice either. Berezan, also a teammate with Gaetz previously in Minnesota, remembers when the Sharks visited Detroit for the first time and Gaetz played forward on his line.

"We go for our first shift and we get scored on. Minus-1," Berezan started. "Go out for a second shift, get scored on. Minus-2. On the bench it's like, 'C'mon guys, let's get it going.' Then the third shift? Minus-3. I looked at Link and he says to me, 'Perry, you know what? I just don't feel like playing tonight.' We go out for the next shift, and sure enough we get scored on.

"Link leaves the ice and goes right into the locker room. 'Are you kidding?' One of the coaches says, 'Go get him.' I'm thinking, *Wait a minute, if you're going to get him, don't put him back on my line.*"

Gaetz was convinced to return, and finished a minus-5. The Sharks lost 11–1.

"He was an exceptional physical specimen. He was a monster. He could shoot the puck, he could skate, he could handle it. He was tough," Kisio said. "Some days he wanted to play, some days, well…."

Kisio was among the veterans who took turns rooming with Gaetz on the road. The thinking was Gaetz would learn better habits if he spent as much time as possible with San Jose's most veteran and strong character types.

When asked how that worked, Kisio said, "I know nothing, I see nothing."

Berezan recalls the sight of Royal Canadian Mounted Police surrounding the team plane upon arrival in the Vancouver airport for a game that night a month earlier. "We all started in, 'Hey Link, they're coming after you.'" Berezan said.

They were coming after him.

The Missing Link no more, Gaetz was arrested on three outstanding warrants.

Like anyone who watched, the Sharks saw so much potential in Gaetz. When he applied himself, the game came easy to him. Too easy.

"A guy like me, I lived in the weight room all summer," said Odgers, who made himself into an NHL player after going undrafted. "Link kind of lifted, and he kind of didn't. He'd come in there, lay down on the bench, put 225 on, and do 10–12 reps as a warm-up. It was like, 'Oh, my God.'"

In what turned out to be Gaetz's final game as a Shark on March 6, 1992, he bolted from the penalty box to engage Pittsburgh's Troy Loney after the final horn during a 7–3 win by the Penguins at the Cow Palace. Gaetz earned an automatic 10-game suspension for his actions, and the team was fined $25,000.

"The one question you always asked: What if Link ever got straightened out or if he got motivated and dedicated?" Odgers said. "It's unbelievable what he could have done."

24 Doug Wilson: The Player

When Doug Wilson joined San Jose for its inaugural season in a trade with Chicago it gave the Sharks a player few expansion teams possess. While his most productive years were spent during 14 seasons with the Blackhawks, the 34-year-old Wilson brought legitimacy, leadership, and a rare outlook to a team trying to establish a foothold in a revived NHL market.

"Doug has a vision few people see in the game. He always says we have enough Stanley Cups in the family. He wants to help the game grow," said Murray Wilson, Doug's older brother who won four Cups with Montreal.

Wilson left behind his 225 goals, 554 assists, and 779 points—three categories that ranked him first all-time among Chicago defensemen—to join the ground floor in building a new franchise. A Norris Trophy winner, Wilson had opportunities to play elsewhere. Yet against the advice of his agent, Wilson was okay with the deal on the eve of San Jose's initial training camp in September of 1991 that sent minor-league journeyman defenseman Kerry Toporowski and a second-round draft pick to Chicago.

"With the Detroit Red Wings, it's Gordie Howe. With the Boston Bruins, it's Bobby Orr. With us, it's Doug Wilson," said Dean Lombardi, at the time San Jose's director of hockey operations.

On the ice, it was a series of starts and stops for Wilson and the first-year Sharks. He missed 17 of the team's first 61 games due to injury or illness. Once he got on a roll by midseason, scoring 15 points on the strength of six goals and nine assists in 16 games, he sustained a knee injury during a game in late February against Calgary that cost him the final 19 games of the season. In all, Wilson was the team's sixth leading scorer, and was tops on the blue line with 28 points on nine goals and 19 assists.

When asked about his favorite memory from Year 1, Wilson responded, "Our first victory, against Calgary—that is history."

Off the ice, the team's first captain was an ambassador for hockey in the Bay Area, giving of his time for appearances away from the rink in addition to raising a young family of four children with his wife, Kathy.

"Athletes come and go, but Doug's the kind of guy who certainly leaves a mark," *Chicago Tribune* columnist Bob Verdi would say a year later. "Anybody who has spent time around him has to have feelings for him. He's always doing things for people.

"I'm supposed to be objective, and I think I am," Verdi added. "He's not only a special hockey player, but a special person as well."

His second year with the Sharks would be his 16th and final season in the NHL. Wilson again battled the injury bug, managing to score three goals and 20 points while appearing in exactly half of San Jose's 84 games. Wilson announced his retirement during training camp the following season.

The night of November 21, 1992, was special as Wilson became the 77th player in league history to appear in his 1,000th career regular-season game. It coincidentally came on a night the Blackhawks were visiting during San Jose's second and final season in the Cow Palace. During the pregame ceremony, he announced the creation of the Doug Wilson Scholarship Foundation, which provides assistance to worthy college-bound Bay Area students and continues today.

"We lost 2–1, but we gave them their money's worth. The team played hard for our captain," goalie Arturs Irbe recalled. "The look Doug gave me, and the embrace, it was more telling to me than later reading what 1,000 games in the NHL meant."

The team's first representative to the NHL All-Star Game in 1991–92, Wilson was twice named the Sharks' nominee for the King Clancy Memorial Trophy awarded annually for leadership and humanitarian contributions both on and off the ice.

Following his playing days, Wilson remained true to his word by continuing to build the San Jose franchise. After four years away from the team, Wilson rejoined the Sharks in 1997 as director of pro development, and was promoted by 2003 as the team's third general manager where he led the Sharks to 10 straight playoff appearances during his first 10 years as the club's top hockey executive.

25 Patty and Whits

Like two peas in a pod, a pair of shinny new sports cars—1992 Dodge Stealth models to be exact—were always parked right next to each other just outside the Cow Palace. One was bright red, the other jet black. Each drew attention away from the less striking vehicles, whose license plates represented states across the northeast and Canadian provinces.

The cars belonged to Pat Falloon and Ray Whitney, the first two players selected by the Sharks during their initial entry draft of 1991.

It was as if a hockey metaphor—the Sharks' future powered by their two young, flashy stars—was on display in the players' parking lot.

"Both were exceptionally skilled," recalled Kelly Kisio, one of the team's many well-traveled vets on San Jose's expansion roster.

Falloon was viewed as basically the consolation prize in the '91 draft, which featured Eric Lindros going first overall. A native of rural Foxwarren, Manitoba, Falloon produced offensive numbers with Spokane of the Western Hockey League that could not be ignored—60 and 64 goals plus 124 and 138 points, respectively, his final two seasons of junior hockey. The Sharks were looking for a dynamic scorer and a marquee young talent to hook a new fan base.

And why not get Falloon's running mate Whitney with their pick in Round 2 (23rd overall)? Never mind his lack of size, the 5'9", 160-pound Whitney outscored Falloon during 1990–91 at Spokane with 67 goals and 118 points for 185 points.

While Whitney matured for a season split overseas in Germany and with San Diego of the International Hockey League, Falloon made the Sharks right out of training camp after leading Spokane to the Memorial Cup crown as tourney MVP the previous spring. Having turned 19 in the preseason, Falloon slotted in as right wing on the Sharks' first line.

The decision was one general manager Jack Ferreira and his staff struggled with because Falloon would have been a nice addition to Canada's National Team and eventual Olympic entry for the Albertville Games of 1992. That's where Lindros played.

"In the end, Jack said, 'Listen, he's good enough to play for our team right now,'" recalls Drew Remenda, a Sharks assistant coach in the early years. "'We've got a brand new location, we've got to bring people to the building. Here's someone to come watch.'…He was, in fact, one of the best players in our camp."

Falloon led a Sharks team that won only 17 times out of 80 tries in goals (25), assists (34), and points (59), a rookie season that included a minus-32 on his stat line.

Surprisingly, however, Falloon would never match those first-year offensive numbers in an NHL career that would last eight more seasons.

"That's a tough situation for anyone to be in, being the first pick of a new franchise," Whitney said. "Chances are you're not going to be a successful team early, you're going to have a lot of lumps and a lot of people questioning the pick."

It's easy to look back after the fact, but Hall of Fame defenseman Scott Niedermayer went No. 3 overall behind Falloon to New Jersey. Peter Forsberg, Alexei Kovalev, and Markus Naslund were other top forwards selected in the opening round.

"I don't know if the Sharks had passed on Patty and taken Niedermayer would their career paths have been different?" Whitney said. "Scott is a great player, and he also got put into a great situation."

Falloon's gradual descent in San Jose started with a shoulder injury that limited him to 41 appearances in 1992–93 when he managed a modest 14 goals and 28 points.

"If he doesn't get hurt the second year who knows what he does?" Remenda said.

Certainly no one was giving up on a talent who had yet to turn 21.

"For me, Patty was all about his release and his shot. His ability to get the puck off from anywhere," said Jeff Odgers, who coincidentally stayed at the Falloon household when attending a hockey school at the age of 10. "He had one of those shots he was either going to score or you were going to make a good save on it."

"Kids get thrown into situations where they're counted on and they're not ready for it," Kisio added. "That might have been one of Pat's downfalls right there."

Falloon bounced back to score 22 goals and 53 points during his third season, and first under rookie coach Kevin Constantine. The new bench boss demanded a 200-foot game. Forwards were expected to focus as much on strong defensive play as putting up offensive numbers.

"Patty wasn't given that same kind of freedom he had when he was a rookie," Whitney said. "The second year he didn't get a chance because of the injury. And the third year, when Kevin came in, that kind of clipped his wings."

Falloon played only 57 more games in San Jose before getting dealt to Philadelphia for a player, who never appeared in a Sharks uniform, and two draft picks San Jose traded. The Flyers were the first of four different teams for which Falloon played over the final five years of his career.

"Patty was so bright-eyed, but he was so young. And he was thrown into a soap opera," said Perry Berezan, a forward on San Jose's expansion roster. "Most of us were veterans who could deal with it, but he looked at it and had to wonder, 'Is this normal?' He didn't know who to listen to—'Should I listen to the G.M., which G.M. should I listen to?'

"As an 18-year-old kid making a lot of money, we never won, he was scoring. He should have had a long, successful career but getting drafted by the Sharks killed him."

Whitney's introduction to the NHL was far different, just as was his progress and length of what turned into an illustrious career. Whitney collected three assists while playing the final two games in 1991–92, a season extended thanks to a 10-day NHL strike allowing time for the then-center's minor-league season to end in time for him to join the Sharks.

A heel injury nagged Whitney, who split the 1992–93 season playing 26 games for the Sharks and 46 for their top minor-league affiliate in Kansas City under Constantine. Knowing what the new coach expected may have helped Whitney become an NHL regular in 1993–94, yet after moving to left wing he often found himself playing a third-line checking role with sporadic time on the second power-play unit.

"They never expected me to be that 185-point guy I had been in juniors," said Whitney, who often played with strong defensive forwards Bob Errey and Jamie Baker. "I think it helped me understand the game in the NHL. It turned out to be a blessing in disguise."

Whitney's teammates sensed he could turn into something special.

"You could tell there was a highly skilled, intelligent player," Berezan said. "If he was drafted or brought in the same time Patty was, and they were swapped out, who knows? Maybe Ray would have been tainted the same way and not had the same career."

"Obviously Ray grabbed it fairly quickly after I left," said Kisio, a Shark for the team's first two season. "And a couple years after that he turned into a special hockey player who played for a long time."

A former stick boy for the Edmonton Oilers during the Gretzky era, Whitney probably enjoyed his finest moment as a Shark scoring the series winning goal in double overtime of Game 7 at Calgary in 1995, a deflection past Flames goalie Trevor Kidd off a pass from Sergei Makarov.

"Whits had been told all his life, 'You can't do this because you're too small,'" Remenda said. "He would take the attitude, 'Oh yeah?'"

After scoring 17 goals, 41 points and saddled with a minus-23 in 60 games in 1995–96, Whitney was no longer in the plans for a rebuilding San Jose franchise. Incredibly, Whitney would go on to play until age 41, win a Stanley Cup with Carolina and finish as one of the league's 65 all-time leading scorers (1,064 points in 1,330 games).

In the end, the highly touted rooks driving two new sports cars sputtered out in San Jose. Funny thing, too, neither Falloon nor Whitney knew the other had the same make of car until they showed up as Sharks. Well, almost the same. Turns out Falloon's black Stealth was more souped up.

"Because he was the second overall pick he had the twin-turbo, and I didn't," Whitney cracked. "It was actually a much faster car than mine."

Patty & Whits Stats

Career statistics for Pat Falloon and Ray Whitney:

With San Jose

Player	GP	G	A	Pts.	PIM	+/-
Pat Fallooon	258	76	86	162	75	-65
Ray Whitney	200	48	73	121	52	-49

After San Jose

Player	GP	G	A	Pts.	PIM	+/-
Pat Fallooon	317	67	93	160	66	-1
Ray Whitney	1,130	337	606	943	413	-30

26 Camp Brainerd

In preparing for the 1993–94 season, the Sharks did something different. They packed their bags, loaded the equipment truck, and headed some 2,000 miles northeast from the Bay Area to train in the Land of 10,000 Lakes.

The Minnesota Hockey Camps, a 2.5-hour drive north from Minneapolis in the wooded and rustic community of Brainerd, Minnesota, provided San Jose with a unique, resort-like, out-of-the-way setting to train. The camps were the brainchild of longtime pals Herb Brooks—of "Miracle on Ice" fame—and close friend Chuck Grillo, an executive member of San Jose's front office.

With a single-sheet ice surface, cabins, offices, and dorm-like accommodations dotting the landscape around a beautiful lake, the Sharks spent the first of two late summers getting to know each other in an otherwise peaceful and quiet setting.

"It was great for team building because the distraction of all the business wasn't around," said Joe Will, a front-office member since Day 1. "You're simply at the lake and at the hockey rink. I think it's comparable [to] what NFL teams used to do, and the same reason why baseball goes to Florida and Arizona."

Brooks had a vision in the 1970s of opening a training facility where youth hockey players could attend a camp while their family members enjoyed the accompanying resort. When demands on Brooks' time took him away from Brainerd, he decided to sell the facility to Grillo, who was promoted to the office of general manager he shared with two others after the Sharks' inaugural season.

"A friend of mine was going to the Brainerd camp and invited me to go when I was 16, and I really enjoyed it," said Brian Lawton, the No. 1 draft pick in 1983 who returned to Brainerd with the Sharks at age 27. "Before I signed with the Sharks I was going in the summers, so I spent quite a bit of time there."

Many of San Jose's draft picks and prospects were familiar with Brainerd as they had attended development sessions prior to the start of the full-team camp, which included approximately 50 players each of the two seasons.

Brainerd was where Latvian goalie Arturs Irbe sat at a wooden picnic table, under the full shade of large trees, and emotionally detailed to reporters how fingers on one hand were badly injured due to a bite that resulted in him having to put his beloved dog down.

"The guys got together and it was almost a different mentality staying in what basically were dorms," Jeff Odgers said. "It was unique. It wasn't glitzy. I'm sure going to Vail or Vegas would have more appeal, but you know what? We made do, enjoyed it and felt comfortable there."

Nowadays, training in Brainerd before the season would never fly. Besides the expense to transport hockey gear to the site, the

NHL's collective bargaining agreement restricts how much time teams have to get ready before preseason games commence.

"With a 20-day of training camp, it's quicker getting ready for the season," said Will, of Bloomington, Minnesota. "I think we had more of a four-week window then. It was a great concept. Teams still want to do team-building concepts, but it's a matter of finding the time. But that was a natural for it."

27 The Joe Thornton Era

Numbers say a lot about a player. In sports, that's always been the best way to measure performance, regardless if it's football, baseball, basketball, or hockey.

In the case of Joseph Eric Thornton, even though the stats are eye-popping, they really only scratch the surface. And that's what people who know him best suggest.

"It doesn't get said enough how unselfish he is as a player and a person," TV voice Randy Hahn said. "To be that elite, and to carry it through to the way he makes others around him better, that's his greatest attribute."

"He's a guy who loves life," ex-teammate Jeremy Roenick said. "He loves going to the rink, he loves playing in games, and he loves being around his teammates. His laugh is infectious; he can't do enough for you. He has a competitive fire that most people would kill to have."

When general manager Doug Wilson swung the three-for-Joe Thornton deal with Boston in late November of 2005, the Sharks knew they were getting a big points producer with a big personality.

Jumbo certainly lived up to his nickname.

Joe Thornton has been a model of consistency and durability since arriving from Boston in the blockbuster trade of 2005 that solidified the Sharks as a playoff contender every season since.

"There is no question, he is the iconic San Jose Shark," Hahn said. "No one has affected this franchise in a more profound way than Joe Thornton. I mean that on the ice, and off of the ice. He gave San Jose a true superstar in the NHL."

The Sharks reached the Stanley Cup playoffs in all of Thornton's first nine seasons in San Jose. Coincidentally, Thornton either led the Sharks in scoring—which he did six times—or was runner-up over the same span.

"Since he got here, Jumbo's kept the Sharks consistently not just in the playoffs but as a Stanley Cup threat," Hahn said. "And without Joe Thornton, that just doesn't happen."

Thornton arrived from the Bruins at age 26, and made an immediate splash. He logged 92 points in San Jose's remaining 58 games, hooking up with new linemate Jonathan Cheechoo to form the most potent offensive duo in the league.

Cheechoo benefited from Jumbo's precise passing to score a league- and career-high 56 goals. Thornton collected 72 assists with San Jose—giving him a two-team total of 96—and also led the league with 125 points and netted him the Hart Trophy as MVP.

And on it went. Employing his style of protecting the puck with his size and reach, displaying patience in the offensive zone, and possessing the skill to put passes right on the tape, Thornton proved to be the ultimate point producer. Thornton led the Sharks in assists in 10 straight seasons.

"Best playmaker in the game, bar none, and has been for many years," Roenick said. "When you look at the best—Wayne Gretzky and Adam Oates—Jumbo is going to go down as one of the best two-to-three playmakers in the game."

"His passing is one of the best in the game ever," Patrick Marleau added. "He sees the ice so well he makes everyone around him that much better."

Durability wasn't an issue. Since debuting for San Jose on December 2, 2005, Thornton played in 675 out of a possible 680 regular-season games through 2014. And he averaged between 18:23 and 21:24 of ice time per game annually. Leadership? Thornton was captain for the final five of his seven seasons as a Bruin. And he wore the 'C' for five more campaigns in San Jose.

"If we had Igor for that long, during the prime of his career, that's the only other guy I can think of that maybe would have had a chance to affect our franchise in the way Joe Thornton has," Hahn said.

"The way he approaches each game, as soon as it's over he moves on," Marleau added. "A lot of great players have that. He doesn't let a bad game lead into two or three."

Thornton and Marleau, the respective Nos. 1 and 2 picks in the 1997 draft, have been lightning rods for postseason blame in San Jose. The Sharks have been an extremely consistent and successful team in the regular season, yet suffered near annual heartbreak in the playoffs.

"Unfortunately, people look at Jumbo and say, 'Until you win something you're not going to be that guy what you probably should be,'" Roenick said. "I'm hoping he can get around it. Not only for him, but also for the San Jose fans. They've been long overdue for a championship."

Jumbo's Career Highlights

A sampling of Joe Thornton's NHL milestones:

First game: October 8, 1997 at Phoenix (with Boston)
First goal: December 3, 1997 at Philadelphia (vs. Garth Snow)
First assist: January 25, 1998 at Washington
100th goal: January 26, 2002 vs. Florida
500th point: February 12, 2006 at Phoenix (with San Jose)
300th goal: February 22, 2011 at Detroit
800th assist: November 2, 2013 vs. Phoenix
1,000th point: April 8, 2011 at Phoenix
1,000th game: October 21, 2011 at New Jersey
1,200th game: March 27, 2014 vs. Winnipeg
Art Ross Trophy: 2006
Hart Trophy: 2006
First Team All-Star: 2006
Second Team All-Star: 2003 & '08
All-Star Teams: 2002, 2003, 2004, 2007, 2008, 2009
Olympics: 2006 & '10 (gold medals with Canada)
World Championships: 2001, 2005
World Cup: 2004

28 Pavelich into the Woods

Mark Pavelich, of "Miracle on Ice" fame, assisted on the first goal ever scored by the Sharks.

Then, poof; he was gone.

Pavelich played all of two games—losses on consecutive nights to the Vancouver Canucks—before abruptly retiring, and literally disappearing into the back woods of Minnesota.

We hardly knew ya, Pav.

"Mark is more comfortable laying [sic] under a tree in the middle of the winter," Brian Lawton said. "That's just his personality."

The expansion Sharks, short on skill, signed the 5'8", 170-pound Pavelich one month before their first training camp. A veteran of 353 NHL games, he last appeared only a dozen times for the Minnesota North Stars in 1986–87 before taking his talents to, of all places, Britain and Italy. General manager Jack Ferreira used his previous Minnesota connections to convince Pavelich to give the NHL another try.

"I remember, specifically, when Mark was driving out with his girlfriend he rolled his car in Wyoming," said Lawton, of the uninjured couple. "So he had like the toughest trip."

A friendship was struck during their brief time together in Minnesota. Pavelich confided with Lawton when the pair reunited with the Sharks.

"Mark is just an incredible human being. But he's very, very shy. He's very standoffish," Lawton described. "He was just a really good player. Mark had been through a lot in his life. I just don't think it was in his heart."

Pavelich was always his own man. During the 1980 Olympics, and as a member of the gold medal U.S. Men's team, Pavelich missed a team bus from the Olympic Village. So he ran six miles to the rink. During five seasons with the New York Rangers, the only way Pavelich would participate in MSG's postgame show after being chosen a star was if the network offered free fishing gear.

He quit in New York, too, when after Ted Sator replaced the fired Herb Brooks and Pavelich didn't want to play a dump-and-chase system. Brooks convinced him to come to Minnesota the following season, but that lasted only 12 games. Thinking maybe he could rekindle his love for the game after years away, Pavelich was wrong.

"There were just a lot of things that made Mark uncomfortable," Lawton said. "It certainly wasn't the group of guys or anything like that. It was just the whole spectrum.

"This was a time when the game was going exactly opposite from where it is now," he added. "Particularly at that time, guys were getting a lot bigger, there was so much hooking and holding. Mark was such a skilled player. He would be easily a 70-point scorer in today's game."

Pavelich grew up in Eveleth, Minnesota, home of the U.S. Hockey Hall of Fame and 3,700 residents. A three-year star at the University of Minnesota-Duluth, Pavelich went undrafted into the NHL, but caught the eye of Brooks, coach of the fateful Olympic team. Fast forward to Lake Placid, New York, and Pavelich assisted Mike Eruzione's game-winning goal in addition to one earlier during the Americans' 4–3 win over the Soviet Union.

"Mark was part of American hockey history—the greatest event ever," Lawton said. "I almost feel like, for a lot of the players on that team, there was nothing they could ever do to match that."

It didn't take long for Pavelich to realize the end had come in San Jose. His departure was swift and unceremonious. He ended up in the Lutsen Mountains of Minnesota, an unincorporated community where he settled in as a land developer.

"We didn't have the skill to support Mark back then," Lawton said of the Sharks' first-year roster. "And I just think the game was going away from what his true skills were. He was a guy who just didn't need to do it.

"He missed Minnesota, he loved the outdoors. This was very, very hard. I was sorry to see him go; he was a great guy."

29 Claude Lemieux at 43

When word spread that Claude Lemieux was attempting a comeback, and wanted to return to the NHL at age 43, it was hard to find anyone who believed it to be anything but a bad rumor.

On January 20, 2009, rumor turned into reality as Lemieux suited up for the Sharks and logged 7:08 of ice time during a 2–1 win over visiting Vancouver. It marked the first time Lemieux appeared in an NHL game in over five years.

"I loved it. Pepe was tremendous," Joe Thornton said. "I stay in touch with him to this day. He's a friend for life."

Lemieux had last appeared with Dallas during the 2002–03 season, playing 32 games for his fifth different team over 20 NHL seasons. He was too banged up to play in '03–04, and when the lockout dragged on to cancel the entire '04–05 campaign, Lemieux was resigned to retirement after he was advised not to take a substantial pay cut to return once the league re-started.

That decision continued to fester and gnaw at Lemieux, who dabbled in real estate, appeared in a television reality show and was briefly president of the ECHL's Phoenix Roadrunners. He also appeared content while helping to raise two adolescent children from a second marriage. But it bothered Lemieux that his son Brendan, an aspiring youth hockey player, didn't have much recollection of his father's NHL career other than unflattering clips on YouTube.

Claude Lemieux was his feisty old self, even at the age of 43, when he made a comeback after being away from the NHL for five seasons. Lemieux appeared in 18 games for San Jose in 2008–09, a feat he called one of the biggest highlights of his career.

In September of 2008, Lemieux went public with his desire to return. He'd shed 25 pounds over the summer with the help of a personal trainer, and he contacted a number of NHL teams to gauge interest. The Sharks were one of those teams.

Lemieux left his job in hockey management to chase his dream, which began in China, of all places. The Sharks sponsored one of seven teams in the Asia League of Ice Hockey, and that's where Lemieux shook off enough rust to earn a tryout contract with San Jose's AHL affiliate Worcester by late November.

General manager Doug Wilson studied tape of every one of his shifts for a month, then extended Lemieux a two-way contract by late December that necessitated him clearing waivers to remain in Worcester. Another three weeks passed—a total of 23 appearances in Worcester—before Lemieux was recalled to San Jose.

"The more I was told this was impossible, the more I wanted it," Lemieux said after his first practice with San Jose.

Realize the Sharks were anything but desperate. They boasted the best record in the league at the time—33–6–5—and were headed to a franchise-first and only Presidents' Trophy. And they certainly weren't making the move to sell more tickets. Lemieux had legitimately earned his promotion, and he fully intended to help the team in its pursuit of a first Stanley Cup.

And why not? The last time Lemieux was promoted from the AHL to the NHL, in 1986, the rookie led Montreal to a Stanley Cup by scoring 10 goals in 20 games. That was only the start of his incredible postseason success. Lemieux won four Cups with three teams, scored 80 postseason goals, and won the Conn Smythe as playoff MVP with New Jersey in 1995 as a third-line grinder.

"I grew up a couple hours from Detroit so I remember those battles," said Thornton, a native of London, Ontario. "I was amazed at some of the stuff he did watching as a kid. He was one of the all-time great competitors of the game."

As for Lemieux, it was simple.

"It's like being a rookie again, and that feels good," he said. "I'm playing now the way I played when I broke into the league."

While the Sharks facilitated Lemieux's comeback, he was expected to supply leadership and playoff moxie in addition to fulfilling a fourth-line role when called upon by coach Todd McLellan, who was two years younger than Lemieux.

"I didn't really know what to expect, but I was pleasantly surprised what a great teammate he was," Patrick Marleau recalled.

"He still had that competitiveness. He wanted to bring that, help the team that way, and have it rub off."

"He was in phenomenal shape," Thornton added. "He enjoyed coming to the rink every day. At 43, he was just a machine."

Lemieux appeared in 18 of San Jose's final 38 regular-season games. On some nights his centerman was Tomas Plihal, who was born in 1983—the same year Lemieux was drafted in the second round by Montreal. Lemieux recorded the only point of his comeback with an assist on February 19 in a 4–2 win over Los Angeles.

Jeremy Roenick was another graybeard on the roster, and he was also close friends with Lemieux.

"Not many players played like him, and he didn't give a shit what others thought about him," Roenick said. "He didn't give a shit if he hurt people, didn't give a shit if he cheap-shotted people. He would do whatever he had to do. And even sometimes his teammates didn't like him."

The Sharks' greatest regular season was quickly forgotten when they lost to rival Anaheim in a six-game, first-round series. Lemieux appeared only in Game 2, a 3–2 loss at San Jose. By early July, Lemieux was ready to call it quits once and for all.

"Many people will think the main highlights of my career will be the Stanley Cups, the Conn Smythe Trophy, and Canada Cup," Lemieux said during his retirement presser. "But, to me and my family, coming back and playing in my first game in San Jose will be remembered as one of the great highlights of my career."

30 Neil Young & Metallica

When it comes to celebrity sightings at pro sports events, there's a good chance that recognizable fan is as much there to be seen as to enjoy the event. And more than a few celebs fit into the category of bandwagon-ers, jumping on or off depending how "their" team is doing.

When it comes to the Sharks, it's a different story. Hall of Fame singer and songwriter Neil Young became a season ticketholder after the Sharks moved into their downtown San Jose arena in 1993. And, for the two years they played in the Cow Palace starting in 1991, Metallica lead singer James Hetfield was a regular in attendance.

Rich Muschell was the team's first director of ticket sales, and he remembers vividly when Young called to inquire about purchas-ing season tickets for the yet-to-open new home of the Sharks.

"We knew he was a hockey fan because he's Canadian, and by law, they have to be hockey fans," Muschell mused.

A native of Winnipeg, Young was the son of a Canadian sports-writer. His arrival to Northern California predated the Sharks by 25 years, but by the time the NHL expanded into the Bay Area, the "Godfather of Grunge" was more than ready to support the new team.

"He wanted to come in and pick his seats, but not with people around," Muschell recalled. "We said, 'Fine, we close at 5, just come in at 5:15.'"

Because he planned to bring a handicapped son to games, Young chose an accessible location and four seats in front of the handicap platform.

"He was great. He said, 'Show me what you've got,'" Muschell said. "He was like any ordinary guy coming in. We shot the bull about hockey. And, as I recall, his son liked a cap we had on a shelf. 'Okay, you just bought multiple club seats; here, you can have the hat.'"

And so began the long relationship between Young, a nearby Woodside resident, and the Sharks. Young didn't ask for security. He wasn't looking for any perks. Young simply blended in with the respectful fans who sat around him, and attended game after game, year after year.

"To my knowledge he never asked to come down to the locker room, never wanted any special treatment," said Ken Arnold, the team's director of media relations for many years. "He just wanted his seat there for his son to watch the game."

Young did not want to flaunt his celebrity, that's for sure. In fact, he ensured he'd maintain a low profile with one simple gesture early on. Noticing his live image being shown on the large video board hanging at center ice, Young playfully flipped the bird.

"That was the last time we did that," Arnold said with a laugh.

"He's always been very low-profile," said Scott Emmert, who followed Arnold. "He's always out there in the same spot. He just comes in on his own, and walks out on his own."

Hetfield and Metallica have enjoyed a slightly more interactive relationship with the Sharks. For many years, San Jose has skated on to the ice through the giant shark mouth with Metallica's 1983 release of "Seek and Destroy" blaring through the arena.

"It's an incredible honor," bass player and California native Robert Trujillo said. "The fact that song has that kind of energy to fuel an entire team and give them the strength to battle to kick butt."

The Sharks presented band members with custom-made Metallica Sharks jerseys on a night during the 2014–15 season that the legendary rock group was honored to drop the ceremonial first puck.

"The fact we're considered a mainstay of this arena, and obviously the Sharks are as well," Hetfield said. "You join it together. It makes sense."

31 Sharks Bad Boys

As a young franchise that came aboard when fists were still flying in the National Hockey League, the San Jose Sharks have had their share of "tough guys" on their roster, especially early on.

It makes sense, too, considering what a raw deal the Sharks got in stocking their initial roster through a dispersal draft with the Minnesota followed by what little was available in the NHL expansion draft. San Jose had little choice but to lift a bunch of plumbers, pluggers, and third- or fourth-line grinders as teams protected their skill.

Glance up and down the team's final statistics from its inaugural season and you find no fewer than four skaters with triple-figure penalty-minute totals, and two more who finished with 99 apiece. Team-leader Link Gaetz barely played more than half the season—48 games—yet ranked fifth in the league with his gaudy figure of 326 minutes, a total that still stands by a wide margin as most on the club for one season.

How much did the Sharks scrap in those early years? San Jose earned 78 fighting majors in 1991–92 and a franchise-high 81 in Year 2 when the team managed only 11 wins in 84 outings. Aside from 73 fights in 1996–97, which featured another last-place team, the Sharks haven't come close to dropping the gloves as often as during the first two seasons. Again, fighting in the NHL has been on a steady decline over the past two decades.

Individually, a number of the game's most reputed pugilists have come through San Jose, most at the end of their fighting days, but still at a time when they made opponents think twice about having a go. The impressive list of early-franchise heavyweights includes Jeff Odgers, Marty McSorley, Tim Hunter, Jody Shelley, Dave Brown, Scott Parker, Jim Kyte, Shawn Cronin, Ron Stern, Brantt Myhres, Lyndon Byers, and the late Todd Ewen.

The aforementioned group—let's tag them the Dirty Dozen—built their reputations with fight after fight, year after year. All told, that group combined to earn 1,562 career regular-season fighting majors in the NHL—undoubtedly a good number against one another. During their time with the Sharks, the same group combined for 257 fighting majors, and maybe a couple more that weren't counted because they came against each other during a practice or in training camp.

The one name missing from this list—or the Missing Link, if you will—was probably the most feared and intimidating player ever to wear teal until an auto accident nearly cost him his life, and certainly prevented a longer NHL career. More on the Linkster in another chapter, but for purposes here he definitely packed the most punch when the Sharks looked for someone to turn up the goon tactics. Gaetz fought 14 times in 1991–92 as a 23-year-old who could line up at forward or on defense. He probably would have played in goal, too, if he wanted. No one would have had the guts to say no.

"One of the meanest kids playing....He's one of the meanest kids alive," said Chuck Grillo, the team's director of player personnel in Year 1.

"Link was big and strong, and he could really move," said Sharks general manager Doug Wilson, who as a player took a turn as Gaetz's roommate on the road.

The Shark who embodied the enforcer role the longest, and with probably the most sustained success, was Jeff Odgers. The native of Spy Hill, Saskatchewan, went undrafted but signed as a free agent with the Sharks in 1991 after attending a development camp at the urging of Grillo. Not overly big—standing at 6'0" and weighing 200 pounds—Odgers was a very strong and determined Canadian country boy pulled right off the farmlands. Odgers logged 97 of his 257 career fights as a Shark, and was their captain in 1994–95.

The argument can be made that Andrei Nazarov belongs on the list. He earned 28 fighting majors while appearing in five different seasons as a Shark, including just one game in 1993–94. Nazarov wasn't projected as an enforcer when selected 10th overall in 1992, a first-round pick that turned many heads at the draft.

The Sharks envisioned the Russian native of Chelyabinsk developing into a power forward who would score first and scrap second. It turned out to be a wild swing and a miss. Nazarov finished a 12-year NHL career spent with seven different teams, scoring only 53 goals and 124 points while piling up 1,409 penalty minutes.

The role of fighting diminished into something that was shared up and down the lineup as time went by, and the Sharks who fought in recent years had other responsibilities, too.

Bryan Marchment and Douglas Murray were two of the toughest Sharks to patrol the blue line, combining for 49 fighting majors. Up front, Ryane Clowe (49), Owen Nolan (33) and Scott Thornton (27) were the busiest to mix it up.

Sharks leading fighting majors (1991–2016)

1991–92: Jeff Odgers, 23; Link Gaetz 14, Perry Anderson 12
1992–93: Odgers 19, Doug Zmolek 14, Dody Wood 9
1993–94: Odgers 23, Zmolek 14, Shawn Cronin 8
1994–95: Odgers 13, Andrei Nazarov 5, Wood 5
1995–96: Odgers 17, Wood 11, Jim Kyte 10
1996–97: Wood 17, Marty McSorley 12, Todd Ewen & Nazarov 11
1997–98: McSorley 12, Nazarov 10, Owen Nolan 5
1998–99: Brantt Myhres 14, Ron Stern 10, Stephane Matteau 5
1999–00: Stern 8, Myhres 7, Todd Harvey & Andy Sutton 4
2000–01: Bryan Marchment 11, Shawn Heins 7, Scott Thornton 4
2001–02: S. Thornton 12, Matt Bradley 7, Mark Smith 6
2002–03: Marchment 6, Jim Fahey, Brad Stuart, Nolan & Bradley 3
2003–04: Scott Parker 15, Rob Davison & Smith 8
2005–06: Davison & S. Thornton 6, Smith 3
2006–07: Mark Bell 7, Ryane Clowe 8, Parker 4
2007–08: Douglas Murray 11, Jody Shelley 7, Craig Rivet 6
2008–09: Shelley 16, Brad Staubitz 8, Clowe 5
2009–10: Staubitz 12, Clowe 11, Shelley 10
2010–11: Jamal Mayers & Clowe 12, Frazer McLaren, Scott Nichol & Murray 4
2011–12: Clowe 9, Brad Winchester 6, Jim Vandermeer 5
2012–13: Desjardins 5, Clowe 3, Murray 2
2013–14: Mike Brown 11, Desjardins 10, Tyler Kennedy & Matt Pelech 2
2014–15: Desjardins 6, Brenden Dillon 4, John Scott 3
2015–16: Micheal Haley 8, Brown 7, Tommy Wingels 5

32 "Hey Lawts, What's Happening?"

Each locker room in every pro sport has one. He's the go-to guy—the athlete media are drawn to because his quotes, insights, and availability are golden.

It was common during the Sharks' inaugural season for Brian Lawton to get approached on a daily basis with the familiar refrain, "Hey Lawts, what's happening?"

Like the vast majority of hockey players, Lawton was approachable, cordial, and accommodating. Unlike the vast majority of hockey players, Lawton had a spotlight on him from a very early age.

As the first American-born player selected No. 1 overall in an NHL draft, Lawton faced the loftiest of expectations for any player born in the United States. And it wasn't easy, especially when the New Jersey native, who grew up in tiny Rhode Island, didn't excel at the game's highest level.

Lawton was selected by the Minnesota North Stars atop a 1983 draft class that included Steve Yzerman, Pat LaFontaine, Tom Barrasso, and Cam Neely, to name a few.

By the time the Sharks signed the free agent Lawton one month before their first training camp, he had played 403 NHL regular-season games for five different organizations.

Lawton had every reason to be withdrawn, even bitter, if he so chose. But those qualities were the farthest traits from his outgoing and positive attitude. And everyone around him picked up on that right from the start.

"It was just a pleasure to be associated with the Sharks at that time," recalled Lawton, who after retirement became a players' agent and later a general manager of the Tampa Bay Lightning.

Lawton contributed 15 goals and 37 points in 1991–92, not that far off his one-season best 21 goals and 44 points accomplished four years earlier with Minnesota. But it wasn't about numbers with San Jose. Lawton credited general manager Jack Ferreira for assembling a cohesive group of veterans, the patience and professionalism of coach George Kingston, and the undying enthusiasm and support of the early fan base.

"They hit all the boxes. This was my ninth year in the league, and the first coach who invited us over to his house," Lawton said of the affable Kingston. "I played on some North Star teams that weren't very good. Playing with the Sharks and losing, it was absolutely nothing like that.

"One of the biggest anomalies was how many people came to San Francisco to visit me. I was just thrilled to be there. And, for me, it was a little disappointing to never get a chance to actually play in San Jose."

Lawton, at age 27, managed only a pair of goals two months into the 1992–93 season when the Sharks began giving younger players an opportunity with an eye to the future that included moving from the Cow Palace into their new digs in downtown San Jose the following season.

One of those players promoted from the minors was rookie winger Rob Gaudreau, who coincidentally grew up in Rhode Island and idolized Lawton despite never having met.

"I remember getting to the locker room and Brian came over to me," Gaudreau recalled. "He could not have been nicer. He said, 'Do you need anything? Make the most of this, congratulations.' And, lo and behold, I think that was the last game he played for the Sharks. I don't remember seeing him another day."

Lawton was assigned to the Kansas City Blades, the club's minor-league affiliate from which Gaudreau was recalled.

"I remember that vividly, and there were a lot of guys going in and out, but I remember thinking *Did I really just take his spot?*"

Gaudreau wondered. "He really didn't need to go out of his way. That's something I will always remember. He could have had kind of a sour attitude, which a million guys have at that time, but he did not."

33 Skating out of the Shark Mouth

Jeff Odgers played the first five seasons of a 12-year NHL career with the Sharks. With 242 career fighting majors and 2,364 penalty-minutes earned, Odgers was the epitome of a hard-nosed competitor. And, yes, that nose wasn't very straight.

Overseeing a fifth-generation cattle and grain farm in tiny Spy Hill, Saskatchewan, during his post-NHL days, there's one memory that turns Odgers into a real softie—skating out of the giant shark mouth before San Jose home games.

"I'm walking through the cows in my pasture, and I'm still getting goose bumps just from that exhilaration and how unbelievable that was," Odgers recalls.

With the Sharks relocated to their permanent home in downtown San Jose after an initial two years in the Cow Palace, the team pondered ways to make a splashy pregame opening. Business and marketing guru Matt Levine loved a show put on by pro soccer's Baltimore Blast, whose players burst through a smoke screen during introductions.

But Levine wanted the Sharks to go one better. He turned to Bob Brand, who had Hollywood connections, and asked what he could do. Brand tracked down a Disney spin-off company that designed a giant, open-mouth, smoke-belching, light-flashing shark head that weighed two tons and stood 17 feet high.

Players have been skating out of the shark head for more than two decades, a tradition that quickly turned from a risky gimmick into a mainstay that helps to define attending games in San Jose.

Just one problem: the $25,000 project wasn't in the budget.

"'Look at it this way,'" Levine recalls telling initial team president Art Savage, "'we can amortize this cost because it's going to last at least three years.'"

The lights dim, the familiar music begins, fans focus on the southwest corner of the rink, the jagged-tooth shark head descends to the ice with red eyes lit and smoke bellowing. Sharks players emerge out of the open mouth as if they were shot from a cannon. And the crowd goes wild. This is the scene that has played out for every home game since Day 1 in San Jose.

"It was one of the things I probably will remember the most about playing in the NHL," Odgers admits today.

"The thing I used to always try to take in was coming on the ice for the beginning of the game—no matter where it was—just take a second to realize you're in the NHL," Sharks forward Rob Gaudreau recalled. "It just made the presentation of the team that much better than just walking out from a tunnel. I don't think anyone thought it was going to be around long. But it just became a part that's woven into the fabric, and now you'd be shocked if it wasn't there."

The shark head was lowered and raised manually in the early days, but that was modified to an automated system after music promoters complained about the building's acoustics with it present during concerts. The shark head needed to be relocated in the bowels of the arena through the Zamboni entrance to keep the peace. But there was no way the shark head would take a night off during a hockey game.

"They were really one of the first teams to have a pregame production," Sharks forward Ray Whitney said. "Having that to skate out of kind of got you amped up as a group. I'm glad it's still there. I think the Sharks were pioneers in respect to that part of the game."

"Other buildings, the fans would just be there or late arriving, but it was always the adrenalin boost no matter what day of the week or what game it was," Gaudreau added. "You never needed to look for any other motivation."

Odgers remembers it always being loud at the outset of a home game, but has a special recollection when San Jose returned from opening its first playoff series tied against heavy favorite Detroit in 1993–94.

"We came back, and no one thought we were going to win a game in Detroit, and we came back 1–1," Odgers said. "We skate through that and it was absolutely crazy."

34 River Overflows, Game Canceled

In the long history of the National Hockey League, there's been exactly one game canceled due to rain, and it happened in San Jose on March 10, 1995.

The Sharks were scheduled to entertain the Detroit Red Wings during the lockout-shortened 48-game campaign. Heavy rains fell in the region, causing the nearby Guadalupe River to overflow its banks.

Flood waters filled the streets leading to the downtown arena, which by late morning appeared as if it were on an island. The adjoining parking lot flooded, streets leading in and out could not be traveled, and even the forecast of early-afternoon clearing wasn't going to save the day.

Getting some 18,000 fans, employees, players, and staff in and out of the arena was not going to be safe. By 1:00 PM local time the decision was made to cancel.

"From upstairs in the arena we could see water just pouring down Autumn Street," recalled Ken Arnold, the team's director of media relations at the time. "If it had come any further it would have gone right down the ramp and into the building where all the equipment, electrical wires, and cables were."

Two blocks northwest sits Henry's Hi-Life, a two-story tavern and steak house in a rustic red, turn-of-the-century building. It's a local favorite for fans and players. To this day, there's a mark on the door to represent how high the water rose on the historic structure.

"I remember our trainer, Tommy Woodcock, going to Henry's to stack sand bags," Sharks radio voice Dan Rusanowsky said. "That was his favorite spot, he didn't want it to go away."

The event coincidentally marked the second failed attempt for the Wings and Sharks to renew acquaintances in San Jose following the Sharks' epic upset of Detroit in the '94 postseason. San Jose was also supposed to host Detroit on October 7, 1994, but the owners' lockout caused that cancellation.

"I remember walking over the Guadalupe River last year and thinking, *This thing flooded?*" said Bob Errey, a television commentator working for the Pittsburgh Penguins.

Errey had a lot going on back then. He had been dealt by San Jose to Detroit just 12 days earlier. As team captain, Errey was a key contributor during the Sharks' Cinderella season of 1993–94 when San Jose improved an NHL record 58 points and eliminated the Wings. Errey was dispatched after only 13 games once the NHL labor strife ended for merely a fifth-round draft pick.

And after scoring a goal, four points, and posting a plus-3 in four games during the first week with his new team, Errey was eagerly anticipating the Friday match-up against his former team. The game wouldn't happen until April 5 when the Red Wings beat the Sharks 5–3.

"I remember when it was rescheduled I did pretty good in that game," reminded Errey, who scored two goals, added an assist and was a plus-3. "The referee, Rob Shick, told me he never saw me play a better game. It was the only time I would tell somebody I deserved the first star, but I didn't get any that night."

For the record, Errey was selected as the No. 1 star—that's how it appears on the official game sheet—but his name was not among the three selections announced in the arena afterward. A sensitive front-office exec executed his veto power.

And thanks to a project completed by the U.S. Army Corps of Engineers to ensure 100 years of flood protection, the Sharks have not—and should not again—experience any similar events of March 10, 1995.

"What a crazy night that was," Rusanowsky said.

35 The Chomp

What first-year fans of the Sharks lacked in hockey sophistication they made up for with creativity.

Taking a cue from team employees, "The Chomp" was born. And it took only until San Jose's second power play ever at the Cow Palace for the fans to remove their training wheels and start a tradition that continues to this day.

The Chomp, for the uneducated, is the practice of Sharks fans extending their arms—one at approximate shoulder height and the other starting just below the hip—and bringing them together, apart, together, apart, over and over—as if to mimic shark jaws as the home team prepares to go on a power play. Accompanying *Jaws* music sets the mood in the arena and adds to the theatrics.

"If you have any concentration whatsoever you're not watching what's going on in the stands, but after a while you couldn't happen but notice," said first-year Sharks forward Kelly Kisio.

The Chomp originated on October. 5, 1991, when the Sharks made their home debut against Vancouver, the same Canucks team that beat San Jose 24 hours earlier on Canadian soil in the expansion team's first-ever game. The first of 40 capacity crowds at the Cow Palace that first season were ready to shower their support.

When it came to hockey etiquette, however, they just needed a nudge.

Long before employees could enjoy the comforts of a suite or secluded press facilities, Sharks staff sat in a portion of the stands in one corner high above the ice at the rustic old building. Basically situated with the crowd, staff members noticed a lack of energy and anticipation as the Sharks were about to embark on their first power play. Several employees motioned a scaled-down version of The Chomp, looking at each other with smiles on their faces.

Well, they got noticed.

And like "The Wave" can grow from humble beginnings to wind itself around and around to create a remarkable visual, The Chomp took off in a similar manner. The crowd needed no prompting the second time a Canuck headed to the penalty box.

"Our power play at the time had no beef to it," Kisio joked. "So for them to do that, it was a whole lot of fun."

First-year assistant coach Drew Remenda, who later gained much popularity as a longtime analyst, often sat high in the stands to provide the coaching staff with an eye-in-the-sky. Remenda, too, couldn't help but notice fans around him doing The Chomp.

"By the second power play I thought, *Look at that*," Remenda recalled.

Sensing an opportunity to promote and even grow the original cheer, the Sharks issued a light-weight, triangle-toothed, jaws-like contraption that fans could incorporate into The Chomp at a select number of games. Again, the visual was unique to the Sharks and the Bay Area specifically, and the game of hockey in general.

"We even published something tongue-in-cheek in the team magazine—'How To Do The Chomp,'" said Matt Levine, the team's original business manager.

It turns out The Chomp wasn't exclusive to Sharks fans. Remenda recalls how a visit by St. Louis offered a sarcastic display of the cheer.

Blues tough guy Kelly Chase was assessed a game-misconduct penalty and was ejected from a 1993-94 game at the new arena in San Jose after fighting Sharks defenseman Doug Zmolek. Chase, the pride of Porcupine Plain, Saskatchewan, played to the booing fans by mimicking The Chomp all the way off the ice.

"It was hilarious," Remenda said.

36 A 13–1 Loss at Calgary

If there was one game that epitomized the Sharks' excruciatingly miserable second season, it came February 10, 1993, inside Calgary's Saddledome when the Flames beat San Jose, 13–1.

"It was one of those games that everything that could go wrong went wrong," said Jeff Odgers, looking back with a chuckle.

In 1992–93, the Sharks won only 11 times out of 84 tries, went 3–38–1 on the road, and allowed 414 goals. A total of 42 different skaters and four goalies went through a revolving-door roster. Things were bad. And they were about to get worse.

"It was a really bad team," Ray Whitney said, looking back more than two decades. "There wasn't much we could do about anything because we weren't very competitive at all."

The Sharks opened a three-game trip in Calgary knowing three more losses would equate to a new league record—18 defeats in a row to eclipse the 17 set by the expansion Washington Capitals of 1974–75.

And, really, this Wednesday night contest couldn't have gotten off to a better start. Jeff Odgers fed Kelly Kisio, whose shot from the left boards rebounded off of Flames goalie Jeff Reese to Johan Garpenlov. He punched home a power-play goal for a 1–0 lead just 2:51 after the opening faceoff.

So much for good beginnings.

Flames defenseman Gary Suter, who years later would be a Shark, beat a screened Arturs Irbe with a slap shot at 12:26 to tie it. And 17 seconds later Calgary scored again with Suter providing an assist. Two more Flames goals followed before the first intermission, and it was 4–1.

"Back then the Sharks were limited in what they could do, and Calgary had a pretty good and established team," Suter said.

The Sharks outshot the Flames 17–11 in the middle period, but Calgary scored the only three goals against Jeff Hackett, who relieved Irbe at the start of the period.

"I always had a bunch of people coming to the games in Calgary," said Odgers, a native of Spy Hill, Saskatchewan. "You have all these people in the stands who know you and it's 'Oh, my gawd.' You were hoping for a power outage or something."

There was no power outage from the Flames, who set an NHL record by scoring three times in the first 53 seconds of the third period to lead 10–1.

"There was one goal, Neil Wilkinson had lost his stick," Kisio said recalling the misfortunes of the San Jose defenseman. "He was standing in front of the net and went to kick it. He missed the puck—you know, like Charlie Brown missing the football—his feet went up, he landed on his butt, and they stuffed the puck into the net."

"And Wilkie threw his back out," Odgers added.

"This is how it went for us that night," Kisio said.

Irbe re-entered after Hackett surrendered six goals on 15 shots, and watched as Robert Reichel and Ron Stern—another future Shark—completed hat tricks on Calgary's next two goals. Finally, a Brian Skrudland tally at 16:00 ended the Sharks' misery.

"I think the only other game that compared was a game in Pittsburgh," Odgers recalled. "We were down 10–0 at the end of the second. And we ended up losing 10–2. So we outscored them in the third period."

Reichel led the way with six points, Suter followed with two goals and three assists. All three of Stern's points came on goals. Theoren Fleury, with a goal and five assists, set an NHL record as a plus-9. Reese set a league record for most points and assists (3) in a game for a goalie. Conversely, every Shark except for forward Perry Berezan logged a minus, led by defenseman Doug Wilson's minus-7.

Berezan was forced out in the first period from what turned out to be the last of his 378-game NHL career. He tore his MCL during a neutral-ice collision with Stern. Berezan laughs now, saying the injury was the only reason that kept him out of the "minus" column, but it was serious stuff at the time.

"I'm laying down in the trainers' room at intermission and I hear, 'Kid!'" Berezan recalls. Legendary Calgary broadcaster Ed Whalen peered in to check on Berezan, a player he remembered fondly when Berezan previously played for the Flames. "He asked how I was doing and I said, 'I can't do this anymore, I'm done, I'm packing it in. I can't play this game anymore.'"

An incredible night it was.

"After a game like that, put it behind you and move on," Odgers said. "When things go that bad where are you going to start?"

"Just throw it away and forget it," added Kisio, who for years has joked with fellow Calgary resident Berezan about the game.

Fortunately for the Sharks, after a 6–0 loss in Edmonton two nights later, they avoided setting the NHL record for consecutive losses as San Jose managed a 3–2 victory at Winnipeg on Valentine's Day.

Most Lopsided Losses

Date	Opponent	Score
2/10/93	At Calgary	13–1
12/5/95	At Colorado	12–2
2/15/92	At Detroit	11–1
11/8/92	Los Angeles	11–4
12/17/91	At Pittsburgh	10–2
1/6/94	Detroit	10–3
11/28/92	At Minnesota	10–3
1/8/92	At Calgary	10–3
10/26/91	At New Jersey	9–0
11/10/95	Pittsburgh	9–1
1/21/92	At Edmonton	9–2
12/5/91	Pittsburgh	8–0
12/30/06	At Phoenix	8–0
3/19/93	At N.Y. Rangers	8–1
12/18/92	At Vancouver	8–1

37 Probert-Gaetz Fight

It's simply remembered as the biggest fight in Sharks history.

People who attended the game played at the Cow Palace on November 14, 1991, still talk about it today. It was brutal. It was primal. It hurt to watch. And everyone knew it was coming.

Link Gaetz was a 23-year-old rookie looking to establish himself as the league's toughest fighter. Detroit was visiting, and on the Red Wings' roster was Bob Probert. At 26, and already with six years in the league, the late Probert was the NHL's reputed, if not mythical, heavyweight champion.

They would have to have a go.

And go they did.

At the 16:01 mark of the opening period, the gloves came off right in front of the San Jose bench.

"Holy you-know-what," recalled Drew Remenda, an assistant coach during the Sharks' inaugural season. "When you watch it on video again, you see (goalie) Jeff Hackett on the bench and he's laughing his ass off. He's got the biggest smile on his face."

The bout was no laughing matter to the combatants.

Gaetz went on the offensive at the outset, throwing a dozen rapid-fire rights that didn't stop until Probert pushed his opponent against the boards. Strong and quick, Gaetz grabbed and held onto Probert's left arm with his right and started throwing lefts as the two moved away from the boards.

A Probert right popped Gaetz's helmet up and off. But Gaetz managed to pull Probert's red jersey, and flimsy excuse for shoulder pads, right over Probert's arms. The two held on while keeping their balance despite turning a few circles on the ice. The linesmen got close, but still kept their distance.

Detroit color commentator Mickey Redmond, a former Red Wing, had a noticeable tone of concern in his voice as he described the bout.

"These two boys can hurt if they happen to hit," he told viewers.

Red Wings play-by-play man Dave Strader chimed in with, "You see a little extra determination on Probert's face that you don't always see."

"No you don't," Redmond concurred.

That's when the linesmen broke the two apart, a good 40 seconds after it started, which in a hockey fight is an eternity.

Gaetz, without his gloves and helmet yet his home white jersey still intact, skated toward the exit and disappeared toward the Sharks' locker room. Probert, down to a gray undershirt drenched in sweat and holding his jersey and pads, did likewise, but labored with a deliberate stroll to the visitors' room.

"Boy, that's the toughest fight I've seen Probert have in a long, long time," Strader told viewers.

Gaetz earned 13 other fighting majors during his 48 games in 1991–92. He squared off with other tough opponents—Gino Odjick twice, Mike Peluso, Kelly Buckberger, Randy McKay, Mike Hartman, and Troy Loney to mention a few. But it was the Probert fight that is remembered.

"That fight definitely sticks out because I don't know how many punches were thrown, but it feels like it went on forever," recalled Perry Berezan, a Sharks forward who watched from the bench.

After the game—fittingly a tie, which coincided with how the fight was objectively scored—Remenda met up with Detroit assistant coach Dave Lewis, a longtime friend who also hailed from Saskatchewan.

"First thing Dave says to me is, 'Geez, that Gaetz is a helluva tough kid,' Remenda recalled. "And I went, 'Yeah, he is.'"

38 Dan Rusanowsky

While growing up in Milford, Connecticut, a young Dan Rusanowsky used to fine tune the A.M. dial on a radio in his bedroom to pick up any hockey broadcast he might find on a given night. He wouldn't give up until he found one. Sometimes, however, the broadcast would be in French. Rusanowsky didn't speak the language, but he knew it was a hockey game. And that's all that mattered.

"He was born to be on the radio calling hockey games," Jamie Baker said.

Rusanowsky is the only play-by-play announcer Sharks fans have known. From the first game in franchise history back in October of 1991 through more than 25 years later, The Voice of the Sharks remains dedicated to his craft and as passionate about what he does as ever.

"It's a script that I'd written a long time ago," Rusanowsky said.

Rusanowsky was hooked the day he walked into Madison Square Garden in the early 1970s to watch the Rangers host the Pittsburgh Penguins. Not only fascinated by the speed of the game he viewed in person for the first time, Rusanowsky was taken by the presentation, the entertaining intermissions, the atmosphere, and the ambience associated with a live NHL game.

"Back then, the Rangers were on a station I needed to turn the rabbit ears around properly to get," he said.

Rusanowsky knew what he wanted from the start, but also realized the path to his goal might be a long and winding one. Making education a priority, Rusanowsky earned a bachelor's degree at St. Lawrence University, a private liberal arts institution located in upstate New York. He got his first practical experience as voice of the school's Division I hockey program from 1979–86.

"There were 21 teams in the NHL before the Sharks; there were a number in Canada so you take a few of them off," Rusanowsky figured, "and there was 250 million people in the United States—my odds weren't very good."

He cut his broadcasting teeth on the professional level by calling games for the New Haven Nighthawks of the American Hockey League, where Rusanowsky knew it was important to learn all aspects of the business.

Then, in 1991, Rusanowsky got his big break with the Sharks and he's never looked back.

"Dan is Mr. Loyal," said Randy Hahn, the team's longtime television voice. "He is 100 percent, all in, passionately loyal about the Sharks."

"If you love your job, it's not a job," Baker added. "This isn't a job to Dan; it's a passion."

The connection Baker and Rusanowsky share is unique. When Baker embarked on his four-year hockey career at St. Lawrence, Rusanowsky was winding up his broadcasting career at the school. Little did anyone know at the time the two would be partners in the San Jose radio booth many years later following Baker's 10-year NHL career that included two stints with the Sharks.

"He made it organic from Day 1," said Baker, who broke in on radio in 2005. "He told me I was going to make mistakes, but be yourself and don't force it. The one thing you learn from him is his preparation. He's so meticulous."

Rusanowsky keeps detailed records, tracking every player on a nightly basis while with the team and even when one departs and plays for someone else. Rusanowsky jokes he'll use the material to write his book the day the Sharks win the Stanley Cup.

"What people might not know is how tirelessly he worked to put the radio network together, allowing the Sharks to be heard outside of the marketplace and how that built a base when radio was almost terrestrial," Hahn said.

Rusanowsky's dedicated work was recognized in 2013 with his induction into Bay Area Radio Hall of Fame. For him, it's simple. Rusanowsky just always wanted to call hockey on the radio.

"It's a dream of a lifetime," he said. "The fact I can do something I love to do is very special and it's just a privilege to be in the NHL as a broadcaster.

"Also, the fact I've been with this team since it started. The equity is a very important piece of my career, and that I could do it with this team for so long is very special."

Ruzzie's Favorite Calls

With more than a quarter century of Sharks broadcasts to draw upon, radio voice Dan Rusanowsky has these favorite memories and calls:

- Patrick Marleau's OT winner at Joe Louis Arena to give the Sharks a 3–0 series lead over the Red Wings during a 2010 West semifinal that San Jose won in five.

- Broadcasting three conference finals (2004, 2010, 2011).

- The wild 2011 first-round playoff series against the Kings, which included San Jose rallying from a 4–0 deficit to win Game 3 in overtime 6–5, and Joe Thornton's series-clinching goal in sudden death of Game 6.

Rusanowsky has what he terms a favorite novelty memory stemming from a series of events when the Sharks beat Anaheim 3–2 in a shootout on April 4, 2007.

San Jose's Ron Wilson was honored the week before for coaching his 1,000th game, and an autographed hockey stick by Teemu Selanne was among the gifts the memorabilia-collecting Wilson received. Even though Selanne was now a Duck, he wanted to show appreciation since Wilson had been his coach with two teams.

Fast forward to Selanne's Ducks playing the host Sharks eight nights later when San Jose was called for a late-regulation minor penalty in a tie game. Wilson asked for a stick measurement, and sure enough Selanne was in possession of an illegal width. Wilson had an inkling because he'd found the autographed stick to be illegal.

Selanne wore a sheepish grin while feeling shame in the penalty box. And after a scoreless OT, he failed to get his shot on goal in the shootout.

"He's not my favorite coach anymore," Selanne joked afterward.

39 The Three-Headed Monster

After original general manager Jack Ferreira resigned following the team's inaugural season—read fired—the Sharks opted for a unique front-office set-up. Director of hockey operations Dean Lombardi, scouting director Chuck Grillo, and head coach George Kingston "shared" the office of G.M. in 1992–93.

Or, as more commonly referred, they formed San Jose's "three-headed monster."

"The Sharks were on the cutting edge back then," said Brian Lawton, who following his playing career served as a G.M. in the league. "They weren't afraid to try things. I think the only reason it blew up was because they were three really different guys."

Three very large egos might be more like it.

"That three-headed monster didn't appear to be on the same playbook," ex-Shark Perry Berezan said. "I felt bad for the long-term kids like Pat Falloon. I was just trying to cling on to my career. They could have said anything to me and it wouldn't have mattered. But you need one voice as a player, or a collective voice that is saying the same things and supporting each other."

A former player agent with a degree in labor law, Lombardi was in his fifth year in the NHL. His strengths included negotiating contracts, understanding the collective-bargaining agreement and evaluating talent. Lombardi was deeply passionate and driven, two characteristics that would carry him years later to multiple Stanley Cups with the Los Angeles Kings.

Grillo, 19 years Lombardi's senior, thrived in the area of scouting and innovative player development. He brought years of experience in both fields to the Sharks from his time with the Minnesota North Stars and New York Rangers. Grillo ran his own resort-style hockey camp in northern Minnesota, a venture he started with the late Herb Brooks, a close friend.

Kingston brought more than 30 years of hockey experience to San Jose, 20 of those years spent as coach at the University of Calgary. He was a patient, well-spoken, positive leader who rarely drifted down the road of criticism despite roster shortcomings.

"The coaching staff did a masterful job of trying to insulate most of us," Berezan said. "But if you had meetings with the general managers, which I never did, then they would come back to practice and hear a different message from the coaches. They just messed them up."

The three heads became two when Kingston was fired after the Sharks went 11–71–2 in Year 2. The team was preparing to move into their new downtown San Jose arena for 1993–94, and they wanted to shed as much of their losing image after two years spent at the Cow Palace.

The Lombardi–Grillo combo appeared to be working when San Jose not only reached the Stanley Cup playoffs, but beat division champions in the opening rounds of '94 and '95. But cracks were obvious early in 1995–96, and not long after Lombardi and Grillo received new, five-year contracts.

Grillo was pushing for more of the franchise's recent draftees to make the roster while Lombardi scrambled to find a balance between youth and experience. He struck a series of early-season trades to try and settle a team struggling with a new identity that managed to win only three of their first 25 games.

By late season, the decision was made that the office of G.M. was big enough for only one person, and that would be Lombardi. Grillo was fired as the franchise went through a front-office overhaul that also included Greg Jamison replacing team president Art Savage following an early-season coaching change.

"Like any business, I think the buck needs to stop at one person," Ray Whitney said. "They realized there can only be one chief here, we can't have two chiefs.

"For the most part they brought in the right people at the start because we made the playoffs," he added. "It worked temporarily. But ultimately, and in the end, it eventually had to be just one."

40 The Red-Haired Fist

Kevin Constantine probably knew he was in for an unpredictable ride the day he first interviewed with the Sharks.

Constantine bumped into George Gund in the elevator on his way to meeting team executives to talk about the head coach opening. The unassuming team owner was wearing a Sharks letterman's jacket and hard-to-ignore skimpy shorts that fit a bit too snug, according to Constantine.

"I remember saying, 'Hi George, hey, you didn't have to dress up for my interview'" Constantine recalled. "And he said back, 'Ahhh' in a way you had to ask him twice because he talked in a mumbling style, 'Well, I'll go back and put my suit on for you.'" At this point Constantine replied, "No, you own the team, you can come to an interview any way you want.

"That was my introduction to George," he said.

Constantine got the job. The 34-year-old was promoted from San Jose's minor-league affiliate after the talent-challenged Sharks won only 28 of 164 games in their first two seasons with George Kingston as their bench boss.

Under Constantine's direction, the Sharks orchestrated an NHL-record 58-point turnaround in Year 3. They not only qualified for the playoffs for the first time, they beat No. 1 seed Detroit, then took Toronto to seven games in the second round.

The city threw Constantine's Sharks a parade.

Kevin Constantine's tenure behind the Sharks' bench was short but never dull. He guided San Jose to its first two postseason appearances only to lose his job early in Year 3 after a 3–18–4 start.

His team reached the playoffs again in the lockout-shortened 1994–95 campaign, and again played the role of David by slaying a Goliath masked as the Pacific Division champs Calgary Flames.

Given a three-year contract extension to start 1995–96, Constantine was gone two days into December after the team won only three of its first 25 games.

Talk about a wild ride.

Along the way, Constantine came off as bright, energetic, prepared, cocky, confident, witty, stubborn and engaging. Those who got to know him—and those he let on the inside—could see what made him successful, likeable and endearing. One San Francisco columnist dubbed him the Red-Haired Fist, a moniker that didn't offend Constantine, and stuck throughout his tenure.

"He had a plan, that's one thing about Kevin, he was prepared," said Jeff Odgers, the Sharks' second team captain. "He wasn't going to waver, he kept believing in himself, and he believed what he brought would work."

Constantine will never forget his first meeting with the team in 1993. He prepared and rehearsed a speech he delivered at the outset of training camp. He knew he had an important message to deliver in an effort to wipe away the memory of losing, and start to establish a belief that anything was possible.

"I gave that speech and I was very nervous just getting through it," Constantine recalled. "I remember when we beat Detroit, Jamie Baker was quoted in the postgame as saying, 'Back when Coach told us we were here to make the playoffs and win the Stanley Cup, there was a bunch of us sitting in the back of the room laughing. We were just hoping to not be an embarrassment. That would have been progress.'"

When they returned from losing Game 7 in the second round to Toronto, Constantine was strongly opposed to plans for the city to throw the Sharks a parade.

"The part that seemed right was to say thank you to the fans. They were a big part of the fact we were a tough team to play against in our own building," he said. "It felt completely wrong in terms of culture and tradition in hockey unless you win it all. I was totally against it."

The fact Constantine could change the culture in San Jose wasn't a surprise to Baker, who signed as a free agent in San Jose after playing for an expansion Ottawa team that won only 10 of 84 games in 1992–93.

"Near the end of training camp I talked to my dad and said, 'Something's up here, and I like it,'" Baker recalled. "I liked the attention to detail from the coaching staff. I liked the way practices were being run. After the year they had, we had no expectations."

Constantine was often treading upstream, caught in the middle of a front-office struggle to rush its drafted talent into the lineup while balancing the youth movement with an ever-changing cast of veterans.

All the while, Constantine rarely lost his sense of humor. He'd sit at the table prepped for postgame press conferences, giving thoughtful answers to the questions he was asked. He had a habit of pinching the plastic bottle of water provided and watching the level rise but not overflow. Every once in a while he'd take a small swig.

Unbeknownst to Constantine, his water bottle had been tampered with by a playful member of the media—some water was replaced with whiskey. Constantine went through his bottle-pinching routine, took a swig, and didn't bat an eye. The anxious group of beat writers, all in on the gag, initially felt let down.

Then, as the press conference ended and Constantine prepared to exit, he stopped, turned back and said, "Next time make it stronger."

41 Love Affair with Euros

It didn't take long for the San Jose Sharks to gain a reputation at the draft.

With innovative and aggressive player personnel director Chuck Grillo calling the shots, the Sharks penetrated Eastern bloc nations looking for untapped talent, and weren't detoured from selecting players others feared wouldn't play in the NHL.

"In terms of technology and video, it wasn't what you can do nowadays," said Joe Will, scouting coordinator early on and assistant G.M. later. "You're literally talking about getting into Communist countries. You couldn't watch or stream games or get statistics. You couldn't cross borders."

Grillo & Co. used everything within their means to reach intended targets, whether it was drawing on the contacts of worldly team owner George Gund or tapping into hockey insiders Konstantin Krylov in Russia and Karel Masopust in the Czech Republic and Slovakia. A staff of nine scouts in 1991–92—typical of NHL teams—grew to an astonishing 16 the following two seasons.

"Chuck went over and beat the bushes in Europe," said Drew Remenda, an assistant coach from 1991–95. "This is where he thought he could make the difference."

Eight years a scout with the Rangers followed by two as director of scouting with the North Stars, Grillo was determined to go where he knew players with high-end skill were being trained. And, as the political climate changed with end of the cold war, Grillo figured it was a race to secure the previously unmined talent.

"I think other teams went to the same tournaments, saw players, and didn't know how they could get them out," Will said.

"Occasionally there were hidden players. The difference was we had the willingness to do it."

The Sharks selected four European skaters among their 13 picks in 1991, and made a statement with the 30th overall pick by choosing 18-year-old defenseman Sandis Ozolinsh, a native of Riga, Latvia, who was playing for Dynamo Riga. A dynamic offensive threat on the blue line, Ozolinsh spent the first four seasons of a 15-year career in San Jose. He scored 564 points in 875 career games.

"When you look at it, you can't argue with Sandis Ozolinsh; he became a heck of a hockey player," Remenda said.

In 1992 the Sharks tabbed seven Euros out of 11 picks—highlighted by the surprising pick of Andrei Nazarov at No. 10 overall—but Grillo took his biggest swing in 1993. Holding the second overall pick, the Sharks traded with Hartford to pick up three selections and veteran forward Sergei Makarov. The Whalers selected Chris Pronger and San Jose took Russian forward Viktor Kozlov at No. 6, the highest of the three choices acquired from the Whalers.

"Chuck believed in the Europeans to the point we traded away the chance to draft Chris Pronger," Remenda said. "We got Sergei Makarov—short-term gain for long-term pain."

The Sharks then picked Czech defenseman Vlastimil Kroupa (45th) and Finnish forward Ville Peltonen (58th) with the other two picks from Hartford. In all, nine of San Jose's 13 picks in the '93 draft were Euros.

"Chuck just knew there were players other teams weren't going to take, or weren't going out of their way to see," Will said. "We considered them freebies. The parallel is baseball going into Cuba, the Dominican and Venezuela. And it's the same value that baseball saw."

Some gambles such as Evgeni Nabokov (9th round, '94) and Miikka Kiprusoff (5th round, '95) paid off handsomely while others—Teemu Riihijarvi (12th overall, '95) and Angel Nikolov (2nd round, '94)—were busts. The Sharks took five Finns in '95, including a pair who sounded like their names were turned inside out—Marko Makinen and Mikko Markkanen.

The European trend continued for two more drafts—a total of 16 Euros out of 24 players chosen by the Sharks in '94 and '95—before Grillo was fired in March of 1996.

All told, 59 percent (36 of 61) of all players drafted by San Jose from 1991–95 were Euros. That figure dropped to 24 percent Euros taken (12 of 51) during the seven drafts with Dean Lombardi as G.M., and 21 percent (21 of 99) during the first 13 drafts conducted with Doug Wilson in charge.

"These days there are no boundaries, and with the Internet there isn't anything you can't get, but back then it was pretty tough," Will said.

42 Gaudreau's Hat Trick

Rob Gaudreau described it as an out-of-body experience. He was on the bench, after having scored his third goal of the game in just his second NHL contest, when assistant coach Drew Remenda told him that was the franchise's first hat trick.

"I think I kissed him on the cheek," Gaudreau said. "I do remember that."

Gaudreau reflected back on the night of December 3, 1992, when the Sharks were playing their 106th game in club history, and a 23-year-old rookie right wing was just hoping to make an impression. A reputed scorer during four years at Providence College, Gaudreau was claimed by San Jose during the dispersal draft, served a short time in the minors and was getting his shot with the second-year expansion team.

Gaudreau was scoreless in his debut two nights earlier, but was excited to be on a line with veteran center Kelly Kisio and skilled Swedish left wing Johan Garpenlov.

"I had two very good linemates and the ability to feed off of them was great," Gaudreau recalled.

His first NHL goal came on a slap shot from the top of the faceoff circle to cap a 2-on-1 after Garpenlov fed him with a pass. Gaudreau's patented strong shot beat Hartford goalie Sean Burke to thrill a sold-out Cow Palace crowd.

"At that point, thought of as an offensive guy, I was looking forward to getting on the score sheet because you never know how long you're going to be there," Gaudreau said. "To score the first goal was amazing. I remember it, but I guess I was somewhat numb."

His second of the game came following a pass from Kisio when Gaudreau waited out Burke. And on No. 3, Gaudreau knew he was working against a backskating Whalers forward, slipped the puck through his legs and beat Burke with another slap shot.

"I got the puck, and I still have the picture where I'm wearing a hat and it's hanging on the wall," said Gaudreau, the president of a family real estate management company in his native Rhode Island. "People here on the East Coast bring it up once in a while, which is really cool. It was certainly a heck of a highlight to my hockey career."

If that happened today, Gaudreau's big night would have traveled everywhere in real time. But without cellular technology, computers or the Internet, it wasn't easy to even view a Sharks game for interested out-of-towners.

"My parents had to go down to the local bar in Providence that had one of those humongous satellite dishes and watch the game until 1:00 AM," Gaudreau recalled.

Afterward, Gaudreau returned to the Hyatt Hotel in South San Francisco where so many of the younger Sharks stayed since they didn't know how long they might be up with the big club, went to his room and placed one call.

"I think my call was, 'Did you see that?'" Gaudreau said. "It would be interesting to see how my phone would have lit up now, but it was a much simpler time then."

The funny thing is, Gaudreau wasn't done. Four games later, when the Sharks hosted Quebec during a Saturday matinee, he scored three goals again. This time it came against Nordiques goalie Ron Hextall. Like the 7–4 loss to Hartford, this was another wild loss, 8–7, when a familiar name—Mike Ricci—scored one goal and added five assists to lead Quebec.

"I had always been a streaky scorer," said Gaudreau, who finished the season with 23 goals and 43 points in 59 games. "(Coach) George Kingston let us play pretty open, which I have to give him credit for because we didn't have a lot of talent.

"I remember calling back to my college buddies after the game. Obviously it was just a great way to get everything going. Wins were hard to come by, but I just wanted to stay there and I was very excited to be there."

43 "We're on the Verge of Something"

The Sharks opened their third season winless in their first nine games. Their roster experienced a thorough makeover from a disastrous 11–71–2 showing in 1992–93. The franchise had hoped to leave their losing behind when they vacated the Cow Palace.

Kevin Constantine, who had been promoted from the minors where he had won a title, replaced the fired George Kingston as San Jose's new head coach. Where the 34-year-old may have been short on pro playing experience, Constantine made up for it with his brash and confident style of leadership.

So, instead of hitting the early season panic button, Constantine delivered an interesting line when asked by inquisitive beat writers what he expected from his team going forward.

"We're on the verge of something," Constantine started. "What? I'm not exactly sure. But I know we're on the verge of something."

Russian great Igor Larionov missed all but San Jose's 1–1 tie against Boston of the first nine games. He returned from injury, scored a goal, and the Sharks finally won—3–1 against visiting Edmonton in Game 10. It didn't happen overnight, but San Jose steadily climbed the ladder, getting to within two games of .500 by season's end at 33–35–16, and clinched a first-ever playoff spot.

So how did Constantine know better days were ahead when he uttered his catchy phrase after just nine games?

"There's kind of a funny story behind that," Constantine admitted more than two decades later.

Constantine had a similar experience the year before while coaching San Jose's top minor-league affiliate—the Kansas City Blades of the International Hockey League. And he learned from it, if not through a little potty humor along the way.

"We were not only losing, but losing after having leads in third periods and when leading at home in the third," Constantine said of the team's November slump. "So this was kind of the first real coaching challenge that I'd ever faced after being really, really successful at lower levels."

During the second intermission of a game at home his team led by a goal, an anxious Constantine turned to assistant coach Jim Wiley and said he needed to deliver just the right message to his team before they took the ice for the final period. He sensed this one was slipping away, too.

So Constantine first went into the bathroom to organize his thoughts.

"I was so nervous when I looked down I had actually lined myself up with the sink, not the urinal," admitted Constantine, whose next concern was whether any players in the adjoining room noticed his faux pas. "I kind of looked, and no one was watching, so I bounced over to the urinal because embarrassment was taking over."

Constantine delivered his speech, but the Blades proceeded to blow their lead and lost for an eighth straight time.

"My funny finish to that story is if I don't know where to take a leak, how can I tell the players where to be on the ice?" Constantine said.

He and the Blades figured it out from there, went 35–7–6 the rest of the way, and did not stop winning until the Western Conference Finals against San Diego.

"If I hadn't gone through that eight-game losing streak the year before, I don't think I would have been able to say we might have some good things ahead," Constantine said. "My memory was fresh enough to see the patterns and believe that there was something that was coming."

44 The "Russian" Five

They were five players with plenty to offer who simply didn't mesh with any other linemates. And they weren't particularly keen on the structured system their rookie head coach was preaching.

So when Russian forwards Igor Larionov, Sergei Makarov, and Swede Johan Garpenlov were joined by the defensive pairing of American veteran Jeff Norton and second-year Latvian standout Sandis Ozolinsh, no one quite knew what to expect.

"I know certain players on certain teams get leeway, but I'm not sure it's ever happened where there's that distinct a system and one group plays one way while the rest of the team plays another," Jeff Odgers said.

"They were different players," Jamie Baker added. "You saw it in practice, they just did different things."

With Larionov quarterbacking the unit from his center-ice position, the group zigged and zagged, held the puck and regrouped if zone entry appeared foreboding. They passed, and passed, and passed some more. They passed to the point where one wondered if any shot was good enough.

The group redefined patience.

Yet when they found their chemistry, they were nearly unstoppable.

"The smart thing would be just allow that thing to happen and, at the end of the year, take credit for putting them together," joked Kevin Constantine, the Sharks' head coach who does deserve much credit.

"It's a credit to Kevin," Odgers added. "He was very strict in the way he wanted to play. It must have taken everything he had to back off of those guys."

"To Kevin's credit he was smart enough to realize, 'I'm not going to win this. I'll worry about the other 15 guys in the lineup and I'm going to let the other five guys do what the hell they want and see where it goes,'" Rob Gaudreau added.

Year 3 was almost like a fresh start for the organization. Two years spent at the Cow Palace—and the fresh memory of winning only 28 out of 164 hockey games over two seasons—had to be wiped away with new personnel, new coaches, and a new downtown San Jose arena.

With a character-laden roster assembled, it was Constantine's job to make the pieces fit. Ozolinsh was the only homegrown talent of the five. He was drafted in the second round (30th overall) in 1991, and at 21 was coming off of 37 games played in 1992–93.

Offensively gifted with size to boot, Ozolinsh possessed star qualities rarely found on the blue line. He was paired with Norton, 28, a slick skater who came via trade from the Islanders where he spent the first six years of his NHL career.

Up front, it was a no-brainer to reunite ex-Soviet standouts Larionov, 33, and Makarov, 35. Larionov was plucked from the waiver wire at the outset of the season three months after Makarov came in a risky trade with Hartford that included four high draft picks getting moved. Garpenlov, 25, showed offensive potential during nearly the first 200 games of an NHL career that started in Detroit and moved to San Jose following a deadline deal in 1992.

"Both those guys were incredibly, positively stubborn about playing the game they wanted and knew how to play," Constantine said of Larionov and Makarov. "It was silly after awhile to resist."

The fact, too, the Norton-Ozolinsh pair would accompany Larionov's line for virtually the entire shift to make it a group of five was unique by NHL standards if not the norm in the ex-Soviet system.

"It was a bit unusual to have a group of five, it still is," Constantine said. "Detroit did it later on again. (Coach) Scotty Bowman did it with even more Russians."

It turned into such a success that come playoff time Canada's legendary hockey voice Don Cherry nicknamed the San Jose coach "Constantinov."

"Igor, in his broken English, he'd always say, 'Coach, the best defense is offense yours,'" Constantine recalled. "The translation is if we have the puck on offense we don't have to play defense. So just let us have the puck.

"It broke a lot of rules. Even in today's NHL with the high, high skill level, the idea is still get it over the red line, put it behind the opposition's defense, play below their goal line and generate your offense," he added. "The idea of going to the offensive blue line, not liking what you have, and going back to try it again made no sense to North American hockey."

Not that numbers told the story of the consistent threat and artistic beauty they brought to the ice, just the same they were impressive.

- Makarov led the team in goals (30) and points (68) and was a plus-11 in 80 games;
- Larionov scored 18 goals, dished 38 assists for 56 points in 60 games, and was a plus-20;
- Garpenlov produced a similar 18 goals and 53 points as a plus-9 in 80 games, a vast improvement from the minus-26 he was in 1992–93;
- Norton was steady with seven goals, 33 assists for 40 points and a plus-16 in 64 games;
- Ozolinsh had a breakout season with 26 goals—two shy of Al MacInnis' league-high 28—and 64 points in 81 games. His plus-16 was topped only during his 15-year career with a plus-17 in 1999–2000 with Colorado.

"We got spoiled. I'd tell people they could charge to watch practice," recalled assistant coach Wayne Thomas. "Even though Kevin let the group go, he still had Igor to be the midfielder to protect Sandis and Norty when they were heading out and up the ice. It was a brilliant strategy."

"There's no two prouder guys who I ever played with in the National Hockey League than Igor and Sergei," Odgers added. "They believed hockey should be played one way, and that's how they were going to play."

The "Russian" Five carried the Sharks from an 0–8–1 start to an eighth-place finish in the West to secure the franchise's first postseason berth. Then, behind Makarov's six goals, the Sharks upset top-seed Detroit in an epic, seven-game, first-round playoff series before succumbing in seven games to Toronto in the second round.

"It was hard for other teams to defend because we were so predictable and then to throw those guys out every third shift and it was such a change of pace," Thomas said. "They made it look easy, but they came to work every day. That work ethic rubbed off on others. They didn't have to agree with Kevin, but they worked for him."

And, in turn, it worked for everybody.

Versions of "The Russian Five"

- **Soviet National Team:** Forwards Sergei Makarov, Igor Larionov, Vladimir Krutov plus defensemen Viacheslav Fetisov and Alexei Kasatonov formed the original and most accomplished unit that dominated national and international hockey during the 1980s;

- **Sharks Russian Five:** Forwards Johan Garpenlov, Larionov, Makarov joined by Jeff Norton and Sandis Ozolinsh was the makeshift five-man unit assembled by coach Kevin Constantine(ov) that took the NHL by storm in 1993-95;

- **Red Wings' Red Army:** At the suggestion of Larionov, Detroit coach Scotty Bowman employed five skaters including forwards Vyacheslav Kozlov, Sergei Fedorov, Larionov plus defensemen Vladimir Konstantinov and Fetisov in the mid-90s that were instrumental in the Wings winning the 1997 Stanley Cup.

---

45 Those Loyal Fans

The Cow Palace. Section 109. Maybe that's where it all started.

The Sharks have enjoyed some of the best local fan support in the league throughout their existence. The enthusiasm was there from the start, and grew despite the team managing only 28 wins their first two seasons. It rarely wavered when playoff disappointments and high expectations were not met. And it remains loyal and strong, standing the test of time in a region that failed to sustain NHL expansion in 1967–68.

It was in one corner of the team's original building the passion is traced.

"A group of people were sitting up in Section 109, very active, sometimes over the top, and their language left something to be desired," said Matt Levine, San Jose's initial marketing expert. "They became something fans were happy to have in the building, just as long as maybe they weren't sitting there."

Instead of trying to tone the group down, Levine figured they should be rewarded. Told to be in their seats early for an upcoming game, Levine presented fans in the section with personalized Sharks jerseys and brought head coach George Kingston to them for a pregame chat that emphasized how much the team appreciated Section 109's boisterous support.

"The fans went crazy," Levine recalled. "You don't usually see that kind of connection between fans and a team in that sort of way. That was definitely a sign of the relationship we had with the fans, and how much we thought of them."

Early-franchise sales of merchandise became a global phenomenon as fan support extended well beyond the boundaries of the Bay Area. That caught one first-year Shark completely off guard.

"I remember our first training camp, we were out in northern Quebec for—God only knows where—a couple exhibition games," recalls Kelly Kisio, a veteran forward at the time. "And there's people in the stands wearing these teal shirts, jerseys, and hats. I was thinking this was unbelievable, the phenomenon this was across the country. It was pretty special and a lot of fun."

Fans packed the Cow Palace at 10,888 strong for each and every one of the team's 40 home dates during their inaugural campaign of 1991–92, a season that was interupted late due to a 10-day players' strike and finished by mid-April with rescheduled games. Nonetheless, Sharks fans were there to the bitter end.

"We lost to Pittsburgh in December 8–0—Mario [Lemieux] got like seven points—and the fans gave us a standing ovation," Drew Remenda recalled. "I said to George [Kingston] after the game, 'Well that's something.' He said, 'How long do you think that will last if we keep playing like this?'"

The sellout streak extended a dozen games into the Sharks' second and final season at the Cow Palace to reach 52 games before getting snapped. The franchise rebounded from winning only 11 of 84 games in 1992–93 to christen their new downtown digs in San Jose with a first-ever playoff appearance by the end of 1993–94.

The fans were so drawn to the team the city threw the Sharks a parade at season's end despite losing in the second round of the Stanley Cup playoffs. And it didn't matter to players the fans were still learning the game.

"I always got a kick out of a power play, maybe there was a broken play in the neutral zone so we'd take it back, re-group and maybe start up the ice again," retired Sharks forward Rob Gaudreau recalled. "A couple times we would do that and they would be screaming, 'Go the other way, the other way!'"

When it came to support, Sharks fans rarely turned away. The Sharks played to 99 percent or more capacity in all but six of their first 24 seasons. There was a sellout streak of 205 regular-season and postseason games from 2009 through 2014. And the building has been filled to the brim with towel-waving supporters for every home playoff game in the team's history.

"They were there every night," Gaudreau recalled. "It certainly helped when you were tired, beat up, lethargic and then show up in front of those fans because you didn't want to let them down and the boost of energy is tremendous."

46 Long Road Trips

No doubt living and playing hockey in Northern California has its perks. The travel involved to play out a typical NHL schedule is not one of them.

The Sharks annually rank among the top five in terms of miles traveled during a regular season, and they've found themselves on top of that list a number of times. San Jose logged a league-record 57,612 miles in 2013–14, were given a reprieve with the fifth-most miles the next season, then shot back to No. 1 in 2015–16 with 50,362.

"Talk to players who came from East Coast teams and they'll tell you they can't believe the difference," said Scott Emmert, a longtime member of the team's public relations department with plenty of travel experience.

There's not a lot the league can do when it comes to producing a balanced travel schedule with a team located as far away as the Sharks. Typically Dallas and Edmonton have faced similar challenges, but not to San Jose's extent over its first 25 years.

Through 2015–16, the Sharks endured 40 road trips of at least six games in length. San Jose had trips of six games or more in all but two of its first 24 seasons. During that time, the Sharks have had 12 seven-gamers, four eight-game trips, two with nine stops, and one in 1998–99 that lasted 10 games, which represents the longest uninterrupted road trip in NHL history.

"At the end of long trips you find yourself walking into the hotel elevator and having no idea what floor you're on, what room you're in, and sometimes what city it is," Emmert said. "I've had players text me, 'I can't remember my room.'"

As much as you'd think the players cringe when they see the season's schedule, you might be surprised.

"You can't do anything about the schedule so you just make the best of it," Gary Suter said. "We enjoyed being on the road together. That's a time where it's just the players. You live, breathe, and eat hockey.

"You play a game, and go out for a beer afterward if there's time," he added. "It's a real close bonding thing."

Not surprisingly, the Sharks struggled to win on the road early in their franchise history. They logged nine straight sub-.500 campaigns before finally winning more road games than they lost in 2000–01. And that started a run of winning records on the road for all but two of the next 15 seasons. So, in theory, the team learned how to deal with long trips and have success.

"I actually loved them; I thought it was a tremendous bonding experience," Bryan Marchment said.

The Sharks fly with a charter company that features a reconfigured 737 jet plane with first-class seating and extra leg room throughout. A familiar flight crew provides a quality meal service. And the team flies from business centers as opposed to crowded airports—no security lines and rarely a delay.

"Now, with the charter and food catering, I don't know if there's as much wear and tear on your bodies as there used to be," said Marchment, who before San Jose played in Edmonton when the Oilers were the last team to ditch commercial flights in favor of the modern mode of pro athletes' travel. "My first real chartering experience was when I came here, and I fell in love with it."

Marchment was a member of the 1998–99 Sharks who, on February 3, embarked on that NHL-record long 10-game, 18-night trip. Stops included Phoenix, Los Angeles, back to Phoenix, Chicago, St. Louis, Tampa Bay, Florida, Detroit, Buffalo, and Washington. In the midst of a playoff push, the Sharks managed to win four straight—Games 3 through 6—lost five, and tied one. San Jose eventually finished seventh to qualify for the playoffs.

With the team gone for nearly three weeks, equipment manager Mike Aldrich started his preparations months in advance. Aldrich packed enough supplies—sticks, tape, medical supplies, etc.—for the first 10 days, then had a second shipment greet him when the team reached Florida for the second half of the trip.

"There's no way you could pack everything for 10 games," Aldrich said.

Vincent Damphousse played in San Jose for the final five full seasons of an 18-year career that, except for 1991–92 in Edmonton, was spent in the Eastern time zone. He enjoyed watching games played in the east before suiting up on the same night out west.

One thing he didn't enjoy was a curfew at the nearby San Jose airport which prevented the team's charter from landing after 11:00 PM—even short hops from Southern California. Instead, a return flight landed in Oakland, where the team boarded a bus and took the near one-hour drive to the South Bay. Players typically didn't get into their own beds until 2:00 or 3:00 in the morning.

"Hockey players are not like a machine; we need our rest, too," Damphousse said. "For us to land in Oakland and have to take a bus to the airport, that takes a toll. I don't remember any other city that had that."

Between the number of extended trips traversing two countries, and the inconvenience of the local curfew, the Sharks face the same challenge annually.

"You're going through three time zones usually, and when we returned I felt completely exhausted the next day. And I don't even play any games," Emmert said. "I can only imagine how the players felt."

47 Magic of Iggy & Mak

Deep into the 1993–94 season, and frustrated with the first 40 minutes of a game, Sharks coach Kevin Constantine told assistant Wayne Thomas to give the team a pep talk during the second intermission.

Thomas emphasized the importance of everyone playing the system and working as a group when he noticed Sergei Makarov stand up and walk his way. Thomas had a fleeting thought he was actually getting through to the superbly talented yet standoffish Russian star.

Instead, Makarov walked right into an adjoining room and turned on the whirlpool so the water would be warm by the end of the third period.

"Mak never said two words the two years when I was around," Thomas recalled. "Professionalism, though, was not a question."

Quiet around everyone, Makarov let his play speak volumes. He was thrilled to reunite with fellow countryman Igor Larionov in San Jose thanks to a series of moves orchestrated by Sharks' management that allowed the former Soviet stars to put their rekindled magic on display for the NHL to see.

"I learned a lot from everyone I played with, but are you kidding me?" team captain Bob Errey recalled. "They'd be out there just toying with other teams. It was ridiculous. That was something special, and you just can't recreate that."

The Sharks acquired the 35-year-old Makarov as part of a trade that would be questioned throughout the history of the franchise. San Jose packaged the second overall pick in 1993 to Hartford in return for the sixth overall pick, a second, a third and Makarov. The Whalers selected Chris Pronger, the franchise defenseman the Sharks have never had, while San Jose chose Viktor Kozlov, Vlastimil Kroupa, and Ville Peltonen with their acquired picks.

San Jose plucked Larionov from the waiver wire three months later, confident with Makarov that it could lure the 31-year-old back to the NHL after having spent a season in the Swiss League when things went south following three years with the Vancouver Canucks.

And the Sharks were right.

"It was special," Thomas said. "Give management credit for getting them back together. It was a little bit of a flashback, but it was happening in the NHL."

With the more outgoing and vibrant Larionov at center, and the stately Makarov manning right wing, the two worked their magic as the third-year franchise's best two offensive threats. Larionov scored 18 goals and added 38 assists as injuries and illness limited him to 60 games. Makarov was excellent, scoring 30 goals and 68 points in 80 games. They were a dynamic duo that fans, media, coaches and even teammates couldn't help watching every time they stepped on the ice.

"The chemistry they had was off the charts," Jamie Baker recalled. "When Igor got injured, I centered for Mak a few games. I didn't like it because I couldn't pass like Igor and he would get mad at me all the time. Mak would give me those looks. 'Jamie, on my tape.' 'Hey, I know I'm not as good as Iggy.'"

Larionov was the engine that fueled the offense. His precision and skill, his patience, his on-ice smarts were unmatched by anything Sharks fans had seen before. Larionov and Makarov implemented the old Russian style into their game to confound opponents and redefine puck possession before the analytics even charted such numbers.

"I guess it reminds me of the Sedins now," Errey said of longtime Canuck twins Daniel and Henrik. "But no one has that kind of chemistry and patience anymore. Everyone wants to move the puck north. Those guys could draw back, go side to side and hold on to the puck. If a play wasn't there they could re-trace their steps. They were in no rush to get where they wanted to get to."

They were also steadfast in doing it their way. Rob Gaudreau recalls countless meetings for personnel on the power play, and how Constantine implored Larionov to accept breakout passes on his forehand when defenseman Jeff Norton was behind the San Jose net. Larionov insisted he circle in his zone the opposite direction, and take Norton's feed on his backhand.

"I remember Kevin ripping into Igor, 'Let's do it my way, I don't care, do it my way, go to your forehand,'" Gaudreau recalled. "Kevin gets up after screaming and yelling for five minutes and, as soon as the door shuts, Igor looks at Jeff Norton and says, 'I will be going to my backhand. I will not be going to my forehand.'"

While Larionov was outspoken, Makarov was 180 degrees opposite.

"Sergei never said anything in the locker room," Constantine started. "Nor did he say anything in a more casual setting when you'd bump into him on the ice, getting a drink on the boards or walking through the parking lot to your car.

"Larionov was more than willing to debate. He enjoyed a good debate."

Constantine remembered one time, and only once, when Makarov was forced to open up. The coach scheduled 30-minute one-on-ones with each player. The idea was to get to know each other in a more relaxed setting. Any topic was up for discussion.

"When Makarov came in I asked him one question, he talked, and kind of told me a bit of his life story," Constantine recalled. "He talked, and he talked and he talked. I was soaking it in like a sponge, still young enough to be fascinated with his story.

"And I'll never forget, kind of mid-paragraph, he stopped and asked, 'Coach, how long were these meetings?' I said 30 minutes. He looked at his watch, 'Oh, it's been 30 minutes and he just cut the story off, got up and walked out in the middle of another fascinating tale."

Iggy & Mak stats

Career statistics for Igor Larionov and Sergei Makarov:

Before San Jose

Player	Team	GP	G	A	Pts.	PIM	+/-
Igor Larionov	Van	210	51	92	143	88	-1
Sergei Makarov	Cgy	297	94	198	292	199	62

With San Jose

Player	GP	G	A	Pts.	PIM	+/-
Igor Larionov	97	23	59	82	54	11
Sergei Makarov	123	40	52	92	118	7

After San Jose

Player	Teams	GP	G	A	Pts.	PIM	+/-
Igor Larionov	Det, Fla, NJ	614	95	324	419	332	94
Sergei Makarov	Dal	4	0	0	0	0	-2

48 Record Third-Year Turnaround

After winning only 11 of 84 games during their second season of 1992–93, the Sharks knew it could only get better. A league-record 58-point improvement—from 24 to 82 points in the standings—certainly exceeded expectations in San Jose, especially after the team failed to win even once out of their first nine games in '93–94.

"When we started 0–8–1," Jamie Baker started, "I thought, *Oh, geez, are we going down this road again?*"

One of five offseason veteran free-agent signings, Baker played for an expansion Senators team that managed one less win than the Sharks that previous season. But these Sharks were bound to win over their fans while moving into a new downtown San Jose arena after having spent their first two years at the Cow Palace.

Rookie coach Kevin Constantine assumed a roster that included 20 players who had not played with San Jose the previous season. Six came via trade before the season, and two more via deals in-season. Four recent draft picks—defensemen Mike Rathje, Michal Sykora, and Vlastimil Kroupa, and power forward Andrei Nazarov—were promoted. And two players, headlined by legendary Russian Igor Larionov, were claimed off waivers.

With all the new faces, and an injured Larionov unable to play at full strength until the ninth game, the Sharks had to dig out of a serious early-season hole.

"Kevin, at the time, was young and wasn't going to leave anything to chance," said Rob Gaudreau, who debuted the previous season but also knew Constantine during time in the minors. "He was telling you what you were going to do right down to what time you were going to have lunch. That was fine for some, but a wake-up call for others because it was out of the norm."

As the Sharks continued to work and improve under Constantine's defensive system, the wins and points started to come, usually in the form of 2–1 or 3–2 victories or low-scoring ties. By early December the Sharks nearly reached .500—11–13–5—then lost six straight and were winless in nine to slip back to 11–20–7.

Despite the pre-holiday slump, there was reason for optimism.

"I think around Christmastime, we were playing some better teams and we were giving them better games," Odgers said. "What was being preached in the system was working.

"And a lot of it, too, teams refused to take us seriously. They didn't believe we were for real. They kept thinking we were going to fall apart and that would be it."

With only one winning month, who could blame them? That would change, however, during a stretch of six nights in mid-February.

"The defining moment when the season turned was the three-game series against Chicago. And we won all three games," Baker said.

Consecutive 4–3 victories were followed by a dramatic 1–0 win thanks to a late third-period goal from defenseman Sandis Ozolinsh to cap the sweep of the NHL's rare baseball-like schedule.

"When we won that third game in dramatic fashion—and they were a good team—that's when in the room we had full buy-in," Baker said. "Igor's line was playing their style. Todd Elik's line was playing their style. My line was playing our style. The identity of the team came through then."

"We just kept building and building and building," Odgers added.

Confidence grew, the offense came to life, the defense remained stingy and the Sharks methodically earned points in all but nine of their final 30 games to finish third in the Pacific Division. And more importantly, they finished eighth in the West to secure a first-ever playoff berth.

"We got on a roll there in the middle and it carried on and on," Gaudreau said. "Kevin got a ton of credit because even though we got off to a slow start he stayed the course."

Constantine finished second to New Jersey's Jacques Lemaire for coach of the year honors. Irbe set an NHL record for most minutes played during the season (4,412) and Sergei Makarov became the club's first 30-goal scorer after getting reunited with fellow Russian star Larionov.

"We had good people," Odgers started, "we had good personalities, and we had guys who cared."

49 Baker Shocks Detroit

He scored the biggest goal in Sharks history, but that's not what Jamie Baker remembers most about his heroics in a Game 7 at Detroit.

"We're excited, obviously, we just scored," Baker starts. "Everybody comes in, and Bob Errey, he was the captain—and this is experience, he's won a Stanley Cup. He looks up at the clock and says, 'Boys? We've got a lot of work to do.'

"I remember that more than the actual play."

The actual play is one Sharks fans will never forget. Baker scored the tie-breaking goal at 13:25 of the third period, and San Jose beat Detroit 3–2 at Joe Louis Arena on April 30, 1994.

The Sharks, only in their third year of existence, were making their playoff debut after improving 58 points in the standings, an NHL record turnaround from one season to the next. Rookie coach Kevin Constantine managed to pull a diverse yet character-laden group together after an 0–8–1 start.

The Red Wings, champions of the Central Division and best in the West with exactly 100 points, were accustomed to lopsided wins. Detroit led the NHL with 356 regular-season goals, 50 more than the next closest team. The Sharks snuck into the playoffs with a 33–35–16 record, the only one of 16 qualifiers with a sub-.500 record. San Jose's 252 goals in the regular season were fewest among playoff teams.

"Every game we went into saying, 'Let's keep it close,'" Baker recalled. "They were blowing teams out all year. We had been in playoff mode since Game 10. If it was tied or a one-goal game entering the third period, we were in our comfort zone."

That was the idea going into the final period of Game 7 in a series the Sharks had three one-goal wins and the Red Wings had three multi-goal victories including the one-sided 7–1 final in Game 6 two nights earlier.

"I remember the dressing room was about 100 degrees when we got there," recalled Bob Errey, the team's captain. "(Detroit coach) Scotty (Bowman) must have turned the heat up in our room. Guys were dressing in the hallways. The game before was a blowout, but as long as you don't lose in overtime it's not that big a deal."

"Everybody kept waiting for the wheels to fall off," added Jeff Odgers, a tough winger on the team. "We had a couple of bad games in that series like, 'Ah, well, here it is. They're done. Finished.' But it was a resilient group."

The sequence that led to Baker's fateful goal started with a Detroit turnover in the neutral zone.

"As soon as the puck was turned over, Todd Elik came off and I jumped over the boards," Baker said. "Whits and Bibs (Errey) were already on the ice."

Whitney picked up the loose puck and dumped it into the left corner, jumped around Detroit defenseman Nicklas Lidstrom to pursue while Errey streaked to the opposite goal post. Red Wings goalie Chris Osgood left his crease to beat Whitney, and blindly backhanded the puck up the near boards.

"Ozzie is the one who gets the most criticism, but there's a turnover at the blue line, Whits jumps by two of their D, so Whits is forcing. Ozzie sees Whits coming to get the puck. Bibsy takes away the behind-the-net play by going to the far post. Ozzie has one play only, and it's to throw it up the boards," Baker said.

Baker had been on the ice for no more than five seconds when the puck came right to him, set up neatly on a tee.

"This is like the hockey Gods were with us," Baker recalled. "It came off the glass flat, which almost never happens because it's usually rolling or spinning."

Baker was also aware backchecking Red Wings forward Vyacheslav Kozlov was closing in fast.

"I didn't take a full swing because I didn't want him to hook my stick," Baker said. "It's a bang-bang play—I knew Bibsy was over there, somebody was behind me and the puck landed flat. I used the heel of my stick, and the rest is history, right?

Sharks history, indeed.

And maybe a little karma, too.

"The first goal of Game 1, I'm battling in front of the net," Baker recalls. "Shawn Cronin shoots and I feel it hit my stick. The only person who would have known was me, and I didn't say anything. To me it didn't matter because we scored.

"So Game 7, the karma came back quickly."

Errey was closest to the puck before it entered the net. He recalls having his foot in the blue paint area of the crease, a no-no in those days.

"Osgood was out of the net so no one really paid attention to it, but I think I had my right foot in the crease and the goal shouldn't have counted," Errey said with a laugh.

It counted, there was more than six minutes to go, and no one figured the proud Red Wings would go without a fight.

"I remember going, 'Holy Shit, we're up 3–2 in Game 7,'" Whitney remembered. "From there on, I think our line was playing against (Sergei) Fedorov's line and we're like, 'Oh, boy, we're going to face an onslaught here. Can we do it?'"

San Jose did indeed hold on thanks to a determined goalie from Latvia some had suggested was too small to excel in the NHL.

"Arturs was just solid back there," Whitney said. "We weren't trying to get the fourth goal, we were clinging to what we had.

"What a great feeling for the organization, just a great goal by Jamie."

50 Discovering "John" Nabokov

On June 29, 1994, Evgeni Nabokov's name was announced on the floor of the Hartford Civic Center as the ninth-round selection by the San Jose Sharks. Half a world away, the 18-year-old Russian goaltender didn't have a clue.

"Someone brought the newspaper to me and said, 'Hey, by the way, you got drafted,'" Nabokov recalled. "I thought, *Wow. Cool.*"

As the story goes, the Sharks drafted Nabokov sight unseen, going off reports and a recommendation that he played for a good team in Russia—and because his father was a longtime professional goalie. That story just might even be true.

Nabokov doesn't remember being approached by the Sharks prior to the draft. Longtime employee Wayne Thomas thought maybe someone from the organization saw Nabokov play as a midget (under 18). And Nabokov recalls at that time playing a series of games in Lake Placid, New York, and Sudbury, Ontario, for a CCCP team. But again, he didn't have contact with any NHL teams. And his inability to speak any English would certainly have been a roadblock.

Recommendation to draft Nabokov came from Konstantine Krylov, a native of St. Petersburg, Russia, who joined the Sharks scouting staff in 1992. Previously a freelance hockey journalist, Krylov owned one of Russia's most comprehensive collections of NHL statistics and publications. Nabokov recalls talking to Krylov.

"I think he was a scout," Nabokov said. "But back in '94 no one really knew what a scout was, and what he was doing there, especially in Russia."

The draft had little impact on Nabokov, who was solely focused on moving from his hometown squad in Ust-Kamenogorsk to Russia's marquee team Dynamo.

"That would tell people he was pretty good if he's going to the team in Moscow," Thomas said of Nabokov, who made that jump at age 19 and led Dynamo to two championships in the next three seasons.

That's when San Jose figured it was time to get serious about its 219th pick a couple years earlier. The late John Ferguson Sr. and Thomas traveled to Turku, Finland, for the European championships to watch Nabokov first-hand.

"He had a good tournament, and we tried to grab some tape on him," Thomas said. "We thought it was worthwhile."

Nabokov had a tough decision to make—venture across the large pond to a land of unknown or stay in Mother Russia where things were going very well. He received help from Anna Goruveyn, an assistant from the office of high-powered agent Don Meehan. Goruveyn's specialty was assisting Meehan's growing stable of Russian clients, and she was good at it.

Ultimately, Nabokov decided it was time. Despite not knowing a word of English, Nabokov took a flight to the States and headed to the Minnesota Hockey Camps where he'd meet up with Goruveyn and goaltending guru Warren Strelow. There was just one problem. When Nabokov landed, he didn't have a stitch of goalie gear with him.

Set up with brand-new equipment he and Strelow picked off the shelf of a store, Nabokov hit the smaller Northern American ice surface and was drilled.

"I was nervous about wearing the gear, and I was kind of upset," Nabokov said. "Even the skates weren't sharpened that well. I didn't want to make a bad impression."

Apparently, he didn't.

"He never missed a beat," Thomas said. "His athleticism was incredible."

"I found out from Warren later they were actually impressed, and liked what they saw," Nabokov agreed.

After Nabokov swapped the gear for a custom-fit in San Jose, he headed to Kentucky of the American Hockey League to embark on the start of a pro career that hardly went the way he expected. Nabokov, 22, found himself playing behind Jamie Ram, a 24-year-old netminder who the Sharks signed as a free agent just before the season.

"I expected to get sent down," Nabokov said. "I understood I needed to learn to play in the NHL. But I was expecting a good chance to play in the minors."

Instead, Nabokov often drew the starts on second nights of back-to-backs, or the dreaded third game in three days. His 10–21–2, 3.92 goals-against average, and .872 save percentage had Nabokov thinking about forgoing the second year of his contract and returning to Russia.

Enter Goruveyn, who would make a better save than Nabokov ever did in Kentucky.

"My numbers were terrible; I didn't enjoy it and I didn't want to have another bad season," Nabokov said. "Anna said, 'Don't you want to stay here and prove you can do it?'"

Nabokov had also met his future wife, Tabitha Eckler, and she, too, was instrumental in talking him through the decision.

His second season was only marginally better. Now Nabokov found himself splitting the net 50–50 with Sean Gauthier, another older free-agent goalie signed by San Jose. Only in the playoffs— and at the end of his contract—did Nabokov separate himself and show the Sharks what they wanted to see.

Two months spent in Cleveland the following season with San Jose's relocated top affiliate now in the IHL solidified Nabokov's standing. Living in the same city for the first time, Strelow and Nabokov drove to practice, ate meals afterward, and basically forged a close bond that remained until Strelow passed in 2007.

"He and Warren developed that relationship and trust, and the rest is history," Thomas said.

"They said they wanted me to be the guy," Nabokov said when awarded one more minor-league deal. "That was what I was looking for because I wasn't sure what they were thinking."

What's in a Name?

His name is Yevgeni Viktorovich Nabokov.

In America, it's Evgeni Nabokov.

His name is not John Nabokov, regardless of what appeared in print for several years in the San Jose Sharks media guide.

How did it start? One version goes that Dean Lombardi—general manager at the time of Nabokov's draft in 1994—struggled to pronounce Evgeni, so the young goalie said, "Just call me John." We'll go with that.

To this day, Lombardi still calls him John. Even Wayne Thomas, the ex-goalie and 22-season Sharks employee who forged a very close working relationship with Nabokov, will slip into the habit of calling him John.

From the day he was drafted, and for four more years, Nabokov's name was listed as "Yevgeni" in the team's media guide. It was changed to John Nabokov in the 1997–98 version.

Once, in the Sharks locker room shortly after Nabokov started to establish himself, a teammate suggested he correct the misidentification and strictly go by his given name. He agreed.

Finally, once and for all, his name was listed as Evgeni Nabokov in the team's 1999–2000 media guide.

51 Taking it Outdoors

Dubbed a celebration of hockey in Northern California, the Sharks and rival Los Angeles Kings took the game outdoors on February 21, 2015, at Levi's Stadium, the sparkling state-of-the-art football facility in nearby Santa Clara that had just completed hosting a first season for the San Francisco 49ers of the NFL.

With outdoor NHL games all the rage in recent seasons—starting with the popularity and uniqueness of an annual Winter Classic every New Year's Day since 2008—the Sharks queued up in hopes the warm California climate wouldn't scare league officials off.

The fact the Anaheim Ducks and Los Angeles Kings put on a successful show at Dodger Stadium the previous January influenced the NHL to return to the Golden State. Also, with the Sharks-Kings rivalry helping to raise the profile of pro hockey in California, it was the right place at the right time.

Game on.

The NHL's 22-wheel refrigeration truck departed Toronto, and took a southern route to reach Northern California 12 days before game day. With the makeshift rink filled with nearly 20,000 gallons of the drought-stricken region's recycled rainwater, NHL ice guru Dan Craig had a week to adjust to weather conditions.

For players and coaches, the experience brought childhood memories rushing to the forefront. Sharks coach Todd McLellan reminisced about his grade school days while growing up in the Canadian province of Saskatchewan.

"We went to school with our backpacks and our hockey sticks," he said. "Every school had an outdoor rink and lights, so we'd play every minute at recess, we'd play after school, we'd go home and eat, then come back....It was always like the best-of-43, so it never ended."

With the Kings-Sharks game set to face off at 7:00 PM, fans flocked in droves early to fill the parking lot with football-style tailgating traditions. They wore jerseys from every era of Sharks hockey—Pat Falloon to Owen Nolan to Joe Thornton.

Inside, the rink fit nicely inside the football stadium's configuration. Designs of mountains, vegetation, and bodies of water—including numerous shark fins for a special touch—dotted the landscape around the outside of the rink to reflect the topography of Northern California.

It was a balmy 57 degrees at game time under a cloudless sky. Barely a whisper of a breeze greeted the 70,205 in attendance—the largest crowd to witness a hockey game of any kind west of the Mississippi River, and the third largest gathering for an NHL game anywhere.

The Kings scored first as Kyle Clifford deflected a point shot past Sharks goalie Antti Niemi. The hosts struck late in the period when Brent Burns slipped a bad angle shot through Kings goalie Jonathan Quick. Tied 1–1 at the first intermission, the players couldn't help but notice the surroundings of the unique event.

"It feels like you're on an island out there because of all the space around the rink," Sharks defenseman Justin Braun said.

"It'd be lying if I said there weren't a couple times where guys were slow jumping on the ice because maybe their eyes were wandering, maybe their minds were wandering, but that's human," McLellan added.

The second period was scoreless, but when Marian Gaborik's shot at 4:04 of the third eluded Niemi's glove following a turnover by the hosts, the Kings had their margin of victory 2–1.

"This was our show. These were our fans. This is Sharks territory," McLellan said afterward. "They showed up in droves. I know there were Kings fans here, and there were just plain hockey fans. That's what made tonight so special. The fact we lost was disappointing, but to be part of it, I wouldn't trade it for anything."

"This was by far the coolest sporting event I've been a part of," Sharks winger Tommy Wingels added.

52 '94 Playoff Run

The octopus hit the ice at Joe Louis Arena as it always does in spring time, signaling the start of what Detroit fans hoped would be another long Red Wings run.

But when Sharks defenseman Jayson More uncharacteristically slammed his stick atop the eight-legged creature of the sea, it suggested maybe the visitors weren't intimidated and feeling as out-of-place as a No. 8 vs. No. 1 seed playoff match-up would otherwise suggest.

"I didn't think we could beat Detroit, but let's see what happens if we make the games close," Jamie Baker recalled. "The belief was there."

No, San Jose was not content just to reach the Stanley Cup playoffs for the first time in its three-year existence, this following a record 58-point turnaround during the 1993–94 regular season. And over the next 27 nights, the Sharks took their loyal fans and surprised national followers on a wildly unexpected ride.

"I remember I had so much adrenalin that I kept a notepad next to me at night to get ideas out of my head so I could sleep," recalled Kevin Constantine, a rookie NHL coach that season. "I was so excited that another idea would come—a line combination, this strategy, a comment to a player, what I'd say to the team—that I couldn't sleep. A thought would come: *I've got to write that down and now go to sleep, please.*"

The incredible playoff run of '94 started with San Jose's 5–4 win at Detroit on April 18. Five different players scored goals and 13 skaters collected a point as only Igor Larionov enjoyed a multi-point outing (goal and assist).

Detroit turned from Bob Essensa to Chris Osgood in goal for Game 2, and the Sharks were shut out 4-0. Osgood made 22 saves in Game 3 as Detroit took a 2–1 series lead when the scene shifted to San Jose. Because the series format was 2–3–2, the Sharks had two more chances at the Shark Tank to make it a series.

"What I remember most is skating out of the sharks head at our first home playoff game," Jeff Odgers recalled. "No one thought we were going to win a game in Detroit, and we came back 1–1. We skate through that and it was absolutely crazy."

The Sharks won the next two, 4–3 and 6–4, to take a 3–2 series lead back to Detroit. Sergei Makarov, who led the Sharks with six goals in the series, potted two in Game 5 and Larionov added three assists.

Detroit routed San Jose 7–1 in Game 6, chasing Sharks goalie Arturs Irbe in the process.

"It was really good we got our ass kicked in Game 6," Constantine said. "If you play Game 6 and barely lose, the mindset is, 'We were just a goal away, let's do the same thing, we'll get a break this time.'"

Johan Garpenlov and Makarov scored early and it was a 2–2 game going to the third when Jamie Baker capitalized on Osgood leaving the net and turning the puck over. San Jose advanced despite putting only 17 shots on goal.

"I remember we got that puck back to neutral ice with like 30 seconds left and you're saying, 'I think we got this,'" Constantine said. "It was a spectacular feeling."

Following the late afternoon win, the Sharks bussed to the airport and watched the conclusion of a Vancouver-Calgary late Game 7 to determine if the flight would head toward Calgary or Toronto. By the time the Canucks eliminated the Flames in double overtime, poor weather prevented the Sharks' charter from departing, so the team bedded down near the airport for the night.

Despite arriving later than expected, the Sharks shocked the Maple Leafs 3–2 in Game 1 on goals from Pat Falloon, Garpenlov and Larionov. Toronto evened the series with a 5-1 win in Game 2, but the Sharks took advantage of home ice by winning two of the next three for a 3–2 series edge.

San Jose's big chance came in overtime of Game 6, but a Garpenlov drive struck the crossbar and offensive-minded defenseman Sandis Ozolinsh passed up a shot from the slot during an odd-man break, passing to an unsuspecting Larionov in the corner.

"I'm like, 'Sometimes the Russians can pass the puck too much. Be selfish once in a while, God,'" Ray Whitney recalled.

Mike Gartner's goal at 8:53 of sudden death—the only over-time game the Sharks played that postseason—won it.

"When we lost Game 6 it was 'Ohhh, boy,'" Whitney said.

Leafs captain Wendel Clark scored two goals and assisted another as Toronto eliminated the Sharks 4–2 in Game 7 on May 14.

"We probably deserved a better fate in the series," Bob Errey recalled. "It was already the greatest turnaround in history. Can you imagine if we had won a Cup?"

"In the end, what happened in Toronto, was just fatigue ulti-mately took its toll," Baker added. "That's 14 games in 27 days and even though it's a 2–3–2 series, that's a lot of travel."

As crazy as it sounds, the city of San Jose threw the team a parade.

"It was one big Cinderella thing," Constantine started, "maybe not for Larionov and Makarov. But probably for Jamie Baker and myself, for the city and the fans."

53 Lombardi Studies for G.M.

When Dean Lombardi found himself no longer sharing the general manager's seat in San Jose, he hit the books. Lombardi sought out team builders—both in hockey and other sports—and interviewed them. He read books. He asked a lot of questions, basically immersing himself in learning how to best fulfill the G.M.'s role.

"He was relentless," said Wayne Thomas, an assistant to Lombardi for a portion of his 22 years in San Jose. "His personality is one that works, and he was trying to gain knowledge all the time. He craves it."

A member of the Sharks' initial front-office staff, Lombardi started as an assistant G.M., became director of hockey operations as part of a G.M. office shared by three in 1992–93, and then became sole possessor of the hot seat on March 6, 1996.

Lombardi said at the time of the front-office purge: "From now on, if there's anybody on this bus, it is because of Dean Lombardi. If a player is here, it's my call. We're going to do it like every other team where coaches coach and managers manage. We all know who's the target right now."

Lombardi was not only busy that offseason overseeing the draft, hiring a new head coach and pursuing veteran free agents to surround a group of promising San Jose prospects, he was going back to school.

He studied the New Jersey Devils, admiring the work of Lou Lamoriello. He studied how the Green Bay Packers were built by Pro Football Hall of Fame G.M. Ron Wolf. He studied the San Francisco 49ers dynasty and particularly the works of famed head coach Bill Walsh. And he talked to all of them.

"Dean really worked hard that summer," said Ken Arnold, director of media relations at the time. "Everything went back to what he learned."

"He not only read about all the builders of sports teams, but leaders that were political figures, too," Thomas added of Lombardi. "He never stopped trying to learn. He never stopped trying to push us in that direction, too, to create knowledge and to get better."

A native of Ludlow, Massachusetts—and a New Englander through and through—Lombardi served as captain during his junior and senior seasons on the University of New Haven hockey team in addition to graduating third in his class.

Lombardi later specialized in labor law while earning a law degree at Tulane University, and initially became a player's agent under the mentorship of Art Kaminsky, who boasted a stable of young American hockey players—many off of the 1980 Miracle on Ice gold medal winners.

Lombardi parlayed his knowledge of law and hockey into management. Coincidentally, his wife, Wandamae, is the foster daughter of Hall of Fame player Bob Pulford, who also coached and enjoyed a long career as an NHL G.M.

"Dean appreciated his Ludlow roots," Thomas started, "but, for instance, people from Saskatoon, who were perceived as knowing more about the game, he just wasn't going to let that happen. If he didn't have the knowledge, he was going to find it."

Lombardi had his vices early on. He was a tireless worker, to the point of obsessive habits. He was nearly a chain smoker for a time, extremely analytical, uneasy around the media if the cameras were rolling, but generous with his time and extremely engaging in small groups.

Lombardi could easily turn a five-minute meeting into a two-hour marathon, and no one went away feeling they'd wasted their time. Lombardi took the description of passion for the game and his craft to an entirely new level.

"He refused to let his guard down, he was always pursuing knowledge," Thomas said. "At times, even to a fault where he might have taken a little more time (off), that's something he's learned as time goes on."

What Lombardi learned—and put into practice during his seven years as the team's sole G.M.—was to have a plan and the steadfast belief to adhere to it. He believed will went just as far as skill in the game. He demanded loyalty, honesty, and a strong work ethic from everyone on staff all the way down to the stick boy.

"Honestly, we needed a shake up and to basically just be more professional," Arnold said. "He deserves a lot of credit from turning the franchise around."

54 A 5:00 PM Firing on 12/2/95

Kevin Constantine was fired as coach of the Sharks hours before a home game on December 2, 1995, just two months after signing a three-year contract extension.

This was the same coach who led the Cinderella Sharks to 11 postseason wins and first-round playoff upsets of division champions the previous two springs with rosters of less talent than San Jose's opponents.

The decision climaxed less than 24 hours after owner George Gund, president Art Savage plus front-office executives Dean Lombardi and Chuck Grillo attended the Sharks' lethargic 7–2 loss to Vancouver.

The move to relieve Constantine, a fan favorite in the midst of his first NHL coaching gig, came as the Sharks were 3–18–4, and it capped a week of public ridicule. Reporters were told at 5:00 PM, just two-and-a-half hours before San Jose was to host Washington.

"In training camp it felt different," recalled Jamie Baker, a key contributor during Constantine's tenure. "We just knew there was a push to bring in all these young guys all at once. Ultimately they were going to replace us. The dressing room didn't have the same chemistry."

"When they fired Kevin it was weird, but it hadn't been right all year and we knew it."

Ten players from the 1994–95 roster were gone by December. Lombardi swung four trades in the three weeks leading up to Constantine's dismissal. Recent Sharks draftees including Marcus Ragnarsson, Ville Peltonen, Jan Caloun, and Alexei Yegorov were on the team or about to debut.

What really happened was a front-office disconnect with the way Constantine was running the team, and the distraction that led the players to basically not work as hard under their red-headed coach as before.

"It's always awkward because as a player you feel some responsibility," Baker said.

Emotions boiled over during the week leading up to Lombardi replacing Constantine with Jim Wiley, coach of San Jose's minor-league affiliate in Kansas City. An in-depth analysis by *San Jose Mercury News* columnist Bud Geracie revealed the front-office dysfunction, basically putting the embarrassed organization in defense mode for the first time in franchise history.

Shortly after the paper hit newsstands throughout the South Bay, Lombardi invited Geracie for a car ride that lasted more than two hours in which the general manager blew off steam, shared information, and dug for whom the inside source was for the columnist's expose—which was never divulged.

Lombardi and Grillo, who was intimately involved in drafting and player development, had each received five-year contract extensions. The decision of Gund and Savage was obviously to back upper management, and swallow the three-year deal recently awarded to Constantine.

After having fired Constantine earlier in the day, Lombardi assembled the team in the locker room to talk to the players, who were largely still not sure what had happened. They knew Constantine was gone, and that's about it.

Lombardi entered the room, head down, and announced, "We had to let Kevin go, it was a tough decision. And Jimmy will do a great job."

With that, Lombardi departed.

Andrei Nazarov, a 21-year-old hulking Russian forward the Sharks made as a surprise 10th overall pick three years prior, stood up and walked over to veteran defenseman Jim Kyte. Nazarov extended his right hand, shook Kyte's and said, "Congratulations. I'll play hard for you."

Nazarov was obviously confused exactly which "Jimmy" that Lombardi had hired.

The Sharks under Wiley beat the Capitals 5–3 that Saturday night. Then, in their next game, they lost 12–2 at Colorado.

55 Super Mario

Clearly, no one was happier to see the San Jose Sharks join the National Hockey League than Mario Lemieux.

After the career carnage the Pittsburgh Penguins superstar inflicted upon the league's 22nd franchise, the nickname Super

Mario just wasn't enough. Then again, the names the Sharks probably called Lemieux aren't fit for print.

Theo Fleury, Scott Young, and Justin Williams feasted on San Jose throughout their careers, but no single opponent was more of a Shark killer than Lemieux. During only 14 career meetings, Lemieux scored 17 goals and assisted on another 32 for 49 points. He was a plus-18, landing in the minus category only two times. Lemieux collected points in every game against the Sharks, and enjoyed multi-point outings in 13 of 14 tries.

"Video game numbers," said Bob Errey, a teammate for the first nine of Lemieux's 17-year career.

Lemieux's first meeting with San Jose—a game at the Cow Palace on December 5, 1991—set the tone for his career-long torture of the men in teal. At age 26, Lemieux scored two goals and assisted on four others during an 8–0 shellacking against the expansion Sharks, who deployed three different sacrificial lambs, err, goalies in the game.

A brief play-by-play of Lemieux's night is in order.

- Lemieux takes a pass at his blue line along the right boards, cuts to the middle as he hits the Sharks' line, splits penalty-killing defenders Jayson More and Doug Wilson before beating goalie Jeff Hackett with a screened backhand shot from the edge of the left circle. 1–0 Pens after one period.
- Working the left point on the power play, Lemieux feeds Paul Coffey who beats Arturs Irbe, Hackett's injury replacement. 2–0 Pens.
- Lemieux's slap pass from the top of the left circle is tapped home by Kevin Stevens on the power play. 4–0 Pens.
- Lemieux chases Irbe with a rebound power-play goal. Enter third Sharks goalie Brian Hayward. 5–0 Pens.
- Lemieux wins offensive-zone draw and feeds Stevens for weak-side tap-in. 6–0 Pens after two periods.

• Pittsburgh converts a fifth power play, as from the left circle, Lemieux sets up Stevens' hat-trick goal with a pass to the slot. 8–0 Pens final.

"Gretzky was the same way," Errey said. "If you have the chance to put up the numbers and you want to get to 200 points, you've got to be ready to play in those games.

"But, still, it's not that easy to get six points!"

The teams met 12 nights later in Pittsburgh, and the Penguins led 10–0 after two periods. Lemieux scored two goals again, and added just one assist this time. Lemieux scored two goals in games five times against the Sharks, who could at least boast they were never victimized for a hat trick by him.

Lemieux faced the Sharks one last time during their inaugural season, scoring a goal and adding three assists during a 7–3 win. It should be noted Lemieux did not play in Calgary during the first stop of a three-game trip—a 6–3 loss by the Penguins—but joined his teammates at the Cow Palace three nights later. Mario wasn't going to miss this one.

Coincidentally, when Pittsburgh visited for the first time in 1992–93, Mario again was a no-show for the team's first stop out West in Los Angeles. But, sure enough, Lemieux was on a plane for a game two nights later when he produced one goal and—count 'em—six assists during a 9–4 victory over the Sharks. The seven-point outing would be Lemieux's best against San Jose.

Stevens was Lemieux's only linemate who didn't manage a point in the game, which came exactly one calendar year after Stevens' hat trick against the Sharks.

"All I can remember is big Kevin Stevens out there, almost crying looking at the score sheet because his linemates had like six points and five points and he didn't have anything," Errey said with a laugh.

After a five-point game (two goals, three assists) during a 7–2 Pittsburgh win in March of 1993—giving Lemieux 24 points in his first five against San Jose—Lemieux averaged just under three points a game over the final nine games against the Sharks.

And not until Lemieux's last of seven visits to the Bay Area did San Jose find a way to beat Pittsburgh with him in the lineup. The Sharks won 5–2 on December 12, 2002, despite the fact the 37-year-old Lemieux scored both Pens goals.

To the very end, Super Mario indeed.

56 Where to Go Before and After Games

It's only natural players miss certain things when their careers end.

What Owen Nolan misses might surprise you.

The Sharks' former captain, who has taken up permanent residency in the San Jose area, enjoyed seeing the sea of teal when he arrived for home games. Nolan would get a pregame adrenaline rush just watching fans arrive early to march in unison to the nearby restaurant district, a ritual often repeated postgame as well.

"It truly is one of the main things I miss being retired," Nolan admitted. "Seeing the mobs of people downtown, walking to the rink, and everyone's wearing Sharks jerseys."

So inspired, Nolan bought a piece of the downtown action by investing as a co-owner of Britannia Arms. One of his two pubs is conveniently located a short walk from the Shark Tank, and features a sports bar flavor whether you're talking the menu or the numerous big-screen HD televisions showing wall-to-wall sports programming. Outdoor seating is also available.

"I've been to a lot of rinks, you see fans with jerseys on, but not to the extent of Sharks fans," Nolan said. "It's hard to find someone who isn't wearing a Sharks jersey. You feel that pride, it's part of the experience."

One of the most popular gathering places is San Pedro Square Market in the heart of San Jose, and located near major highways 280, 17, 101, and 87. It can also be reached by light rail and public transportation. A number of pay lots dot the surrounding streets.

With more than a dozen food outlets and another half dozen bars, San Pedro provides a convenient gathering place for a casual start to the evening. Fans rave about the micro beers available at this destination. And you might luck out with some live music provided depending on the night of the week.

In addition, there are a number of sit-down restaurants in the neighborhood along Santa Clara Street to visit before and after Sharks games. The most popular spots, all located in downtown San Jose, include:

- Back A Yard (80 N. Market Street): Carribbean American grill is what to expect
- Bluefin Sushi and Japanese Restaurant (754 The Alameda): Full bar with a solid sushi selection
- Billy Berk's (99 S. 1ˢᵗ Street): Features American fare and a sports bar
- Gordon Biersch (33 E. San Fernando Street): German-style menu in a casual setting
- Farmers Union (151 W. Santa Clara Street): Boasts modern American cuisine
- Henry's World Famous Hi-Life (301 W. St. John Street): Enjoy BBQ and steak, and you might run into an ex-Shark or two
- La Victoria Taqueria (131 W. Santa Clara Street): The hot sauce has everyone talking

- Old Wagon Saloon & Grill (73 N. San Pedro Street): The name says it all
- Paesano Ristorante Italiano (350 W. Julian): Looking for Italian? This is it
- Peggy Sue's (183 Park Avenue): A retro 1950s style diner
- Poor House Bistro (91 S. Autumn Street): Features Cajun and Creole

"It's almost like a pilgrimage from downtown with all these people coming from the restaurants to walk to the Sharks game along Santa Clara Street," said Scott Emmert, a longtime member of the team's public relations staff. "It's pretty neat to see before and after games."

57 Sharks Open in Japan

When it was announced the Sharks were selected as one of two teams to open the 1998–99 NHL regular season in Japan, pretty much everyone was excited and honored. It marked the second straight year that two NHL teams played their first two games at Tokyo's Yoyogi arena as part of the league's enterprise known as GAME One.

The Vancouver Canucks and Mighty Ducks of Anaheim played the first two games outside of North America in Japan to open the previous season just as the sport was enjoying global popularity. And the series would whet the appetite of the Japanese preparing to host the Nagano Olympic Games that included the NHL's participation in the men's hockey tournament.

Marco Sturm greets a Far East hockey fan, who displays the winger's hockey card during the Sharks' season-opening two-game series in Japan in 1998.

Frank Nakano, the director of international marketing for the NHL, termed GAME One 1997 a resounding success. Commissioner Gary Bettman complimented the enthusiasm shown by the Japanese, and saw this as a continued opportunity to bring the game to more people throughout the lucrative Pacific Rim. Senior vice president of hockey operations for the NHL at the time, Brian Burke, said, "This was a great trip. Not a good trip, not an okay trip—a great trip."

So, yeah, everyone was excited about playing in Japan.

Everyone except the San Jose Sharks.

Like the Canucks and Mighty Ducks, the Sharks had an already challenging travel schedule. It's the plight of all West

Coast-based teams playing in a league where the majority of opponents are situated east of the Mississippi River. More travel means less time to recover, more wear and tear on the body, and less time to practice.

Seeing their new season would start abroad against Calgary didn't sit well with veteran center Bernie Nicholls, who was embarking on his third season with the Sharks and final campaign of an 18-year NHL career.

"It's (expletive) ridiculous," Nicholls blasted. "Two NHL teams playing in Japan, why are we going over there? It's not fair to the organizations. My question is why?

"I'm all for promoting the game by going to cities in the U.S. or Canada that are going to have a team. One day, are we going to have a team in Japan? I don't think so," he added. "I have no problem with the country or anything. We're not going over there sightseeing—we're going to work. I just don't understand why we're doing this."

Darryl Sutter was starting his second season behind the San Jose bench. He guided the resurgent Sharks to the Stanley Cup playoffs after a two-year hiatus the previous spring. Sutter was familiar with Japan, too, since he began his professional career as a player skating 20 games for the Iwakura Tomakomai as a 20-year-old in 1978–79. Just the same, he wasn't looking forward to revisiting his past.

"We logged the second-most miles in the league last season," he said. "So, I suppose what's another 5,000 miles?"

Not all of Sutter's public comments were appreciated by the league, who suggested to team owner George Gund III he tell his coach to keep his comments positive. That didn't stop Sutter from suggesting "off the record" that the Sharks and Flames should agree to a split beforehand because "no one will know otherwise."

The Sharks and Flames made the trip, indeed, yet Sutter didn't get his wish. One night after the teams battled to a 3–3 tie, Theoren

Fleury collected a hat trick and two assists to offset goals from Tony Granato, Patrick Marleau, and Bill Holder for a 5–3 Calgary victory, leaving the Sharks with a season-opening 0–1–1 record for all their travels and tribulation.

As was the case the year before, the games were played at a converted swim center that even featured the high-dive platform hovering over the makeshift rink. Unlike the previous year, the Sharks–Flames series failed to enjoy the level of corporate support hoped for—presumably due to the economic downturn.

Nicholls would be somewhat vindicated as the league traveled back to Japan only in 2000 when Pittsburgh and Nashville played two regular-season games. After that, the NHL concentrated its overseas efforts in Europe.

San Jose's original 1998–99 schedule had the Sharks returning home from Japan to play three nights later. Because the Sharks requested more time off, a revised schedule meant an eight-day break before the Sharks hosted the Boston Bruins, which indeed resulted in a 3–0 loss, and a game added later in the season. To complicate matters, San Jose headed back out for a three-game road trip that started in Philadelphia.

Their stumble from the gate extended to a 1–6–2 start before San Jose slowly turned things around. The Sharks battled uphill all season, finishing 31–33–18, yet still managed to slip into the play-offs as the West's No. 7 seed. San Jose was eliminated in six games in the first round by Colorado.

Neutral-Site Games
How the Sharks have fared in games in non-NHL venues:

Date	City	Opponent	Result
• 1/4/93	Sacramento	Montreal	L, 4–1
• 2/22/93	Sacramento	N.Y. Rangers	L, 4–0
• 10/21/93	Sacramento	St. Louis	L, 5–2
• 2/8/94	Sacramento	Chicago	W, 4–3
• 10/9/98	Tokyo	Calgary	T, 3–3
• 10/10/98	Tokyo	Calgary	L, 5–3
• 10/8/10	Stockholm	Columbus	W, 3–2
• 10/9/10	Stockholm	Columbus	L, 3–2 OT
• 2/21/15	Santa Clara	Los Angeles	L, 2–1

58 Make-a-Wish for Tageson

Sam Tageson just couldn't hold back any longer.

Dressed in hockey gear from head-to-toe, and wearing the uniform of his favorite team—the Sharks—Tageson stood alongside the team's bench moments before puck drop on a regular-season game between San Jose and the visiting Florida Panthers.

With thunderous applause raining down from 17,562 fans, Tageson glanced up to acknowledge the adoring sellout crowd when he caught a glimpse of his live image on the video board above center ice. He quickly wiped his eyes with the hockey glove on his left hand, recognized Sharks assistant coach Jay Woodcroft, and then it happened.

The tears came flooding down Tageson's face.

And they wouldn't stop. Tageson continued to wave to the crowd as he retreated down a narrow hall leading to the Sharks' dressing room before disappearing out of sight.

Out of nowhere, a teenager's realized dream provided one of the most emotional moments of any season in San Jose.

"No way to top today," Tageson said. "Once-in-a-lifetime experience."

Lifetime experiences take on a more heightened priority, especially considering the fact Tageson goes through each day with a life-threatening heart condition.

As much as he may want to, Tageson will never play professional hockey. He was born with two chambers in his heart instead of four, a medical diagnosis referred to as hypoplastic left heart syndrome. He had played the sport he loved—hockey—since the age of 6, this against the advice of doctors.

"It's supposed to be debilitating," his mother Lisa Mills explained. "They said he would be the child that would never ride a bicycle, never do any of that. The doctors all through the years have said, 'Give him golf clubs, take the hockey stick away.' We tried. It doesn't work."

On this special day of March 18, 2014, through the joint effort of the Make-A-Wish foundation and the Sharks Foundation, Tageson would enjoy the spoils very few, if any, had experienced with the team.

Tageson's day started with the formal signing of a one-day NHL contract, presented by general manager Doug Wilson. That allowed the 17-year-old to participate in the team's morning skate as they prepared to take on the Panthers that evening. A mid-day press conference followed the team's routine skate-around that was hardly routine on this day.

"You see the smile," Wilson said. "There's a universal language in our business, you can tell when someone really loves something. Seeing Sammy around here, I think everybody feels pretty good about him being here and him having a great day."

Looking to take a quick break from the skate, Tageson sat on the bench right where Joe Thornton normally sits. He heard a low, but friendly voice nearby.

"Jumbo told me to scoot over a little bit," Tageson said with a laugh. "And go out and score on Al."

Al would be Alex Stalock, San Jose's backup goaltender, who was fending off breakaway moves from teammates as the practice wound down. Tageson used a couple of his favorite moves to beat Stalock between the legs for a practice goal.

But the best was yet to come.

Dressed in full gear, Tageson became the first person in any walk of life who wasn't a Sharks player to skate out of the giant Sharks mouth that allowed San Jose's players to enjoy a dramatic entrance to the ice before each home game. He stood on the blue line with the Sharks' starters for the National Anthem before departing the ice for his emotional exit.

The Upper Deck trading card company even went as far as to produce a "rookie" card featuring Tageson adjacent to the famous Shark head.

The Sharks lost the game 3–2, but not before the Sharks cut the deficit in the third period to one goal off a faceoff play that resulted immediately after Tageson's image was again shown in the video board that drew a huge ovation from the fans.

"Everyone spent some time with him, talked with him," Sharks forward Logan Couture said. "You could feel how excited he is. It's awesome."

59 Buster Beats the Blues

Minutes before the puck was dropped on the Sharks–Blues Western Conference quarterfinal playoff series in 2000, the beat writer for St. Louis' paper of record was asked why he was working alone. The respected veteran scribe answered, "I'll get more help by the third round."

That pretty much capsulated the feeling around St. Louis when the Presidents' Trophy winners appeared almost inconvenienced having to play the No. 8 seed from San Jose. Three of the Blues regulars dyed their hair white and another—Jamal Mayers, who in later years played for San Jose—went as far as to color his eyebrows in the manner of tiger stripes. All the buzz around the city and the team was anticipating the opportunity to host the Stanley Cup Final.

A 5–3 Blues victory in Game 1 did nothing to kill the feel-good vibe. Mayers even kept the friendly ribbing at arm's length by contributing two assists. Maybe these Blues really were ready for a long springtime run.

And then things changed.

After two idle days, the Sharks caught a big break in Game 2. Defenseman Gary Suter's shot from the point during an early-game power play struck Blues defenseman Marc Bergevin in the stomach. A well-reputed prankster off the ice, Bergevin had no intention of joking around when he gloved the puck and inadvertently threw it into his own net, badly misjudging his intended toss toward the corner. The Sharks went on to win 4–2.

Or as a female television reporter at ice level put it while wrapping up a live postgame interview with Sharks forward Scott Thornton: "Here's to continued sex in San Jose." She meant to say "success."

Yes, this series was starting to get weird.

Back inside the intimidating confines of the Shark Tank, San Jose won a pair of one-goal games in regulation—2–1 and 3–2—to send the series back to St. Louis with commanding lead. The Blues beat the Sharks 5–3 in Game 5, and then appeared to seize the momentum with a 6–2 road victory in Game 6 on the strength of a Scott Young hat trick.

It was back to the Gateway City for a deciding Game 7.

Sharks coach Darryl Sutter ignored the critics and went right back to Steve Shields in goal despite his struggles two nights earlier with a chance to clinch at home. Grinding forward Ron Stern gave the visitors a 1–0 lead in Game 7 with a backhand shot just 2:51 after the opening faceoff. That set the stage for a late-period back-breaker.

Team captain Owen Nolan skated alone through center ice, intending to dump the puck into the St. Louis zone and change, but heard someone shout "Shoot!" Just as Nolan hit the bottom of the blue note logo at center he unleashed a hard, rising slap shot that caught Roman Turek off-guard, the puck deflecting off of the goalie's right glove and into the net.

Kiel Center went silent—2–0 Sharks with 10.2 seconds left in the first period.

"I didn't even see what happened," Nolan confessed. "I just shot it and turned toward the bench."

"It was a bad goal, I can't explain it," said Turek, who struggled throughout the series. "I feel so bad. You cannot win in the playoffs if you have goaltending like I played these games."

Jeff Friesen made it 3–0 before the Blues cut the deficit back to two on Young's goal early in the third, and had a chance late with a 29-second two-man advantage on the power play. But Nolan spearheaded a huge kill by sliding to block a shot off the stick of Blues defenseman Al MacInnis, who possessed the hardest shot in the league in those days.

"Those types of plays are bigger than people think," Nolan's teammate Mike Ricci said. "Owen showed a lot of courage."

The Sharks upset was complete. Nolan scored six goals in the series and displayed his leadership skills at the biggest time of the season on a national stage.

"I'm pretty damn proud of these guys," Sharks general manager Dean Lombardi said. "There's a big difference. In the three stages of development there's hope, think, and know. This team knew they could win. That's a big difference from hoping or thinking."

"They withstood all the Chicken Littles who said they couldn't," Sutter echoed. "It should have been a seven-game series, and the right team won."

60 Tennyson's Historic Goal

Matt Tennyson was 14 years old when his family relocated from Minnesota to Northern California. Moving away from a youth hockey hotbed to the sunny climes of Pleasanton, a quaint hamlet tucked among the San Francisco Bay Area's cluster of family-friendly suburbs, Tennyson wasn't quite sure how to react.

"When my dad told me we were going to California, I was like, 'Oh, really? That's good for the weather, but I don't know how the hockey will be,'" Tennyson recalled. "I was kind of on the line thinking it could be good or I could try doing something else."

Soccer, baseball, football, and basketball were huge. Hockey? Well, there was an old, single-sheet rink one town over in Dublin. Attending a new high school, Tennyson found just enough classmates to make a ride pool and venture 35 miles to the south where the San Jose Jr. Sharks ice hockey program offered an opportunity for youth players to pursue their dreams.

Little did Tennyson know that destiny was waiting for him.

Fast forward 10 years to the 2014–15 NHL season when Tennyson, a recent recall from the minors, was getting a second crack at making an impression with the San Jose Sharks. In addition, Tennyson made history.

Tommy Wingels made a splendid cross-ice, tape-to-tape pass through the neutral zone to spring Tennyson across the blue line and past Edmonton forward Boyd Gordon. Oilers defenseman Andrew Ference didn't have an angle or the speed to deny the right-handed shooting Tennyson from launching a low wrister from the right circle that eluded the blocker of goalie Ben Scrivens.

Tennyson's first career goal at 8:39 of the third period tied a game the Sharks would eventually win at home, the same site where 10 of his former Amador Valley High School classmates were on hand to watch Tennyson's first career game three years earlier.

The celebration of his first goal, however, extended well beyond the traditional group hug teammates James Sheppard, Tomas Hertl, and Marc-Edouard Vlasic shared with Tennyson immediately afterward.

It was divulged that original and late team owner George Gund III had a dream.

"His goal was really special for our organization and, actually, for the city," Sharks coach Todd McLellan recapped. "I know when Mr. Gund was still alive, one of his dreams was to have a San Jose-bred player, and somebody who played in the Jr. Sharks system actually play for the Sharks, score a goal.

"Hopefully he's looking down and he's really proud of bringing the team here and it finally happened after 24 years."

Gund loved hockey played on all levels. He understood the business aspect that future generations needed to help sustain and grow his expansion team's fan base would likely come from those who were intimately close to the game. The romantic side of Gund was pure and simple, he just wanted people to have every opportunity to play the game and enjoy it.

The birth of the Sharks quickly inspired a Bay Area-wide boom in youth participation, and the San Jose Jr. Sharks quickly became Gund's obvious organization of choice.

For Tennyson, the organization provided a springboard toward a circuitous route to his eventual pro career. After two years with the Jr. Sharks, Tennyson played two seasons of junior hockey in the U.S.—one with the Texas Tornado in the North American Hockey League and the other with the Cedar Rapids RoughRiders of the United States Hockey League.

"It elevated my level of play," Tennyson said of his time with the Jr. Sharks. "It was the first time I ever played AAA hockey and everyone was great. I had really good coaches and really good teammates and I think the experience helped me move on to the next level."

Tennyson played three years of college hockey at Western Michigan University, then signed as an undrafted free agent with the Sharks in March of 2012. He made his NHL debut in 2012–13 with the Sharks and played a total of four games—contributing two assists, including one on a Joe Thornton goal during Tennyson's first game—but didn't score a goal and wound up in the minors for another 97 games between 2013–15 before his fateful second promotion.

Other Jr. Shark grads beat Tennyson in scoring an NHL goal—Alec Martinez (Kings), Stefan Matteau (Devils), Casey Wellman (Wild), Viktor Tikhonov (Coyotes), and Brett Sutter (Flames)—but Tennyson will always remain the first to do it in teal, again fulfilling Gund's wishes.

"This was one of his stated dreams," Wilson said. "The thought of having a player that played in the Jr. Sharks program wear a

Sharks jersey and score a goal. I'll tell you what, it was kind of emotional."

"It validates what we're doing here," Jr. Sharks advisory board chair Jon Gustafson added. "He's a great role model for the kids that are up-and-coming. Since Matty's local and playing for the Sharks that certainly puts the exclamation point on it for the kids."

Jr. Sharks in the NHL

Players who appeared at one time during their amateur career with the San Jose Junior Sharks:

Player	Pos.	NHL teams
• Stefan Matteau	F	New Jersey, Montreal
• Alec Martinez	D	Los Angeles
• Brett Sutter	F	Calgary, Carolina, Minnesota
• Matt Tennyson	D	San Jose , Carolina
• Viktor Tikhonov	F	Arizona, Chicago
• Casey Wellman	F	Minnesota, Washington

61 Mike Vernon

When he wasn't providing staunch goaltending and veteran leadership, Mike Vernon let his mischievous side show. Kelly Hrudey was often the target of Vernon's pranks, and it worked for a while until his netminding partner caught on.

"Mike liked to look over to me at the bench and pretend he had something bugging him," Hrudey recalled. "I'd get a little nervous, 'Oh, Geez, I've got to get ready and go in there now,' And then I figured out he was just pulling my leg."

Then, during a late-season game in 1997–98 with the Sharks nursing a one-goal lead in the third period at Toronto, Vernon appeared in discomfort while skating to the bench during a break. Hrudey waved him back, saying, "Yeah, yeah, forget about it."

The Sharks held on for a 5–3 win, but Vernon was diagnosed with a slight groin pull afterward. San Jose coach Darryl Sutter summoned Hrudey to his office. He wondered why the veteran backup wasn't prepared to jump in.

"I had to tell him, and Darryl had a bit of a laugh over that one," admitted Hrudey, who relieved Vernon at the start of the third period in San Jose's next two games.

Vernon had his fun side, but the Calgary native was all business when it came to his craft. Acquired for a pair of draft picks two months after leading Detroit to the Stanley Cup—and winning the Conn Smythe Trophy as playoff MVP—the 34-year-old Vernon brought a wealth of experience to a San Jose team looking to rebound from consecutive last-place finishes.

"Vernie brought that winning attitude," Tony Granato said. "He brought a confidence not only in himself, but expressed to his teammates that we could win there. And that was big at the time."

"I don't know what they listed as his height, but when he stood in net his chest seemed higher than his head," Wayne Thomas said. "He gave you that persona."

The former goalie Thomas had a relationship with Vernon that began in 1986–87, long before either joined the Sharks. That's when Thomas was coaching Calgary's secondary affiliate in the IHL, and an unhappy Vernon was sent all the way down to Thomas' team after bouncing around the Flames' system.

"He never forgot that I helped him, too. It's one of my most fond memories as a coach, and as a player being appreciative," Thomas recalled. "I told the guys in Calgary he doesn't belong here."

Vernon certainly belonged in San Jose where he won 30 games while making 62 appearances in '97–98 and led the Sharks back into a playoff spot for the first time in three seasons. Vernon's first season in San Jose was Hrudey's last of 15 in the NHL. And he couldn't think of a better way for it to all come to an end.

"Mike was an awesome teammate," Hrudey said. "That might have been one of the things that topped off my career—playing in San Jose the last couple of years and playing with Mike."

Vernon was a bulldog between the pipes, belying his 5'9" frame. He played much bigger. He played strong. He played with a swagger and an attitude.

"Stubborn," Thomas said. "He just refused to be beat."

"He knew how to protect a lead better than anybody in the game at that time," Hrudey added. "Once our team started getting better, and we put together streaks, if we were tied or led at some point in the second period, Mike never gave it up. He was lights out at that point."

As the last playoff qualifier in the West, the Sharks met Central Division champion Dallas, the Presidents' Trophy winners who had earned 31 more points than San Jose in the regular-season standings. Vernon played all but 20 minutes of the six-game series that was tied 2–2 before the superior Stars closed it out.

During 1998–99, his last full season in San Jose, Vernon saw his workload trimmed to 49 games with the emergence of Steve Shields. Vernon, however, played five of San Jose's six-game playoff series loss to Colorado.

With Shields having established himself the starter in 2000, Vernon (then 36) was dealt in late December, but not after having left an indelible mark on the San Jose franchise.

"He's was a gamer," Granato said. "He was a different type of teammate than most goalies. Usually goalies like to isolate themselves from the rest of their teammates, but he was right there with us. He was one of the ringleaders.

"Fun, fun guy."

62 Nolan for Ozolinsh

Owen Nolan was already nine years old the first time he slipped into hockey skates, a second-hand pair purchased for $10 at a flea market. His mother was leery her son wouldn't get enough use to justify buying a brand-new pair.

Ready for his first organized game, Nolan volunteered to arrive early and play goalie. But when another youngster beat him to the rink to fulfill the role, Nolan was relegated instead to lining up at forward. Nolan scored a hat trick that fateful day, and his coach told him to forget about ever strapping on goalie gear.

Nolan was in the National Hockey League only nine years later, the first overall selection by the Quebec Nordiques in the 1990 entry draft. During Nolan's first five NHL seasons he was part of a young and talented core that included Joe Sakic, Peter Forsberg, Mats Sundin, Mike Ricci, and Adam Foote that gave a relocating franchise to Denver the hope of competing for a Stanley Cup.

Playing now as the renamed Avalanche in Colorado's mile-high capital city, the team knew it was close yet needed a couple of pieces to complete the championship puzzle. Scoring was not the problem. Goaltending and finding a puck-moving defenseman were the priorities.

Meanwhile in San Jose, the Sharks were embarking on only their fifth season after wildly varying results in their first four campaigns. The Sharks followed two laughing-stock seasons with consecutive appearances in the second round of the playoffs. But San Jose's roster was hardly complete as an 0–7–4 start would suggest.

The Sharks had what the Avalanche needed, and vice versa.

Less than one month into the 1995–96 season, San Jose sent young defenseman Sandis Ozolinsh to Colorado in exchange for Nolan, the skilled and powerful winger in a 1-for-1 deal on October 26, 1995, that would significantly impact both franchises for years to come.

"We had a ton of great forwards and Dean wanted me bad," Nolan said of then-Sharks G.M. Dean Lombardi. "I became the man to trade. You look at our team, we were all coming into our own. Unfortunately I was the player who had to go."

The Sharks had made Ozolinsh a high second-round pick (30th overall) in 1991. The native of Riga, Latvia, familiarized himself with North American hockey during a season spent with Kansas City of the IHL before earning regular shifts on the San Jose blue line as a 21-year-old in 1993–94. Ozolinsh was a special talent, scoring 26 goals and 64 points, but he sometimes cheated more toward the offensive end for the coaches' tastes, and it wasn't an easy habit to break.

The Avalanche could afford Ozolinsh's gambling style thanks to a number of trusted defense-first rearguards. And after Colorado took advantage of Patrick Roy's falling out in Montreal to acquire the goaltender in late December, the Avalanche were well on their way. Ozolinsh contributed five goals and 19 points as Colorado won the Cup at season's end.

"A lot of people think I was mad that they won the Cup, but I wasn't," Nolan said. "These guys were like brothers, I was happy to see them win."

San Jose was 0–4–3 at the time of the trade, didn't earn its first win until Game 12 after going 0–7–4, was 1–14–4 two weeks later, fired coach Kevin Constantine in early December, and continued to sag all the way to a 20–55–7 last-place finish.

Twenty-three years old, Nolan said he knew within three months he could get used to the Bay Area. The hockey part might take longer. In retrospect today, he calls the trade a blessing.

"The only tough time I had to go through was the realization I was starting over again," he said. "It was five years of playing hard to get our team where it had a serious shot. And to come to San Jose—nothing against the city or the organization—it was a fact I had to start over again."

Ozolinsh went on to score 253 points in 333 regular-season games with Colorado. He represented the Avs three times in NHL All-Star Games. And he set team records for most career goals by a defenseman (72), most points by a defenseman in one season (68), and most points in the playoffs for a career (67). Before he was traded again in 2000 to Carolina, Ozolinsh was a finalist for the Norris Trophy in 1997.

Despite the team's struggles, Nolan became an instant fan favorite in San Jose thanks to his hard-nosed and determined style of play. He scored 124 points during his first 144 games as a Shark, made three All-Star Game appearances and served as team captain from 1998 until his trade to Toronto late in 2003.

63 Evgeni Nabokov

It's hard to imagine a more improbable start to an NHL career than the one Evgeni Nabokov experienced.

Viewed by some as a long shot since the native of Ust-Kamenogorsk, Kazakhstan, was a ninth-round draft pick the Sharks selected sight unseen, Nabokov was promoted three months into his third minor-league season to back up Steve Shields after San Jose traded established veteran Mike Vernon just days before.

Nabokov made his NHL debut in relief, stopping all four shots in 15 minutes at Nashville on New Year's Day of 2000. Ten days passed before Nabokov next saw the net—again in relief of Shields—but this time for 36:25 in a home loss to St. Louis. The rookie was credited with 14 saves on 15 shots. The one that represented his first career goal surrendered he never had a chance to stop.

Evgeni Nabokov, who didn't know a word of English when he joined the Sharks'
system, left as the franchise's leader in most goaltending categories after spending
10 seasons in San Jose.

That's because it came off the stick of teammate Stephane
Matteau in the form on an own goal. Nabokov had vacated his net
for an extra skater on a delayed penalty against the Blues.

Then it really got unpredictable.

Two more games passed before coach Darryl Sutter decided to
give the player who affectionately became known as "Nabby" his
first career start—a daunting game against Colorado where Patrick
Roy loomed large in goal for the host Avalanche. The Sharks were
dominated throughout, managing only 15 shots while surrendering
39 in a game that went 65 minutes.

Final score: Sharks 0, Avalanche 0.

"Looking back, that's what started it," Nabokov admitted just months after retiring from the NHL in 2015. "That game showed me maybe I could play at this level. That's when the Sharks started to believe maybe I could do something.

"Before that they weren't even sure what was going on with me."

Shields injured an ankle during the second game of the following season, and Nabokov assumed the starting job. By season's end, Nabokov was selected to the All-Star Game, led the Sharks to the playoffs and won the league's Calder Trophy as Rookie of the Year.

"He was so athletic, all he needed to do was adapt," said Wayne Thomas, who coincidentally posted a shutout with Montreal during his first NHL start in 1973. "There's guys who are a flash in the pan. They don't try to get better every day. And if they do try sometimes they don't get it."

Working closely with goaltending coach Warren Strelow, Nabokov employed a combined butterfly and stand-up style that was unique during a period when goalies were otherwise quick to drop down on shots and try to cover the bottom of the net. Unlike most goalies, Nabokov was vocal and opinionated. He knew how he wanted the defense to play in front of him, and he wasn't shy about telling them.

"You never had to worry about what he was thinking, he'd always let you know," Patrick Marleau said. "Defensemen loved playing with him—he was their eyes basically. Nabby made it easy for the D to play in front of him."

"I just liked talking to him," Joe Thornton added. "He had a lot of opinions about hockey and how it should be played. It was always interesting. He's just a smart hockey guy."

"Guys trusted him," Thomas said. "Goalies aren't supposed to say anything. You know, your job is just stop the puck. Nabby was a guy who was a leader of our team, and he was right."

While numbers jump out—nine full seasons spent as San Jose's starter, a litany of franchise goaltending records set that stand today, and a love affair with fans who serenaded him with chants of "Nab-by, Nab-by, Nab-by"—the undercurrent for Nabokov's success was the strong relationships he held on to dearly.

It started in his youth when his father, a pro goalie for a team in Kazakhstan named "Torpedo," mentored Evgeni until age 18. Nabokov wore No. 20 not in honor of Soviet great Vladislav Tretiak but because his father, Viktor, wore that number. He first had Strelow in San Jose, then Thomas. And he had Sutter as his first coach. Sutter reminded Nabokov what drove him in Russia.

"Darryl was basically exactly what I needed," Nabokov said. "He would say things the way they are, not sugarcoat. I liked that. Darryl would tell you straight up you sucked. And I liked that. I knew exactly what the coach was thinking.

"Now, looking back, I realize without all those people—and maybe even more who were involved—I wouldn't have been able to achieve what I did," he added.

The one thing Nabokov & Co. were not able to accomplish in San Jose was reaching a Stanley Cup Final. While disappointing, he dwells on the positive.

"People focus on the negative, but as a team and an organization we never cheated the fans," Nabokov said. "That's the biggest thing. We were always on the ice with a good team and no one ever took a shortcut."

Nabokov Franchise Records

Sharks club records set by Evgeni Nabokov, who played in San Jose from January 2000 through the 2009–10 season:

Games played: 563

Career minutes: 32,492

Career wins: 293

Career decisions: 537

Career shutouts: 50

Career goals allowed: 1,294

Career shots against: 14,757

Career goals scored: 1

Career assists: 9

Career penalty minutes: 100

Consecutive games started: 50

Longest unbeaten streak: 16 (15–0–1)

Games played (season): 77

Minutes (season): 4,561

Wins (season): 46

Decisions (season): 75 (46–21–8)

Shutouts (season): 9

Playoff games played: 80

Playoff career minutes: 4,820

Playoff wins: 40

Playoff decisions: 78

Playoff shutouts: 7

Playoff goals allowed: 184

Playoff shots against: 2,118

Playoff assists: 2

64 Visit the Hockey Hall of Fame

Of all the Sharks-related mementos collected and displayed by the Hockey Hall of Fame, nothing draws as much attention as Brian Hayward's stylish goalie mask first worn during San Jose's inaugural season of 1991–92.

The artistic depiction of an open-mouthed, jagged-toothed, great white shark—airbrushed in the team colors of teal, black, and white—is one of four San Jose related artifacts that can be viewed on a daily basis. A number of other Sharks items are housed in the Hall's Resource Center.

A visit to the Hockey Hall of Fame should be on every Sharks fan's bucket list. Located at 30 Yonge Street in bustling downtown Toronto, the Hockey Hall of Fame and museum houses enough of the game's memorabilia and trophy display to keep the hockey fan of any age intrigued for hours.

Additional Sharks pieces on display besides Hayward's mask include a 1992 Doug Wilson jersey, a Joe Thornton jersey from 2011–12, and the stick Jeremy Roenick used to score his 500th career goal on November 10, 2007.

Hayward finished his 11-year NHL career with two seasons as a Shark before turning to a long broadcast career, and still gets asked about wearing the intimidating mask to this day.

"It was my only chance to get in the Hall of Fame," Hayward cracks.

Hayward's attention-grabbing protective head gear was born as much out of necessity as to make a statement. Hayward sustained two head injuries while wearing the more popular two-piece style mask with Montreal. He began researching an alternative after getting claimed by San Jose in the 1991 dispersal draft from the

Minnesota North Stars where he had been traded by the Canadiens seven months earlier.

Hayward got in touch with Greg Harrison, a Toronto-based manufacturer of the new baseball-style, one-piece mask. Proven to offer more protection with a slightly bigger and heavier design, the mask also provided Harrison with a blank canvas to produce a creative look.

"It was pretty easy when we knew I was coming to San Jose, we jumped on that pretty fast," Hayward said of incorporating the look of a shark. "I knew what I wanted, and just let him run with it."

Hayward envisioned jaws and an open-mouth shark with his face peering out of the front. That's really all of the input the Toronto native passed along. Hayward sensed this was Harrison's project, and he would have final say.

"Greg was an artist by the true definition of the word," Hayward said with a laugh. "I told him what I envisioned, he said he was thinking the same thing and said, 'It will be awesome.' I didn't see it again until I used it for the first time."

Hayward tested another one-piece mask made by a competitor during the preseason before that first season, but found Harrison's mask a better fit in addition to its more striking look. That mask was worn when Hayward authored San Jose's first win in franchise history with 36 saves—including 20 in the first period—during a 4–3 victory over the Calgary Flames on October 8, 1991.

That was the only win Hayward earned in five decisions and seven appearances during the Sharks' inaugural season. A back injury forced Hayward to miss 59 games. He returned to play 18 times in 1992–93 before retiring at season's end at the age of 32. While he didn't have a huge impact, his mask lives on.

"It was a great design," Hayward said. "Toward the end of my career, I actually started a company where we made miniature replicas of hockey goalie masks, and it was quite successful for a couple of years."

65 Mike Ricci

Pick the one Shark who displayed the most grit and determination throughout the years and it'd have to be Mike Ricci.

Dealt by Colorado less than a year after winning a Stanley Cup, Ricci joined the Sharks in his prime and went on to enjoy the most productive seven seasons of his 16-year NHL career.

"Ricci is a complete player," G.M. Dean Lombardi said after making the trade. "When people talk about Mike Ricci, the first thing they say is, 'He's a competitor and plays every night.'"

Coach Darryl Sutter chimed in with, "It's a hell of a trade."

The Sharks reached the Stanley Cup playoffs each of the first five seasons Ricci pulled on his familiar No. 18 sweater in San Jose—and during six of his seven years in all. He was the heart and soul during an era in San Jose defined by teams with strong character that continued to battle higher-salaried opponents.

"A couple years in I really thought if there was a salary cap we would have had a chance," Ricci recalled. "We had really good chemistry on those teams. We always lost to teams with huge payrolls."

Standing at 6'0" and 200 pounds, Ricci wasn't the biggest player on the ice, but he could always be found either in front of the net or in the corners. Pound for pound, no one sacrificed as much and worked as hard as Ricci, often recognized as much for his long black hair and wide, toothless smile.

"Where do I start?" Owen Nolan offered.

"I've known Mike for a long time, we used to play in junior against each other, played together in Quebec for as long as he did, too," added Nolan, Ricci's roommate on the road in San Jose. "He's quite a character. He competed at the top level, gave everything he had and fought through everything."

Selected fourth by Philadelphia in a 1990 draft when Quebec took Nolan first overall, Ricci was part of one of the biggest deals in league history. He was joined by four Flyer teammates, along with two first-round picks and $15 million, to Quebec in exchange for Eric Lindros. Ricci was a key figure when Quebec relocated to Denver and won the Stanley Cup in 1996.

Ricci coincidentally set a record for most goals scored by an opponent against the Sharks—five on February 17, 1994—during his first season with the Nordiques.

While he didn't enjoy the same kind of offensive success as a member of the Sharks, he was a consistent performer on the score sheet nonetheless. Ricci logged double-figure goal totals during his first six years in San Jose, eclipsing the 20-goal plateau twice with a high of 22 in 2000–01.

In all, Ricci scored 101 goals and 263 points while appearing in 529 career games with San Jose. He scored 14 goals and 42 points in 59 Sharks playoff games.

"He never had the hardest shot and he wasn't the fastest skater," Nolan said. "When it came to dedication there was no one better. He was willing to do anything it took—block shots—and it didn't matter if he had to do it three times on the same shift. He sacrificed his body, anything to do to win that game."

Years after retirement and involved with San Jose in player development, Ricci still remains a fan favorite. Attending a non-hockey event in San Jose with ex-teammate Bryan Marchment, Ricci couldn't escape the grasp of adoring followers.

"We went out one night and couldn't move," Marchment said. "Everywhere we went it was pictures and autographs. I played with tons of elite players, but Reech? He's the biggest rock star."

66 Playoffs Pause for Littleton

"What's a sport compared to life?" Sharks winger Joe Murphy said. "Sports are nothing. These kids had all of their lives ahead of them. They could have become doctors, lawyers, anything they wanted. And it was taken from them because of a senseless act."

Murphy spoke while surveying a sprawling memorial that filled Jefferson County's Robert F. Clement Park next to Columbine High School in Littleton, Colorado. Nine days earlier, on the eve of San Jose's first-round playoff series against the host Colorado Avalanche, a horrible tragedy took place—12 classmates and a teacher were shot and killed by two students, who turned their weapons on themselves and committed suicide on April 20, 1999.

The NHL ultimately decided to delay the start of the best-of-seven series, and open with the first two games in San Jose instead of nearby downtown Denver with Commissioner Gary Bettman adding, "If this series goes seven, you know there will be four games in five days, but it was more important, we thought, to slow down the schedule and to move it out to San Jose."

"Bottom line, it's the right thing to do, the right decision. Flat out," Sharks coach Darryl Sutter said.

Northwest Division champions with 98 points and No. 2 seeds in the West, the Avalanche beat the host Sharks 3–1 in Game 1 four days after the shooting and went up 2–0 with a 2–1 road win two nights later. Now came the hard part—Colorado returned home to its broken community and tried to maintain focus.

"Reminders are going to be there," Avs captain Joe Sakic said. "It's going to be there for a long time. Nobody's ever going to forget that."

It was on the off day after the Sharks won Game 3 at McNichols Arena that Murphy and seven teammates took a 20-minute drive into the heart of the devastation to pay their respects. The players placed a 50-foot banner on a chain link fence surrounding the tennis courts adjacent to Columbine High School. The banner, which read, "Our Hearts & Our Prayers Are With You," included thousands of signatures and well-wishes from fans collected during the first two games in San Jose. The Sharks Foundation added $10,000 to the $6,000 in donations collected by fans in San Jose.

"I was very impressed with our fans," Sharks president Greg Jamison said. "The messages they wrote, I was very touched by that. And the players have been very supportive, too."

Sharks teammates Tony Granato, Bill Holder, Dave Lowry, Stephane Matteau, Jeff Norton, Mike Rathje, and Ron Sutter joined Murphy and Jamison at the outdoor memorial dotted with the cars of several deceased students covered in floral bouquets, photo collages and sympathy cards.

"Sports is a very minute part of our society," said Sharks goalie Mike Vernon, who dueled Patrick Roy in the series. "This hits too close to home for me. I can't imagine what it's like for the people involved. It's going to affect this community for a long, long time."

The Sharks evened the series with a 7–3 victory in Game 4. But when the Avalanche became the first team to win on home ice, 6–2 in Game 5, they had a chance to wrap things up two nights later in San Jose. Colorado's Czech rookie forward Milan Hejduk scored his second overtime goal of the series—this one at 13:12—to send the Avs on to a 3–2 win and six-game victory over the Sharks.

"We feel good about the way we played," Sharks center Vincent Damphousse said. "If we didn't give it our best, then I would be ticked off. We gave it everything we had. Overtime can go either way."

67 "Hazy Had to Go in There"

Old Chicago Stadium was the site of the Sharks' first game against an Original Six opponent—the host Blackhawks—on October 13, 1991. It was only San Jose's sixth match of its inaugural season, and the middle stop on the team's first multi-game trip.

"Oh yeah, I remember it like it was yesterday," Brian Hayward said more than two decades later.

The 31-year-old goalie, claimed by the Sharks in a dispersal draft to share the wisdom and experience from his nine NHL seasons, was between the pipes for only his second start and for the first time since backstopping the club's historic first victory three games earlier.

This was a special game for three veteran Sharks—captain Doug Wilson, fellow defenseman Bob McGill, and forward Wayne Presley—who all were making their first return to Chicago after having played for the Blackhawks the year before.

This one didn't go so well for San Jose. The Blackhawks broke from a 1–1 tie after the first 2:41 with three straight goals against Hayward to take a 4–1 lead into the intermission.

Then it got a little chippy in the second stanza.

"The Hawks were spanking us pretty good when a fight broke out in front of my net," Hayward recalled. "And Chris Chelios, who I knew fairly well, went around behind our guy, who was fighting one of their guys, and grabbed the back of his jersey with both arms. So he was defenseless."

Never mind friendships—Chelios was a teammate during all four seasons Hayward played from 1986–90 with the Montreal Candiens—he knew he had to do something. Hayward left his crease and joined the melee.

"Hazy *had* to go in there," exuberant Sharks teammate Steve Bozek said afterward, coming to the defense of his goalie.

Hayward's act was viewed as an illegal third-man-in to the fight, and referee Paul Stewart sent the goalie to an early shower by assessing a game-misconduct. Turns out Stewart and Hayward had history.

"It was the referee who I hated more than any ref," Hayward said of Stewart. "I was thrown out of three games during my career and he threw me out of all three."

On his way off the ice, Hayward didn't take kindly to a heckler and narrowly missed the fan with a swing of his goal stick before descending down a flight of stairs that led to the visitors' room below.

"I'm sitting in the locker room all by myself, I'm pissed off, and I'm also worried because I just took a swing at a fan," said Hayward, realizing he'd put himself at risk of a possible suspension.

He also wouldn't have to watch the rest of a 7–3 loss in a game the Sharks' power play went 0-for-9.

It was about then that Mark Stulberger burst into the room. The Sharks' director of telecasts told Hayward, "That was great; we were able to catch all of that with a tight shot!"

Fantastic, that just means I could get suspended, Hayward thought.

Meanwhile back in San Jose, Hayward's wife, Angela, was entertaining new neighbors, and they were watching the game on television.

"My wife tells me our neighbors were in shock watching all of this. They caught it all on camera," Hayward said. "She told them, 'He's really not like this.'"

68 Randy Hahn

Randy Hahn's passion for the NHL was sparked while working for a radio station late during his teen years in Vancouver, B.C. Hahn was assigned to the visitors' locker room to tape one-on-one interviews with stars such as Rogie Vachon, Phil Esposito, and Bobby Clarke.

"To take the time to sit and talk to a snot-nosed, 18-year-old, little radio reporter for five minutes, and be a real good guy about it, that's what fused my passion," Hahn said.

That passion pushed Hahn to pursue a career in broadcasting—familiar to Sharks fans as the team's primary television play-by-play voice for more than two decades—even if it didn't happen in the NHL overnight. Hahn later worked briefly in his native city of Edmonton, Alberta, and in San Diego before relocating to the Bay Area in the late 1980s. It was there Hahn read a newspaper blurb that a group of enthusiastic hockey fans were meeting at a local pizza parlor to discuss a grassroots effort to bring pro hockey to San Jose.

Hahn's attendance would prove fortuitous.

"Three or four guys there were the type to throw on a jersey, stand in front of City Hall, and chant, 'We want hockey,'" Hahn recalled. "Others saw it more as a business or promotional effort, and that might be taken more seriously."

Hahn connected with Jim Hager, a lawyer in San Jose, and the two spearheaded the formation of a non-profit corporation—Pro Hockey San Jose. The venture started with potential fans offered a T-shirt and newsletter for $20.

Approval for a downtown San Jose sports arena had already been granted before Hahn & Co. got involved, but their grassroots efforts to spread the word and try to influence the NHL to select the

South Bay city as the next expansion designation couldn't be ignored by Howard Baldwin.

The former owner of the Hartford Whalers was itching to get back into the sport, and Baldwin represented a figure who could finance the $50 million expansion fee. Hahn and Hager put Baldwin in touch with San Jose city officials.

When San Jose was awarded its franchise within two years of that initial pizza parlor meeting, Hahn applied for the play-by-play job but was disappointed to receive a "thanks, but no thanks" response. That's because Baldwin ended up taking ownership of Minnesota while the North Stars' previous owners—George and Gordon Gund—moved West to head up the Sharks.

"I was so excited this thing we thought up actually happened— San Jose got a hockey franchise—but the bad news was I had all my eggs in the Howard Baldwin basket," Hahn said. "When the Gunds came in my status disappeared, and I wasn't hired as the television announcer."

The team's first director of video production, Mark Stulberger, was familiar with and supportive of Hahn's work in Southern California. Original TV voice Joe Starkey had a split allegiance with 49ers and Cal football, so Stulberger recruited Hahn for the occasional conflicts.

After providing color on several radio broadcasts, Hahn's first television assignment came in New Jersey during the opening month of the Sharks' inaugural season.

"The first game he ever did, and we lost 9–0," radio voice Dan Rusanowsky reminded.

Hahn replaced Starkey in Year 3 and has been the TV voice ever since.

"To me, you talk about the voices of the San Jose Sharks, there's Randy and Danny," said Drew Remenda, pairing Hahn and Rusanowsky. "They're as much a part of the Sharks as Joe Thornton, Doug Wilson or Patty Marleau. And the fans identify with them."

"When people ask what's the dream job, I have it," Hahn said.

Jamie Baker is one of five former NHLers to work alongside Hahn as analysts. He marvels at Hahn's work to prepare for his next telecast. Baker describes Hahn as having a great sense of humor, and a passion that runs deep for his job and the team.

"Randy really understands the entertainment value of sports," Baker said. "If it's a huge game he'll call it a certain way. If it's mid-season, or we're playing a team lower in the standings, then he'll try to be a bit lighter and entertain the audience with his humor."

It's that humor that often had longtime sidekick Drew Remenda in stitches.

"There wasn't a day with him I wasn't laughing," Remenda said, "hysterically laughing."

Hahn sums up his time with the Sharks with the fact he was there when Patrick Marleau arrived at age 17, and hopes to still be there when Marleau retires.

"That's the great thing for us—players come and go, coaches come and go—but we get to see whole careers in front of us," Hahn said. "To be part of something for so long is a privilege, not only broadcasting, but in any line of work."

Hockey Is in His Blood

Randy Hahn's passion for hockey was rooted in his upbringing in Edmonton, Alberta. His team of choice as a youth was the Edmonton Oil Kings, the junior team playing in the Western Hockey League as the Oilers were not part of the NHL yet.

"We got special tickets, they were something like $1 a game," Hahn said.

Hahn returned to Edmonton to take his first television job, working on a Sports Tonight show in 1981–82 when Wayne Gretzky racked up 50 goals in only 39 games for the Oilers.

"If you wanted to talk to him you'd just call him," Hahn said of Gretzky. "We had his home phone number. It was no big deal. The world was different."

69 Turning to the Vets

If there was one thing about Dean Lombardi, he had a plan.

The team's second general manager believed the lifeblood of an organization is success through the NHL entry draft. The key, he felt, was turning that young talent into players who would eventually accept the mantel of winning at the NHL level.

The trick was getting the Sharks' coveted homegrown players into position where they would not fail. Too much time, energy and work had gone into bringing them this far along.

As part of rebuilding after two surprising playoff runs in the franchise's third and fourth years, Lombardi scoured opponents' rosters in search of veteran players whose pedigree included past success, strong character traits and those who were ready to accept a role on a team that wouldn't contend for a season or two.

Lombardi was aware, too, he might have to pay more to lure vets to San Jose. That was possible because a salary cap wouldn't be part of the NHL for another decade.

The team's 1996–97 roster included seven players the Sharks had drafted in the first or second rounds—Shean Donovan, Jeff Friesen, Viktor Kozlov, Vlastimil Kroupa, Andrei Nazarov, Mike Rathje, and Ray Whitney—in addition to lower-round picks (Marcus Ragnarsson and Michal Sykora), who had developed into regulars.

Now it was a matter of surrounding the promising core with veterans who possessed the qualities Lombardi sought. And he did his homework to find it.

"That was the thing about Dean, he really got to know people," said Kelly Hrudey, one of five significant free-agent signings.

Hrudey, a 36-year-old goalie with 13 years in the NHL, including the previous eight with the Los Angeles Kings, recalls meeting two hours with Lombardi and Sharks assistant G.M. Wayne Thomas the first day and two hours the next.

"They knew exactly what they were getting in me, and vice versa," Hrudey said.

In short order, Hrudey signed in San Jose where he was joined by free agents Tony Granato and Marty McSorley, all Kings teammates the year before. Veterans Ron Sutter, Tim Hunter, and Todd Ewen also signed, dotting a roster that already included quality vets Bernie Nicholls and recently acquired Todd Gill.

"All of us knew what our roles were," Hrudey said. "It was very important for us to lend experience to these guys, who were starting to make the Sharks' roster, that we knew were going to carry the franchise forward."

The '96–97 season was a rough one in the standings as the Sharks finished last in the Pacific Division for a second straight year. But more veterans were on the way just in time to help support four more first-round draft picks—Alexander Korolyuk, Patrick Marleau, Marco Sturm, and Andrei Zyuzin.

Shawn Burr, Murray Craven, Stephane Matteau, Mike Ricci, and Mike Vernon—quite the offseason haul—all came via trade in time for 1997–98, in addition to head coach Darryl Sutter who replaced the fired Al Sims.

That's not all. Dave Lowry and John MacLean were acquired in November and December. Then Bryan Marchment and Joe Murphy came aboard in deals at the March trade deadline.

While pausing in February to allow the NHL's participation in the Olympics, the Sharks took a side trip of their own for a mini-camp in the picturesque Canadian resort town of Banff, Alberta.

"Wow, did we bond," Hrudey recalled. "We practiced hard, but enjoyed each other's company away from the rink equally as well. I was 37 years old and really in a different place than those kids. You don't often see guys 36 to 37 hanging around with guys who were basically 20 years old."

After grabbing the last playoff spot in the West, the Sharks returned in '98–99 with Lombardi's plan working well. As six vets either retired or moved on, free agents Jamie Baker, Bob Rouse and Ron Stern were signed as replacement, and Vincent Damphousse was acquired at the trade deadline.

"And all of us guys were great about it, no egos, let the kids play and help them with things," Hrudey recalled. "And it was a really cool dynamic because there was just such good chemistry between all of us."

Amazingly, no less than 10 of Lombardi's chosen veterans ended in San Jose what had been long, multi-year careers including Craven, Damphousse, Ewen, Granato, Hrudey, Hunter, Nicholls, Rouse, Stern, and Gary Suter. Five others—Burr, Lowry, Matteau, Ricci, and Ron Sutter—moved on to play for only one more team.

Certainly what Lombardi did worked, and it would be hard to duplicate.

"I'd be tough," Hrudey said with a laugh.

70 Wayne Thomas

The Sharks knew they were getting experience in ex-goalie, minor-league coach, and NHL assistant Wayne Thomas when he was hired in 1993–94 to assist new bench boss Kevin Constantine. The Sharks didn't know they were getting someone who would become an assistant G.M., goaltending coach, and an executive vice president who would stick with the organization for 22 productive years.

Yeah, that was a pretty good hire.

"You get attached to a logo, and you think you're going to be there forever," Thomas said. "But I was traded twice, changed organizations twice and got let go in New York and Chicago. So you get a little gun-shy.

"Had I known, I would have bought a house in San Jose the first year," he deadpanned.

Robert Wayne Thomas turned to coaching when an eight-year playing career with three teams ended in 1981. Four years in New York were followed by head coaching stints in the IHL for four of the next five years. And two years as an assistant coach with the St. Louis Blues preceded Thomas' move to San Jose where he initially interviewed for the job Constantine accepted.

The two were familiar with each other from Thomas' days spent at the Minnesota Hockey Camps where Constantine was employed by Herb Brooks and Chuck Grillo, San Jose's first director of player personnel. As often is the case, the hockey community is a close-knit, tight group where relationships in the past lead to opportunities in the future.

Soft-spoken, respectful, and driven, Thomas made an immediate contribution for Constantine, who as a rookie NHL coach appreciated having someone to bounce ideas off of that first year. When Constantine found himself at wits end with five high-end talent players—Igor Larionov, Sergei Makarov, Johan Garpenlov, Sandis Ozolinsh, and Jeff Norton—the coach turned to his assistant for help.

"I remember telling Wayne, 'I'm going to give you five guys who won't do it the way we want it done. I'll take the rest of the guys who are at least trying to do it. You take those five guys. I don't care what you do with them. I won't tell them anything unless they're a minus. Other than that, they're doing it their own way anyhow,'" Constantine recalled.

Led by the magical play of reunited Russians Larionov and Makarov, the unique five-man unit not only led San Jose to an improbable postseason berth in the team's third year of existence and a massive first-round upset, but they formed the most interesting and creative group in hockey.

"They were really unstoppable, or at least pretty unstoppable," Constantine said. "I don't know that Wayne did anything other than buffer them from me, but that was a tremendous contribution."

When young G.M. Dean Lombardi needed assistance he turned to Thomas in the offseason. When foreign goalies—first Arturs Irbe and later Evgeni Nabokov—needed guidance and on-ice coaching, Thomas was summoned. When the team's top minor-league affiliate Worcester came aboard in 2006, Thomas managed the team by logging hefty air-mile trips between the two cities located on opposite coasts.

The Sharks reached the playoffs in all but four of his 22 years. Thomas worked for only two G.M.s—Lombardi and Doug Wilson—and especially enjoyed his time with who he classified as smart and savvy head coaches including Darryl Sutter, Ron Wilson, Todd McLellan, and Constantine.

"To think it was 22 years, it flew by," Thomas recalled after retiring in 2015. "We've had an amazing run. We felt we could win most years, and that's a privilege in this game. Ownership was wonderful to work for, and both general managers let you do your own job. That's not true everywhere."

With all the many hats worn, Thomas most enjoyed his time as a coach and interacting with the players. And because he had nine years of NHL experience as a goalie for Montreal, Toronto, and the New York Rangers, Thomas was most comfortable dealing with those who wore the most pads and were expected to stop the puck.

Kelly Hrudey distinctly recalls his early days in San Jose when as a 36-year-old free-agent signee he was pressing early in 1996–97 to impress his new team.

"I really struggled my first year there right out of the gate," Hrudey recalled. "We were three to four games into the season and I was grinding away, trying to find my game. You're proud, you just got signed and you want to do well.

"Wayne came to me, re-assured me, saying, 'Hey, it's no time to panic, we'll work with you to get your game back,' and it sort of turned there for me."

Above all else, Thomas went about his tasks in a quiet professional manner. But don't let that fool you; he could produce the timely unexpected zinger. Like this one.

A reporter recognized a dated tune playing in the elevator he shared with Thomas and suggested, "This is from your time, huh?" Without hesitation, Thomas measured his words, paused for effect and replied, "I like to think...it still is my time."

71 Hit the Road with the Sharks

Few can complain about the fan experience at the Shark Tank, which after use for 23 years was already targeted to be the third oldest NHL building behind Madison Square Garden and Calgary's Saddledome with the opening of new arenas in Edmonton (2016) and Detroit (2017).

Fans can, however, broaden their hockey viewing pleasure—and get a feel for what the Sharks experience—by hitting the road just like the team. We're not suggesting shadowing the Sharks on one of their infamous seven games in 12-night specials. If you're selective, do a little research and plan ahead; it's definitely a memory to savor, whether done solo or with a group.

Every NHL destination offers a different experience, both inside the host city's arena and out on its streets. See what hockey really means in Canada by visiting any one of the seven Great White North outposts. Don't be afraid of the cold or snow; it only adds to the Canadian flavor. Pick up a paper and don't be surprised to see the first six pages of the sports section contain hockey-only stories.

Walk into any Canadian pub on a Saturday night. As soon as Coach's Corner and Don Cherry pops on the screen, listen to the place go silent and all eyes focus on the big screen. Think hockey is a big deal in Canada? It's much more than a religion; the game is woven into the fabric of this friendly nation. And it's awesome to experience.

"You hear that all the time," traveling Sharks fan Chris Shuttlesworth said. "But once inside you can just feel it in your soul."

The United States has its hockey-mad pockets—Detroit, Boston, Philadelphia, Chicago, Pittsburgh, and the New York area boast loyal support. Sun worshipers won't be disappointed with either of Florida's two stops—Sunrise and Tampa—along with other Sun Belt destinations in Dallas, Southern California or the Phoenix area.

All it takes is a little imagination and creativity.

That's what Shuttlesworth has learned in her more than 15 seasons of select hockey travel. It all started in late January of 2002 when she chose the final three stops of San Jose's five-game Eastern swing to visit historic Montreal, Toronto, and Pittsburgh when the Penguins were still skating in the Igloo.

Shuttlesworth visited the Hockey Hall of Fame and got her picture taken with the Stanley Cup while in Toronto. She hopped aboard Canada's clean and efficient Via Rail to reach fabled Montreal where going to a hockey game is truly a unique experience. Several blocks from the modern Molson Centre is where the Habs used to play—a mall sits on the site of the old Montreal Forum where the red and blue lines remain when the surface was ice.

"It's not just fun to support my team, but it's a good way to visit places I wouldn't otherwise have a reason to see," Shuttlesworth said. "Why would I visit Detroit? What would be the reason to go to Denver? You get there, and they're lovely cities that all have their interesting things about them."

Taking the train throughout Canada, or the Red Arrow bus between Calgary and Edmonton, allows for views right into backyards where you'll spot homemade rinks. The train is an excellent way to get around the U.S. Northeastern cities, too.

Nashville might not be close to another NHL city, but it's a must-see destination. The Country Music Hall of Fame and Museum, the Ryman Auditorium, and the lively bar scene on

Broadway are just a slap shot away from where the Predators play.

Experiencing the National Anthem at a sold out United Center in Chicago is alone worth the price of admission. Guaranteed goose bumps result regardless of your level of patriotism.

Think Buffalo doesn't have anything to offer? Guess again. It's a short drive to Niagara Falls, and only 90 minutes from Toronto. The building is tremendous, the fans are loyal yet friendly, and they play both the Canadian and U.S. anthems no matter where the opponent comes from.

Best building in the league? This vote goes to the Xcel Energy Center in St. Paul, Minnesota. More affectionately known as the Lodge, the Wild's home has the feel of a huge cabin in the woods with perfect sight lines and all the modern amenities.

Is it safe to wear your visiting team's colors?

"That question comes up a lot—do you feel unsafe?" Shuttlesworth said. "I've never really felt unsafe. I probably got the most chatter in Boston, all in good fun. As long as you're not looking to pick a fight you're fine.

"It's a little rough when you travel and your team loses. You have to be prepared to wear it," she added. "It always makes for interesting conversation. 'What are you in town for?' 'I'm here to watch the Sharks play.' 'Really?'"

Top-6 Food Cities

(Editor's note: Victor Chi served 10 years as the Sharks beat writer for the San Jose Mercury News. Because he doubled as a food connoisseur on the road, Victor provides the following recommendations.)

If you're looking to hit the road with the Sharks, here are some considerations that offer the best blend of scrumptious food and a robust hockey environment.

For the purposes of creating this short list, I established some ground rules, just so nobody looks at these picks and thinks, *Whaddya nuts? How can you not include Boston? Or Toronto?* Or wherever. I get it.

There is incredible food everywhere on the NHL circuit.

- **Rule 1:** List is limited to six cities, a nod to the Original Six
- **Rule 2:** Equal split between U.S. and Canada
- **Rule 3:** Because travel was unbalanced, four are from the Western Conference and two are from the East.

Here goes:

Montreal: This is one of the world's best food cities. It is famous for its smoked meat in the same way that New York is known for its pastrami. Poutine, an original Quebecois concoction of fries, cheese, and gravy, is best described by *Esquire*'s Chris Jones: "If bacon ate, bacon would eat poutine." A good way to start a conversation (or argument) in Montreal is asking who has the better steaks: Gibby's or Moishes? Our advice: try both; there are no losers in this game.

Edmonton: The *Hardware Grill* puts a Canadian twist on food that's fresh, modern, and local. Example: Bacon-wrapped elk and slow-braised beef rib. It is considered fine dining, so budget appropriately. But the atmosphere is lively and neighborly, not too formal, the way some high-end places can be. *Cafe Praha* is a Czech establishment, specializing in comfort food, and that's a huge plus on those nights when you feel like your eyelids are going to freeze off. Go for the roasted goose, one of its signature dishes.

Calgary: *Caesar's Steak House* is a classic old-school steakhouse with leather seats and very little lighting. Whatever steak you pick, get the sautéed mushrooms as a side. *River Cafe* is Calgary's version of the Hardware Grill: A little pricey but the freshness, taste, and innovation make it worthwhile. *Joey's* is a chain that has undergone some re-branding. Originally Joey Tomato's, which had an Italian sensibility, it transitioned to Joey's Mediterranean, and apparently it has now settled on just Joey's. But the food was always zesty, its portions were generous, and the kitchen stayed open late.

Chicago: In a world-class city that has become even more puck-centric since the revival of the Blackhawks, there are many options. Here are two worth noting. In keeping with the theme of steakhouses, *Gene & Georgetti* is a Chicago institution that opened in 1941.

There's a reason why it's still so popular. *Tufano's* is a neighborhood Italian restaurant on Vernon Park with chalkboard menus and a no-credit card policy. It is popular with Blackhawks fans and players, so if you want to get into the local hockey ambiance, this is the place.

Denver: The *Buckhorn Exchange* has been open since 1893, and the number of its Colorado state liquor license is 1. Steaks are great, but wild game is the specialty with choices including buffalo, elk, and quail. It's not always on the menu, but I've had yak here. Rocky Mountain Oysters is the featured appetizer, and if you're unfamiliar with this dish, let's just say it has nothing to do with seafood. Lots of animals are stuffed and mounted on the wall, so the joke goes that part of your dinner is watching you eat the rest of it. *My Brother's Bar* had a location that was the perfect lunch stop as we walked from the arena back to the hotel after the morning skate on game days. It is unmarked. No signs. No awnings. Just fantastic burgers and a healthy beer selection.

Philadelphia: Picking New York—and I love New York—seems like a cop-out, so I'm going with Philly largely because of *Jack's Firehouse.* This is where I once had pan-fried bear in a sauce made with lime and Coke, and its pulled pork is fantastic. Jack's also features a chef's choice menu where adventurous types are willing to be surprised based on what's fresh and tasty that day. Want lunch options? Go to *Reading Terminal Market,* which has more than two dozen restaurants, plus other food stores, under one roof.

Ninja Hertl's Four-Goal Game

Tomas Hertl skated around a flat-footed defender at the blue line, danced through the left circle, glided into the crease with a wide stance, stick-handled the puck behind his left leg and flipped a trick shot into the upper part of the net.

Goal No. 4 of the night.

Tomas Hertl burst onto the scene with a Saturday night special: four goals with a highlight-reel doozy during barely 11 minutes of play in only the rookie's third career NHL game.

Joe Thornton swiped at the puck in front, not knowing it had already gone into the net. He flashed an incredulous smile toward the referee, then whipped his head around to the find Hertl already celebrating on the near boards.

Hertl's mother and girlfriend were attending their first game—only Hertl's third in the NHL. The telecast caught mother and girlfriend in a poignant embrace. Both wore teal Sharks jerseys, Hertl's mother sporting the No. 12. That's the jersey Hertl was given to wear when drafted 17th overall a mere 16 months earlier in June of 2012. Replica No. 48 jerseys were not available to the public yet, but they would be soon.

After a 9–2 win over a New York Rangers team playing the second of back-to-backs during a season-opening nine-game trip, there was Hertl standing in front of his locker trying to answer questions, and put what had just happened into perspective, in his best broken English.

"It's crazy," Hertl said. "This is a dream. Four goals. I never (scored four) in the Czech League. I never had three. In the NHL, it's crazy."

Goal No. 1 came at 9:19 of the second period on a breakaway and chased Rangers superstar goalie Henrik Lundqvist.

Goal No. 2 came at 12:32 of the middle period against Lundqvist's reliever, Marty Biron. Hertl's hat-trick goal, a turn-around effort in front of Biron, came at 9:02 of the third.

Then came the stunner, the goal that got national attention, the goal at 12:05 of the final period that was the ultimate show stopper.

"That's something I don't have in my bag," Joe Thornton said of Hertl's unique move. "He likes to score goals, and you can see that by his celebrations. He loves to put pucks in the back of the net, and as his teammate it's fun to watch."

Hertl put himself in the record books, too. Tying a team record set by Owen Nolan during his seventh season in the league, Hertl became the youngest NHLer to score four goals since Jimmy Carson did so with the Kings in 1988 at the age of 19 years and 254 days. The Czech native was 19 years and 330 days on his fateful night of October 8, 2013, for which he was quickly dubbed the Teenage Mutant Hertl.

The database at Hockey-Reference.com listed only Jussi Jokinen with Dallas in 2007 (11:04) and Michael Nylander with Chicago in 1999 (10:41) having scored four goals with less than 12 minutes of ice time like Hertl (11:12).

It had been a whirlwind week for Hertl. He collected his first NHL point with an assist as San Jose's first teenage rookie to dress on an opening night in seven years. He scored his first two goals in Game 2. Living out of a local hotel while bumming rides from teammate Alex Stalock because Hertl at 21 was too young to rent a car, he inadvertently stepped into controversy by using such a flashy move to score and celebrate in a game that was long decided.

"He's a passionate young man and I'm not even sure if he realizes where he is," Sharks coach Todd McLellan said. "He's innocent out there."

Not that Hertl was the reason why, but Biron played only one more game—four nights later for the Rangers—before calling it a career after 17 NHL seasons.

The four-goal game thrust Hertl into the national spotlight, and he continued to pace NHL rookie scorers through the season's first couple of months as inquiring media in each outpost was eager to detail Hertl's story.

The best nugget may have come through a translator when Hertl was asked about his childhood idol, Jaromir Jagr, and if he tried to pattern his game after the established superstar and ageless fellow countryman. "Both of us have big bottoms and I just try to use my big bottom as Jagr does," Hertl was translated as saying.

Hertl's breakthrough rookie campaign, however, took a dramatic turn.

Late in the first period of a game on December 19 in Los Angeles, Hertl collided knee-on-knee with Kings captain Dustin Brown, who was assessed a major penalty but was not suspended. Hertl was injured. Surgery was needed to repair torn ligaments in his right knee, yet Hertl surprised the medics by returning in time to appear in the season's final two regular-season games and all seven contests in the playoffs.

73 "Let 'Em Try It Against Pitt!"

It started innocently enough.

Following a 7–4 loss to the Rangers at Madison Square Garden to open a seven-game trip during the 1995–96 season, several Sharks players were joking about going back into Manhattan as the team bus headed the opposite direction through the Lincoln Tunnel. San Jose would bed down in nearby New Jersey since it had a game the following night against the Devils.

A short time later, back at the Embassy Suites near the Meadowlands, roommates Owen Nolan and Ray Sheppard were watching television in their bedrooms at the back of their suite.

"I guess Jim Kyte had come and knocked on our door," Nolan recalled. "We didn't hear it. So he went and told the coaches we went to New York."

That put interim coach Jim Wiley in a tough spot. Wiley had been promoted from San Jose's minor-league team in Kansas City to take over behind the Sharks' bench in early December to replace the fired Kevin Constantine.

The former NHL defenseman inherited quite a mess. San Jose had won only three of its first 25 games after reaching the second round of the playoffs each of the previous two springs.

Wiley was very much interested in turning his interim tag into "head coach," so he had to weigh the risk of creating a ripple or keeping the peace. But from what Kyte had told him, Wiley felt some form of discipline was in order. He decided to scratch Nolan and Sheppard, two of the team's biggest offensive threats, for the game in New Jersey.

"We couldn't figure out why we weren't playing," Nolan said. "We weren't getting an explanation.

"It was bizarre, I've never seen anything like that."

The Sharks managed to snap a seven-game losing streak with a 2–1 win over the host Devils. But two nights later the Sharks were scheduled to visit the powerhouse Pittsburgh Penguins. San Jose was not only an NHL-worst 3–15–2 on the road, but 0–6–2 lifetime against the Pens—one of four franchises the Sharks had yet to beat. And Pittsburgh had the second-best home record in the league at 18–3.

"That's why that quote came out—'Let 'em try it against Pitt,'" Nolan admitted.

And who said that?

"Oh, I can't remember. It could have been me, I said a lot of dumb things in my career," Nolan offered with a laugh.

Re-inserted into the lineup, Sheppard collected his seventh career hat trick by scoring three goals and Nolan added two more. Each chipped in an assist to combine for five goals and seven points. The Sharks rallied from a three-goal deficit and beat the Penguins 10–8, a game that stands as the franchise's best offensive output on the road.

While getting set for a rink-side interview for viewers back home, Sheppard reminded the team's public relations director, "You know, Buster and I had half of the goals."

"I don't think I can explain this game," Wiley said at the time. "I know this sounds kind of stupid, but I didn't really think we played that open (of a game). If we had, God knows what the score would have been—18-to-something, probably."

The Sharks lost the last four games of the trip, went 10–25–3 the rest of the way, and finished last in the Pacific Division. Wiley returned to coaching in the minors the following season. Nolan finished with 61 points, one behind Craig Janney for the team lead. And Sheppard, acquired in October from Detroit for Igor Larionov, was dealt again before season's end to expansion Florida.

Yet, how do you explain that one crazy night in Pittsburgh?

"I don't know," Nolan said. "We played hard every night so I think the cards just fell where they were and we had a good night."

74 All-Star Calls His Shot

By 1997, the once competitive NHL All-Star Game had transformed itself from an anticipated midseason showcase to little more than a three-hour game of shinny hockey.

The event had turned into a non-contact match played by million-dollar stars. They certainly weren't going to risk injury for an exhibition to cap off a weekend of events geared to involve and captivate new and old fans of the sport.

Fans had grown accustomed to final scores as 12–7, 16–6, 11–5, 10–6, and 9–8 leading up to the 47th annual event hosted by San Jose.

The game played on January 18, 1997, followed a similar pattern as the Eastern Conference built a 10–4 lead over the West by the late second period. That changed dramatically, though, over the final 22 minutes and you can thank a hometown hero for injecting life into this All-Star Game.

"I still to this day get people saying, it was one of their favorite moments in hockey," said Owen Nolan, the author of a called shot.

To set the scene, Nolan was a blossoming star in the league. He scored 33 goals the previous season, 29 after the Sharks acquired the burly right wing from Colorado in an early-season trade. Nolan was the home team's lone rep until veteran forward Tony Granato was made a late special selection by NHL Commissioner Gary Bettman to replace the injured Joe Sakic.

Held off the score sheet for nearly two periods, Nolan redirected a feed from Calgary's Theoren Fleury past New Jersey goalie Martin Brodeur. Then Nolan beat Brodeur with a blast from the wing eight seconds later to set an All-Star Game record for the two quickest goals by one skater.

Buffalo's Dominik Hasek went into the East goal to start the third period. The Dominator stopped Nolan on a breakaway 25 seconds into the final period, and denied him on four more shots as West teammates tried to set Nolan up for a hat trick.

With time ticking down inside the final three minutes, Nolan knew he had precious few chances left.

"I just had had enough," Nolan said at the time. "He's an incredible goalie, he does the same thing during the regular season."

Nolan pounced on a turnover in the neutral zone, and set his sights directly on the goal. Skating unmarked, Nolan took a couple strides to the top of the left circle, pointed in Hasek's direction and wired a hard wrist shot over the goalie's left glove, off the far post and into the net.

The sold-out crowd went nuts as hats reigned on the ice.

"I'd never been in an earthquake to that point, and I honestly thought I was in one and that the roof was going to come down," Nolan recalled.

It would be the only puck out of 21 directed on net that escaped Hasek.

Granato said afterward, "That's something he can use to elevate his game and realize the kind of player he is."

Granato's words proved prophetic.

Nolan went on to play 11 more seasons in the league, and enjoyed his career-best campaign three seasons later when in 1999–2000 he scored 44 goals and 84 points to finish fifth in the league's MVP race. In all, scoring 212 goals and 468 points during 707 games in the seasons that followed the '97 All-Star Game. That brought his impressive career totals to 422 goals, 463 points, and 885 regular-season points during an even 1,200 games.

And his called shot could very well be traced to Nolan's jumping off point as one of the game's more recognizable stars.

"For me? It was nothing planned," said Nolan looking back. "It was spontaneous. It just felt right.

"I had two goals already, it was at the home rink. When you look back at it, if it happens it's great—everyone's going to remember it. If not, then you look like a fool for trying it."

75 Colossal Collapse

The 1942 Detroit Red Wings. The 1975 Pittsburgh Penguins. The 2010 Boston Bruins.

It's an inglorious list, one no team would want to join. And it's a list almost exclusive to the National Hockey League. It's a list of teams that won the first three games of a best-of-seven playoff series only to lose four straight and suffer elimination.

Major League Baseball didn't have such a list until the Boston Red Sox did it to their bitter rivals, the New York Yankees, in 2004. So rare, the National Basketball Association has no such list.

The San Jose Sharks rolled into the 2014 Stanley Cup playoffs for a franchise-record ninth straight season. On the strength of a 13–5–3 record over the final two months of the regular season, the Sharks boasted a 51–22–9 record, good for 111 points. In historical perspective, San Jose eclipsed 51 wins only in 2008–09 when 53 victories and a franchise-high 117 points added up to the club's only Presidents' Trophy. It marked the third time the Sharks landed on exactly 51 wins.

Feeling good about their game and feeling good in general because the roster was injury-free, the Sharks had the added motivation facing the Los Angeles Kings to open the 2014 Stanley Cup playoffs. It was the same Kings who bounced he Sharks during a home-dominated, seven-game series the previous spring.

Things started well enough. The Sharks scored three times in the first period and led 5–0 after two on their way to a 6–3 win in Game 1, chasing goaltending nemesis Jonathan Quick in the process. Game 2 was more of the same. After spotting L.A. two first-period goals, the Sharks roared back to score the last seven—three in the second period and four in the third—to cap a dominating 7–2 victory and a 2–0 series lead.

"Success has only been two games. We've got a lot left," Sharks coach Todd McLellan said, keeping the big picture in mind, afterward.

Two nights later at Staples Center, Game 3 went into overtime tied 3–3 and the host Kings pressed hard by putting the first five shots of sudden death on goal. San Jose's first on net went into the net courtesy of veteran Patrick Marleau, who with his fourth career playoff overtime goal took a step toward shedding his almost annual postseason label as an underachiever.

"They had the bat in their hands, and they were going to swing it," McLellan said, using a baseball reference to describe the desperate Kings' attitude. "They had us on our heels, but sometimes it goes that way. We will take that break."

There was disappointment in the Los Angeles locker room, but no sense of panic. This was basically the same team that won the franchise's first Stanley Cup two years prior. Their veteran coach Darryl Sutter kept things in perspective, saying, "Our better players were better. That was noticeable. That will give us a chance next game."

Next game came two nights later in L.A., again in front of a cautious sellout crowd. The Kings scored first, and the Sharks answered. The Kings second again in the second, and the Sharks answered. The Kings scored two more times late in the second, and there was no answer. It ended 6–3 in favor of the Kings, making it three one-sided results out of four games, a vast departure from the previous spring when five of the seven games were decided by one goal and the two other finals were 2–0 and 3–0.

Still, the Sharks headed home for a potential clinching Game 5.

A raucous sellout crowd, many in teal from head-to-toe, enthusiastically greeted the hosts skating out of the giant Shark mouth before the opening faceoff. It seemed only a matter of time before the night would end with a celebration, one more win to dispatch their SoCal rivals who were on the verge of extinction.

Then the Sharks laid an egg. The Kings scored twice in the opening 13 minutes. There was no pushback from San Jose, which appeared amiss emotionally. Outshot 41–30, the Sharks fell victim to Quick, who was now back, as were the Kings.

Uh oh.

"We did a lot of good things for 3½ games. Tonight was red rotten," McLellan said afterward. "When we started the series, we talked about leaving games behind, closing the book on it. There's no doubt we'll look at it. We have to improve. But it's put in the bank and we'll move on."

Moving on meant a change in goal for starters. Rookie Alex Stalock, who relieved in Game 5, replaced starter Antti Niemi again for Game 6 back at Staples. The Kings scored in the first, and the Sharks scored in the second. It was a 1–1 game still with less than half of the third period to go.

Justin Williams, who has a flair for playoff dramatics, untied it at 11:56. San Jose didn't like the tiebreaking goal. McLellan claimed "we got cheated" after video review upheld the good-goal call. The Sharks protested there was a whistle before Williams' shot. No dice. And the Sharks unraveled. Anze Kopitar scored 91 seconds later. And it was Kopitar again after another 75 seconds passed.

Los Angeles won 4–1. There would be a Game 7.

"In my mind, if it gets to Game 7, it doesn't matter how it gets there," Sharks forward Logan Couture said. "It gets there, and you're going for one game. We played all year for home ice. We've got to turn this thing around and win that game."

With Niemi back in goal to duel Quick, the deciding game was scoreless after one period. When defenseman Matt Irwin blasted his first goal of the series past Quick it was 1–0 Sharks 28 seconds into the second period.

Exhale.

Not so fast.

Defenseman Drew Doughty's power-play goal tied it at 4:57. Kopitar's even-strength strike at 18:39 untied it for the last time. Forwards Tyler Toffoli, Dustin Brown and Tanner Pearson scored goals in the third. The Kings won 5–1 to advance, and the Sharks were stunned, shaking hands on home ice with their season suddenly over.

"It's hard to put into words," San Jose forward Joe Pavelski said afterward. "It's really tough."

"I look at it as they fixed their problems, we didn't," McLellan added. "Our problems got progressively worse. I'm in charge, I'm responsible for the group that performs on the ice. I have to accept that responsibility."

"Every year you lose is pretty low," Couture concluded. "But this one is the type of series that will rip your heart out. It hurts. It's going to be a long summer thinking about this one, and what we let slip away."

The 1942 Detroit Red Wings. The 1975 Pittsburgh Penguins. The 2010 Boston Bruins.

And, now, the 2014 San Jose Sharks.

76 Only the Equipment Guy Knows for Sure

Mike Aldrich's job is pretty simple. The longtime equipment manager for the Sharks is prepared with everything a player might want or need to perform his best.

"We had a player who liked purple gum," Aldrich said. "So we pack purple gum."

Aldrich has spent more than two decades with the National Hockey League team. He's the first person to arrive at the rink in the morning, and the last to leave after a late-night game. Day after day, month after month, year after year, Aldrich grinds away. Players come and go. Coaches are hired and fired. The one constant is Mike Aldrich.

"There is nobody in our organization that works harder," said Randy Hahn, that team's longtime television voice.

Aldrich disagrees. He proudly hails from Michigan's Upper Peninsula and the tiny town of Hancock, the northern-most city in the state where logging and mining is how inhabitants make their living.

"My grandparents' generation mined underground. I have really close friends there, and they work hard," Aldrich said. "I've said it a million times. We don't work hard, hard. I just work stupid hours."

You decide.

Aldrich and his staff are responsible for everything a player needs—freshly sharpened skates, a healthy supply of sticks, altered equipment which is different for virtually everyone, a clean jersey, and socks, whether for practice or games—and that's just the tip of the iceberg.

The season stops for no one, especially Aldrich. There is a constant need for supplies. Basically, from weeks before the start of training camp until several weeks after the postseason, the equipment and training staff's work is constant and unrelenting.

"For me, I need 8½ hours of sleep a night," Joe Thornton said. "Most nights he gets 4–5 hours, and there's no complaining. He just sucks it up. Mikey's the first guy you see at the rink, he's got a smile on his face and he's ready to go."

"It's almost inhuman the kind of work schedule those guys keep," added Scott Emmert, a longtime team spokesman. "Home games are one thing—Mike's probably here by 7 in the morning on game day, and certainly one of the last to leave. But it's the travel where it really gets crazy."

The Sharks are notorious for having long road trips with many stops—the curse of being a West Coast-based team. Aldrich has been part of all 29 trips consisting of six or more games during his time with the team. That included a league record 10-game trek for nearly three weeks in February of 1999 featuring 7,123 nautical miles of travel by air and countless bus trips to arenas from airports and hotels.

"We land in a city at 1:30 in the morning. There's a bus for us that goes straight to the Ritz-Carlton, and there's a big white truck with all the equipment where Mike Aldrich sits up front and goes to the arena," Hahn said.

"They hang wet gear for an hour and a half before they get to bed, and knowing they'll be the first ones back in a few hours before anyone else arrives," Emmert added. "And it's day after day after day."

"He just motors away every day," Thornton added.

Why in the world would anyone get into this kind of racket?

After chasing a dream to play hockey at a high level died, Aldrich considered the Air Force before opting to remain at Michigan Tech where he was coaxed to leave a mailroom job he enjoyed to reluctantly become equipment manager for hockey and football. With sights set on the NFL someday, Aldrich turned down a job offer from the University of Michigan because it didn't make economic sense.

Not long after, Aldrich returned to his desk one day to find a scribbled note telling him to phone Doug Soetaert.

"A student took the call, and when I asked if this was the former NHL goalie and he said, 'I don't know,'" Aldrich recalled. "The name wasn't even spelled right."

It indeed was the retired 12-year vet, now general manager of the IHL's Kansas City Blades, who was in need of an equipment manager. Aldrich had a verbal commitment to take a similar job at Denver University, but the school's athletic director—an acquaintance of Soetaert—recommended his would-be employee because Aldrich was trying to advance the right way: college, minors, then pros.

Aldrich spent three seasons with the Blades, where he grew close to owners Russ and Diane Parker along with members of the coaching staff that included head man Jim Wiley and assistants Drew Remenda and the late Vasily Tikhonov.

"I loved Kansas City; I had no intention to ever leave there," Aldrich said. "My family loved it there. I wanted to buy a house and kind of live happily ever after."

Times were changing in San Jose, however, and the parent team wanted Aldrich, who only agreed when Dean Lombardi was named G.M. Even so, the 1996–97 season was a challenge.

"My first season was miserable," Aldrich admitted. "We had a young coach who was tough. There was really no direction. Then they added Darryl (Sutter) and I knew this was what I wanted to do forever."

Now, with close to 2,000 NHL games under his belt, Aldrich's resume also includes work for Team USA at the Winter Olympics, World Championships, World Cup of Hockey, and during the '97 NHL All-Star Game in San Jose for the Western Conference.

"He does it all," Thornton said. "He sharpens skates, he fixes things, he's a therapist. He does so much for the guys. And he's not appreciated as much as he should be, but we all do love him."

Short Takes with Mike Aldrich

Questions and answers with the Sharks' longtime equipment manager:

Q. How much sleep do you need?

A. "Once I'm on a schedule I want five hours of sleep max. If I get more than that I feel rotten."

Q. How do you handle odd requests?

A. "The answer from me is never no. But it may not happen immediately. If that's what it takes for a guy to be ready to play, he'll have it."

Q. How do you remain patient?

A. "I was probably a little on the fussy side, too. I would mess around with my own stuff. Being a small person I always had to alter my gloves, pants, and jerseys. Between myself and my grandmother I used to do a lot of that stuff on my own."

Q. How do you find time to work out, too, every day?

A. "That's my priority. I'm not a napper. I'd rather get a workout, and I'll feel better."

Q. What was Darryl Sutter like behind closed doors?

A. "Darryl was tough to work for, but not in my position. I'd sometimes look in the room and think, *God I'm glad I'm the equipment manager and don't have to put the pads on.* He knew the people who were important to him. He pushed you, too, but he also patted you on the back."

Q. Who are among your favorites?

A. "Every manager has had great guys they can use as an example. Mine are Gary Suter, Tony Granato, Rob Blake, and Patrick Marleau. They stand the test of time because they never change anything. They're always nice to people. They always trained their bodies and took care of themselves the same way."

Q. How do you give everyone their space yet be available always?

A. "It's delicate. I don't work for the CIA or the government. I have a lot of pride working for this organization, but I don't get wrapped up in the drama."

Q. What's the best part of your job?

A. "I still love walking out to the bench. I'm a big-time sap for the National Anthem."

Woody: The One and Only

Before Mike Aldrich, there was Tom Woodcock—or, as he was more affectionately called, "Woody."

"I came in the league when there was characters," retired Sharks forward Murray Craven said. "Woody was the last of the characters."

Woodcock was actually the team's original head trainer, brought to expansion San Jose in 1991–92 with 23 years of NHL experience. He remained in a full-time capacity for 13 years before making cameo training camp appearances for several more seasons.

Woodcock worked more than 3,000 NHL games over his 37 years, and was inducted into the Professional Hockey Trainers Society Hall of Fame in 2003.

"I was scared to death of him when I first game in," Aldrich admitted. "There was never a question who was in charge of the equipment managers, the trainers, and the auxiliary staff. He made sure everything ran smooth. And he was 100 percent an athlete-first guy."

He will forever be known for a concoction he called "Woody's Rub-Dub," a rubbing balm that he would liberally apply on an injured player's sore spot. No one knew what was in it, but the players swore by the stuff.

"Oh, it burned like you cannot believe," Craven said. "But the reason it was so good is that it lasted so long." Woody made container after container, always labeling them with the words "Rub-Dub" on hockey tape that circled the container. When a player got traded, he would request Woody's rub-dub, and that's how it would get into other teams' locker rooms.

"I used to needle his wife, 'Tina, some day you've got to sneak the secret to us.' She said, 'No way, that's like Colonel Sanders' secret recipe,'" Aldrich said. "Tina was an Italian from the East Coast. She'd say, 'You'd have an easier time getting my spaghetti sauce recipe from me.'"

Craven did his best to describe it. "It was kind of orange, kind of red. You had to put on gloves otherwise you'd have it on your hands and you might touch your eyes." "He would tell guys, 'Be careful with that; it might kill you,'" Aldrich added.

77 Nabby Scores Historic Goal

The Sharks-Canucks game at Vancouver on March, 10, 2002, had just about everything.

San Jose captain Owen Nolan notched a season-high five points on the strength of a goal and four assists. Nolan's 17th goal of the season came with two-tenths of a second left in an opening period that saw the Canucks jump out 2–0 while outshooting the hosts 14–1.

The late goal provided the impetus for three more in the span of five shots during a 2:38 span of the early second period for a lead the Sharks would not relinquish. Scott Thornton topped his previous year's career-high by scoring his 20th goal to cap the three-goal explosion. Then, even before the end of the period, Thornton fought for a third time in the game to earn an automatic game misconduct.

Enough yet? Not nearly.

Frustrated Canucks forward Jarkko Ruutu planted an elbow in the ear of Bryan Marchment late, a deliberate and cheap-shot act that invited a major penalty and ejection. Moved by how the Sharks defenseman remained motionless on the ice for a brief period, Vancouver coach Marc Crawford accused Marchment of overdramatizing the moment.

"I think the play was a disgrace," Crawford said. "There's some sour grapes there because we lost the game....It was bush. He deserves everything he gets."

Marchment was ready in his team's locker room when Crawford's quote was relayed to him: "He's gutless. He does a lot of things around the league that guys don't respect. He was gutless as a player, and he's still gutless."

All that, and we still haven't gotten to the headline of this game.

That moment came at 19:12 of the third period, Vancouver with its goalie pulled trying to rally from a 6–4 deficit and the Sharks still on a power play thanks to Ruutu's penalty.

Let's let Randy Hahn's call on the telecast describe the event: "Nabokov knocks it down....He'll try and SCORE!...Evgeni NabokovvvVVV!...HE SCORESSSSSS!...Evgeni Nabokov has SCORED the first goal in his NHL career. And THAT puts the cherry on top."

That's right. A power-play goal from Nabokov, who thus not only became the seventh goalie all-time to fill the opposing net, but the first European-born netminder to do so on the power play.

"I saw how their defense was really split wide so I thought, *Go for it*," Nabokov said. "It was exciting."

Rewinding a bit, Vancouver's Markus Naslund gathered a loose puck in the neutral zone, skated a semi-circle from the left boards to center and backhanded the puck on net just as a linemate hit the San Jose blue line with the intent to chase it down.

Nabokov calmly gloved the dump-in, dropped it to the ice five feet in front of the top of his crease, made a quick fake to his left as if he was going to dish to Sharks defenseman Brad Stuart, and instead saucered a shot maybe 15 feet off of the ice and over center that dropped back to the clean sheet midway into the Canucks zone. With the crescendo of crowd noise growing with anticipation, the puck slid flat on the ice into the lower right corner of the vacant net.

Goal.

Stuart, bearing a wide grin, was first to hug Nabokov. Then Vincent Damphousse, Niklas Sundstrom, and finally Stephane Matteau joined in the unexpected celebration.

"Really, the goalies weren't very sharp in terms of stopping the puck," Sharks coach Darryl Sutter said. "It was great to see that. You could tell that's what he was trying to do."

78 Vincent Damphousse

Vincent Damphousse spent all but one of his first dozen seasons in the NHL under the intense media scrutiny and fishbowl-like atmosphere only the hockey-centric cities Montreal and Toronto could offer.

Things were different, however, on his first day as a Shark. Damphousse had to talk his way into the building past security, who failed to recognize the team's newest acquisition.

Welcome to San Jose.

"For me it was a welcome change," Damphousse recalled after leaving his hometown team. "It was getting kind of stale with the Canadiens. And the key for me was going to a team that really wanted me, and they liked what I brought to them."

The Sharks were looking for offense. They had been held to two or fewer goals in 43 of their first 70 games. San Jose was executing second-year coach Darryl Sutter's defensive system to perfection and, despite riding a six-game unbeaten streak, needed a boost to ensure reaching the playoffs.

General manager Dean Lombardi also wanted to reward his team that opened the season with a taxing two-game trip to Japan, and survived a record 10-game road trip in February. But risk came with dealing three draft picks to acquire the 31-year-old Damphousse, who could walk as a free agent in the offseason.

"With Darryl, we had a good relationship," Damphousse said. "I felt he knew what I could bring. He gave me a lot of ice time. He's someone I wanted to play for."

Between that first impression and scoring seven goals and 13 points in 12 games, Damphousse was convinced to sign a five-year deal.

"Not that it was difficult, but it was different," said Damphousse comparing his time in Canada with San Jose. "To always be looked after or followed, they knew who you were everywhere you went. In San Jose you could do other things. The sunshine, the good weather outside of the rink, it keeps you energized."

Classy and well-spoken, Damphousse fit in well with the Sharks, who were screaming out for a No. 1 center in addition to the infusion of leadership and experience. Sutter had a player he could trust, and Lombardi had someone younger players could emulate. Damphousse had a new home where he could continue to be a solid contributor.

"I didn't sign to be a mentor, per se," Damphousse said. "Even though I had been in the league a while, my role was to perform, not to be there as just a second fiddle."

Damphousse scored 92 goals and 289 points in 385 games over those five-plus seasons in San Jose. Including the season he was acquired, Damphousse helped the bounce-back Sharks reach the playoffs for four straight seasons. He scored 20 or more goals three times, and was known for a deadly backhand shot that often confounded opposing netminders.

"He was a high-scoring guy wherever he played," said ex-Sharks defenseman Gary Suter. "When he came to San Jose he was put in a leadership role. I know Darryl respected, talked to him a lot and was in his ear about different things."

79 Teemu Selanne

Teemu Selanne's tenure in San Jose was brief, but not without substance. The Finnish Flash wore teal for basically two seasons, and left his usual indelible mark on the organization despite his short stay.

"I don't know if he was always 100 percent when he was here, but he still loved coming to the rink every day, playing hard and having fun," Patrick Marleau said. "You saw that."

The Sharks acquired Selanne at the March 5 trade deadline in 2001 in a surprising move considering the star-power player they were receiving, and the fact San Jose engineered a significant deal with division-rival Anaheim. Then known as the Mighty Ducks, Anaheim sat last in the Pacific and moved its leading goal-scorer in the 30-year-old Selanne for respected goalie Steve Shields, popular forward Jeff Friesen and a second-round draft pick.

Selanne's debut in San Jose was delayed a couple weeks following a procedure to remove loose cartilage from a knee, but he finished strong by scoring 13 points in 12 games as a Shark.

The highlight came on March 29 when the Sharks faced Selanne's ex-teammates for the first time since the trade. Selanne recorded a hat trick during a 7–4 win. Coincidentally, and almost poetically, Selanne's longtime running mate in Anaheim—Paul Kariya—scored three goals in the game as well. Not only that, after Selanne scored his first of the night (his first as a Shark), he turned and inadvertently bumped into Kariya, looking for a moment as if they would share an awkward embrace.

"It was a big relief," Selanne said afterward.

Selanne was without a goal and had managed three assists during his first six games with San Jose before that emotional night against the Mighty Ducks.

There weren't as many big nights in San Jose as Selanne would have liked. Injuries, or feeling less than 100 percent, plagued him during his tenure.

Selanne broke his right thumb in the opening game of a first-round playoff series against St. Louis just months after his acquisition, an injury that was not disclosed until the eve of the Blues' clinching win in Game 6. Selanne heard criticism for his lack of production—no points until the first of two assists in the series that didn't come until Game 5.

"I can't do anything with the puck," Selanne said at the time. "It's frustrating for me because I want to help the team. It's tough when you can't even feel the puck."

Selanne had decent, if not spectacular numbers, his two full seasons in San Jose. Selanne's 29 goals in 2001–02 and 28 in 2002–03 led the team, and he was third and first among San Jose scorers with 64 and 54 points, respectively.

And, just as was the case in Anaheim, when the Sharks fell out of the playoff race in 2002–03, they looked to deal Selanne to the New Jersey Devils. Selanne blocked the deadline deal, decided not to pick up a $6.5 million option to return to San Jose, and signed a $5.8 million pact to play one season with Colorado.

And just like that, the Finnish Flash was gone.

Even if Selanne didn't make as big of an impression on the ice as San Jose had hoped, he was the life of the party in the locker room and a steady leader off the ice.

"If it was quiet, all of a sudden Teemu would get up and do something no one thought would happen to keep things light," Marleau recalled. "I don't know if he was trying to do it on purpose or that was just his personality."

Watching his rambunctious sons turn San Jose's locker room into their personal play pen on select practice days was always entertaining. Selanne's close friend, a pilot in the military, was another frequent visitor to the room. They joked about racing from the Bay Area to Selanne's Orange County home—Selanne in one of the fast cars in his collection and his friend via jet. But they weren't kidding.

What would you expect from someone whose first job was teaching kindergarten for three years in his native Helsinki, Finland.

"The biggest thing I learned from Teemu was always having passion for the game and life," Marleau said.

80 Darryl Sutter

Think of Darryl Sutter and the words *taskmaster*, *demanding*, *driven*, and *intense* come to mind. Sutter will tell you exactly what he thinks. He won't mince words, and he won't sugarcoat.

But there's another side to Sutter not everyone is privileged to see.

"We're talking about a guy who's bark is worse than his bite," said Drew Remenda, a former coach and television commentator in San Jose. "Such a big heart."

That big heart is what pulled Sutter away from hockey, and brought him back again as the Sharks' fifth head coach in eight years of existence. And the story begins long before Sutter was hired on June 9, 1997, by general manager Dean Lombardi.

Late in 1992–93 as a first-year coach of the Chicago Blackhawks, the only NHL team for which he also played, Sutter became a father for the third time. His wife, Wanda, gave birth to their second son, Christopher, who on March 30, 1993, entered the world with Down syndrome. The Sutters were told Chris faced long odds to live, and if he did, he'd likely be blind, deaf, and need to be institutionalized.

Multiple surgeries got Christopher through his early years, putting his early prognosis in the rearview mirror. After another two years behind the Blackhawks' bench, Darryl felt the need to give his youngest son two parents providing full-time support instead of one. He returned to the family farm in Viking, Alberta, and drove young Christopher 50 miles each way to therapy three times a week.

The itch to return to coaching and Christopher's medical needs intersected as the Sharks, who needed a new bench boss, played in a city that is world-renowned for medical services for Down syndrome patients. It was a perfect match.

"People think of Darryl and the Sutter brothers as being tough, but the thing I remember about him is what a wonderful father and a family man he is," said Adam Graves, who played parts of two seasons under Darryl in San Jose. "That's what always resonated with me."

Tending to family challenges off the ice was one thing. Picking up the pieces of a Sharks team that had finished last two seasons in a row and changing fortunes was quite another. On the first day of training camp, Sutter observed how the Sharks were used to doing things and said to a nearby reporter, "I'm not here to run a hockey school."

"He knew he had to be the bad guy. He had to change the culture," Remenda said. "He had a plan from the get-go, this is how I have to be."

"Darryl is obviously a competitor, and I think that's an understatement," added Gary Suter, a defenseman who played for Sutter in Chicago and San Jose. "And he demanded that everybody works their tail off. When you play Darryl Sutter teams you know they're going to keep coming and coming. And they're going to battle, scratch and claw."

Saying one time players had to look good on the ice, not just good in a suit off of it, Sutter instituted a system that stressed playing hard and responsible from the goal out. Players bought in, or they were shipped out. Sutter would lead the Sharks to respectability in the only way he knew how.

"I liked Darryl because he was fair to everybody. It didn't matter if you were a young guy or a veteran," said Vincent Damphousse. "Ice time needed to be earned, it wasn't a given."

"If you own a team, you might not agree with everything he does, but you're not going to find a guy who gives more than the 100 percent Darryl gives every day," said Bernie Nicholls, who played under Sutter both in Chicago and San Jose.

Under Sutter's leadership, the Sharks established an identity and rode that nightly hard-work ethic to five straight playoff appearances for the first time during each of Sutter's first five seasons behind the bench.

"I'll never forget; he'd be in the dressing room with his hands on his knees, swaying from side to side while looking around the room," Graves recalled. "He saw everyone else getting ready for the drop of the puck. He wanted to win so bad. That is not manufactured, that comes from within."

"There's not a more intense person than Darryl," Nicholls added. "Game day, it doesn't matter if it's the 50th game of the season, the first game of the season or the final game of the season, he's so intense."

His game and player analysis was expressed in short sentences with simple terminology, but Sutter hit an intellectual side and he was known by those on the inside for his preparation and complete understanding of the game.

"The team we're playing tonight could have a new kid up, his first game," Nicholls illustrated. "I remember Darryl asking a player, 'Do you know anything about this guy'? It's his first game, players have no clue. But Darryl will tell you what he had for breakfast, who his first girlfriend was, where he's from, what his mum and dad do for a living."

Behind the scenes, Sutter treated his locker room like the inhabitants of his cattle farm—they were family. Sutter cared to make good players great. He cared for them on and off of the ice.

"I loved Darryl," Owen Nolan said. "He really made me look at the game in a different way."

Nolan arrived in San Jose two years before Darryl, having shown flashes of the potential that made him the No. 1 overall draft pick in 1990 by Quebec. But Nolan was inconsistent, he was moody. Maybe Sutter saw a little of himself in Nolan.

"I remember going through a tough time, something like 13 games without scoring," Nolan said. "He called me into his office, looked at me straightforward, and said, 'I don't care if you don't score another goal for the rest of the season. But you won't let another goal in when you're on the ice.'

"And that kind of set in with me, 'I really should be a better two-way player.' I just thought offense all the time. That small little speech really helped me become a better two-way player."

Nolan enjoyed the most production of his 18 NHL seasons while playing for Sutter, who made him team captain in 1998.

"I really respected him for doing that," Nolan said. "It was an honor. I was ready to take that leadership role, and really push the team in the right direction."

When the Sharks were 8–12–2–2 after 24 games into 2002–03, Sutter was surprisingly fired after easily racking up the decade-old franchise's best numbers as a coach (192–167–75).

Sutter was out of work for less than a month, hired by Calgary to coach the Flames. And that meant living not far from the family farm in Viking where his wife and Christopher, now in a much better place, felt good about moving back home.

"The thing with Darryl, it's sincere," Remenda said. "He's a real cowboy, and he's a real person."

81 From Brain Surgery to Masterton

Tony Granato was a Shark for the last five seasons of his 13-year NHL career, something made possible only by a life-saving procedure performed on Valentine's Day in 1996.

Granato underwent delicate brain surgery to remove a blood clot that had been causing pressure and bleeding from his left temporal lobe. A member of the Los Angeles Kings, Granato experienced severe headaches and memory loss for several weeks, tracing back to a game in Hartford on January 25. Granato played two nights later, but knew something was wrong when he awoke the day after attending a Super Bowl party at Wayne Gretzky's home.

"I don't think any of us realized in what bad shape he was until that night in L.A. he was rushed to the hospital, and he almost didn't make it," said Kelly Hrudey, a teammate of Granato's that season, and for the next two in San Jose. "At that point, it was like, 'Oh, my God, how could we have not recognized the signs and known that something was going on?'"

Granato not only missed the remainder of the 1996–97 season, but his career was in question. He was 32 years old, married with four children, and at a crossroads.

"I really wanted to come back and play, and I wasn't sure if I was going to be able to," said Granato, who with a modified helmet was determined to play again. "I put down a priority list if I was going to play I wanted to make it closer to home, or make it with a team that I thought could win the Stanley Cup."

The native of Downers Grove, Illinois, targeted his hometown Chicago Blackhawks along with Cup contenders Detroit and Colorado. A chat with agent Jeff Solomon added one more team to the mix.

"He convinced me to meet with Dean Lombardi because he was my old agent," Granato said of San Jose's general manager. "Dean had talked to Jeff and said, 'If Tony is going to come back to play, don't let him sign before he comes to me and I can explain what we're doing here in San Jose.'"

Long before the constraints of a salary cap, Lombardi had a budget to overpay for character veterans who had a resume of winning and leadership but might sign elsewhere for less.

"Dean had a plan in place, he showed me respect, and that he wanted me to help him change the culture in San Jose," Granato recalled. "Really, Dean made it easy on me. With the presentation he made it really flipped me from where I thought I wanted to go instead to San Jose."

Besides supplying leadership and a veteran presence, Granato proved he could still produce on the ice. He scored 25 goals, third most on the team, and played in 76 games for the Sharks in 1996–97. He was selected to play in the NHL All-Star Game, hosted by San Jose, and was a slam dunk winner for the Masterton Trophy for his display of perseverance, sportsmanship, and dedication to hockey.

"When he came to San Jose, Tony showed the young players how hard you have to play," Hrudey said.

Granato's time in San Jose, however, was not without incident. While standing in front of the opposition's goal, Granato was struck in the face with a puck shot by a teammate from the point early in his second season with the Sharks. Granato managed still to appear in 59 games despite having his jaw wired shut and plastic surgery required to repair facial cuts.

"Tony left it all on the ice every single game," Hrudey said. "I can't think of a single game where I thought he dogged it. That was just not part of his makeup."

82 Going for the Gold

Joe Pavelski was three years old the first time National Hockey League players were allowed to participate in the Winter Olympics at Calgary in 1988.

When the United States won gold at Lake Placid to cap the Miracle on Ice, accomplished without the help of the NHL's professional talent, Pavelski was still four years away from birth. All the San Jose Sharks forward has known about hockey and the Winter Games is if you're one of the best players in your country, you could get a chance to play.

During the 2010 Olympics Games, hosted in Vancouver, British Columbia, Pavelski was one of a league-leading eight representatives from the Sharks to pack their bags while the NHL shut down for 18 days to give way for the men's ice hockey tournament to play out.

Team Canada summoned San Jose linemates Joe Thornton, Patrick Marleau, Dany Heatley, and puck-moving defenseman Dan Boyle. In addition, goalie Evgeni Nabokov (Russia), rugged defenseman Douglas Murray (Sweden), and backup goalie Thomas Greiss (Germany) joined Team USA member Pavelski to participate in the most prestigious tournament.

Dressing in the same room for nights, months, and seasons on end, then facing those same close teammates now wearing enemy colors, invited all kinds of interesting reactions.

Boyle scored a goal on Nabokov during Canada's quarterfinal win over Russia. "It was weirder to jump into Ryan Getzlaf's and Corey Perry's arms," Boyle said, referring to Canadian teammates who were bitter division rivals with Anaheim. "What was I thinking?"

Thornton and Pavelski were two of San Jose's most accomplished performers in the faceoff circle during the season. Now they opposed each other looking to win the same draw when USA faced Canada in the gold medal game.

"We practice a lot against each other in faceoffs. I think it was pretty even. It probably went 50–50," Thornton said. Pavelski interrupted to crack, "About 60–40, maybe."

Thornton and his Canadian teammates earned what they were after—the gold medal—but it wasn't easy. Fending off the ever-present pressure when playing in Canada, the host country led the rival Americans 2–0 early, but couldn't celebrate until Sidney

Crosby's goal at 7:40 of overtime gave Canada a 3–2 win over Team USA in what was universally depicted as one of the great deciding games in international hockey history.

"It was complete pandemonium there after the game," Marleau said. "In the streets of Vancouver, it took three greens to get through a light. Everybody was excited. Everybody was honking their horns. People were hanging out of windows. It was spectacular to see. Those are the moments you really cherish your nationality."

Pavelski, a native of Madison, Wisconsin, had designs on ruining Canada's party, of course. His team came close. With one-time Sharks coach Ron Wilson at USA's helm, the Americans won Group A with a 3–0 record while the Canadians finished second at 1–1–1. Team USA shut out Switzerland 2–0 in the quarters and routed Finland in the semis 6–1 while Canada handled Russia 7–3 in the quarters and edged Slovakia 3–2 in the semis.

Trailing 2–1 late in the gold medal game, and with their goalie pulled for an extra attacker, Pavelski put a shot on net that triggered a goal-mouth scramble for the Americans that culminated with Zach Parise tapping home the rebound of a Patrick Kane shot to tie it with 24.4 seconds left in regulation.

The euphoria of a near miracle late-game goal turned to indescribable disappointment shortly into sudden death.

"It's one of those things where you realize the excitement of the game, and it was in Canada and meant so much to the hockey world," Pavelski said. "To be part of it was awesome. We came up short, ultimately one goal shy. Down the road, it'll feel good. But we still didn't win."

Sharks in Olympics

2014 at Sochi, Russia: Patrick Marleau and Marc-Edouard Vlasic, Canada (gold); Antti Niemi, Finland (bronze); Joe Pavelski, USA (no medal)

2010 Vancouver, B.C.: Dan Boyle, Dany Heatley, Marleau and Thornton, Canada (gold); Pavelski, USA (silver); Douglas Murray, Sweden; Evgeni Nabokov, Russia; and Thomas Greiss, Germany (no medals)

2006 at Torino, Italy: Ville Nieminen, Finland (silver); Christian Ehrhoff and Marcel Goc, Germany; Thornton, Canada; Nabokov, Russia (no medals)

2002 at Salt Lake City: Owen Nolan, Canada (Gold); Gary Suter, USA (silver); Niklas Sundstrom and Marcus Ragnarsson, Sweden; Marco Sturm and Ehrhoff, Germany; Teemu Selanne, Finland (no medals)

83 A Minor yet Major Move

In 2015, the Sharks said so long to the "Worcester Shuttle."

Thanks to the creation of an all-California division of the American Hockey League, the team's top minor affiliate relocated from suburban Boston to San Jose. Now, players promoted or re-assigned no longer had to climb aboard a six-hour commercial flight and travel cross-country. They simply walked down the hallway and parked their equipment bag in a different locker room.

"The foundation of what we do is drafting and developing players," Sharks general manager Doug Wilson said. "To have access to your players, to be able to truly have your developmental staff be involved on a day-to-day basis is crucial.

"You can talk about the time zones, you can talk about the logistics moving players up and down, the disadvantage we've been at for so many years. Giving all of our players all the tools to succeed is magnified by having them out here," Wilson added.

The Sharks had never enjoyed the benefits and convenience of having their young players so close by. From Kansas City, Missouri (1991–96), to Lexington, Kentucky (1996-2001), to Cleveland, Ohio (2001-06), to Worcester, where it remained for a franchise-long nine years, San Jose management had far to travel to keep tabs on the development of prospects.

"We wondered if they believed we were watching, but everybody has an eye on them now," development coach Mike Ricci said. "It works both ways. We're watching everything they do, and they have a chance to watch our big club play."

Ricci and Co. constantly reinforced what style of play and expectations the Sharks had for their prospects when in Worcester. Players, however, had to wait until 10:30 PM in the East to tune into a Sharks home game, and then needed a satellite dish or the NHL package to watch it.

"There's no excuse now," Ricci said. "When the big club plays they'll be able to watch. Our job is to tell them to play the way the coaches want. They're able to watch guys who they know they want to be like more often."

The 2015–16 season was the first for the San Jose Barracuda, and four other affiliates that made the westward move. The new division placed teams in the California cities of Bakersfield (Edmonton Oilers), Ontario (Los Angeles Kings), San Diego (Anaheim Ducks), and Stockton (Calgary Flames). San Jose played at SAP Center and shared the parent team's practice facility a few miles away at the expanded Sharks' Ice.

"This doesn't happen 10–15 years ago," said NHL deputy commissioner Bill Daly. "It's really the effort of our franchises in California growing hockey in their communities. This becomes reality now because of those efforts."

"Relocating five teams is a complex process," AHL president David Andrews said. "The Western-based NHL clubs had been in dialogue with our league for almost three years. This launches a new era for the AHL and for professional hockey in California."

The AHL began in 1936 when the Canadian-American Hockey League merged with the International Hockey League to form the AHL, which has grown from eight to 30 teams. More than 88 percent of today's NHL players are graduates of the AHL, home to more than 100 honored members of the Hockey Hall of Fame.

Fans of the Barracuda paid less for AHL games, but had the unique opportunity on a number of weekend dates to attend both an afternoon minor-league game and a Sharks contest in the evening.

"It's one of those things our original owner, Mr. (George) Gund, would have been very proud of to see this day in addition to our present owner, Mr. (Hasso) Plattner," Wilson said. "It's a celebration of California hockey."

84 Buster Runs Belfour

When Owen Nolan decided to send a message, he did so loud and clear.

The San Jose captain's hit of Dallas goalie Ed Belfour put an exclamation point on Game 2 of the 1998 Sharks-Stars first-round playoff series, which was a nasty affair for the first three games.

The No. 8 seed Sharks in the West, under .500 during the season, lost Game 1 to the Presidents' Trophy-winning Stars, and were trailing 4–0 four minutes into the third period of the second game.

"You know what? Dallas was a much better team than us," said Bernie Nicholls, capping the second of his three years with the Sharks.

With the puck dumped into the right corner, Nolan began his pursuit. He moved around back-skating Dallas defenseman Craig Ludwig while gaining a full head of steam with Belfour right in his sights. A strong and aggressive puck-handler, Belfour left his crease to play the puck, something he'd done hundreds of times in his career without incident.

Just as Belfour rimmed the puck toward the point, Nolan made contact. Belfour was flattened, though he stayed on the ice only long enough to regain his balance and get back to his feet. Stunned and surprised, Belfour struggled to adjust his mask with both hands while the Reunion Arena crowd was coming apart at the seams.

As a whistle stopped play, Nolan wandered out front, fully aware retribution would follow. Ludwig threw his gloves off and tackled Nolan after defense partner Sergei Zubov played matador by barely touching the offending Shark in hopes help would arrive.

"Well...that's Owen," Nicholls said.

"He was on top of his game and I was just trying to think of a way to rattle him," Nolan recalled. "The opportunity presented itself. Still, going in there, I wasn't sure if I was going to do it. It just got to the point where I said to myself, 'I'm just going to ram this guy.'"

Nolan was quickly escorted to the sin bin on a night the Sharks compiled a playoff club-record 72 minutes in penalties. The Stars cashed in on four of a ridiculous (and franchise-record) 15 power plays for an eventual 5–2 victory.

"Eddie is such a competitor, he just rolled off and continued to play well," Nolan said.

Belfour, coincidentally, bolted San Jose the summer before to sign with the Stars, and quickly became arch enemy No. 1 during all subsequent visits to San Jose.

"I'm not sure what Owen's intent was, maybe it was to get Eddie out," Nicholls speculated. "He might still have been pissed at Eddie because he left us to go there.

"But that's playoff hockey. I don't think it really did anything for us. If anything, it kind of pissed them off and we expected that. Owen is probably our best player, he's going to do whatever he can to light it up for us and try to get us going."

The Stars were fuming. They'd lost Joe Nieuwendyk to a serious knee injury courtesy of a Bryan Marchment hit in Game 1, and Mike Modano—Dallas' $6 million man—sustained a "mild concussion" when he got dinged by a Marcus Ragnarsson stick in Game 2.

"Both teams are bordering on running over the top emotionally," Stars coach Ken Hitchcock said at the time. "The emotions are ripe to top out."

And that's what happened in Game 3. With Nolan avoiding a possible suspension off his team-high 24 penalty minutes, the Sharks were on the receiving end of 14 power plays during a 4–1 win in Game 3 that ended with Belfour kicking Ragnarsson to ignite a melee. Again, no suspensions followed.

As San Jose evened the series on rookie Andrei Zyuzin's overtime goal for a 1–0 win, things predictably calmed down as the series evolved into a best-of-three.

After combining for 55 power plays in the first three games, the Sharks and Stars compiled only 38 penalty minutes over the final two games, both won in one-goal, 3–2 fashion by the superior Stars.

"We did all we could, we needed obviously to get lucky because they were the better team," Nicholls said.

85 Cheechoo Train

Most players who reach the NHL have overcome long odds to achieve their ultimate goal. When you live on an island that requires two modes of transportation to reach depending on the time of year—train followed by either a plane, helicopter, or boat—your dreams of reaching the NHL are not realistic in the least.

Good thing no one told that to Jonathan Cheechoo.

The native of Moose Factory, Ontario, not only beat everything that stood in his path to play in the best league in the world, but Cheechoo left an indelible mark on the game. He authored a dream season in 2005–06 when he led the league with 56 goals to win the Maurice "Rocket" Richard Trophy.

Not bad for a kid who didn't skate on an indoor rink until the age of nine.

Cheechoo grew up on the five-square-mile island reservation located near the mouth of the Moose River at the southern end of James Bay. Moose Factory is approximately 500 miles north of Toronto. Moosonee is the nearest community located on the mainland across the Moose River, which is navigated by water taxi unless the river is in some degree of freezing, unfreezing, or frozen altogether. Then it takes a chartered helicopter to reach Moose Factory.

During a six-year career with the Sharks, which had a spectacular rise and dramatic fall, Cheechoo was the first and only member of the Moose Cree First Nation (formerly known as the Moose Factory Band of Indians) to sign and play in the NHL. Even before his rookie season of 2002–03, Cheechoo's minor-league jersey was presented to the Hockey Hall of Fame in recognition of from where he came.

Jonathan Cheechoo beat long odds coming from Moose Factory, Ontario, to not only reach the NHL but lead the league with 56 goals in a remarkable 2004–05 season when he was united with center Joe Thornton following the Sharks' blockbuster trade with Boston.

Ted Nolan, the former NHL coach, knows what kind of long odds Cheechoo battled. Nolan is an Ojibway Indian who was born and raised on the Garden River Reserve, located near Sault Ste. Marie, Ontario. Injuries ended Nolan's brief pro career as a player.

"There are a lot of problems in the native community with a high unemployment rate, lower self-esteem, obvious drug and alcohol problems," Nolan said. "I bet 98 percent of the (NHL) players never had the hurdles Jonathan's had to overcome."

Cheechoo, who moved away from home at age 14, enjoyed a productive junior career with the Belleville Bulls of the Ontario Hockey League. He wasn't a smooth skater and didn't possess a polished game, but Cheechoo had a nose for the net and that's what caught the eyes of Sharks scouts. San Jose made Cheechoo the 29th overall pick in the 1998 entry draft. Cheechoo spent two seasons in the minors before making his NHL debut with the Sharks in 2002–03, scoring a modest nine goals and 16 points during 66 games.

Cheechoo showed dramatic improvement in Year 2, scoring 28 goals and collecting 47 points while playing mostly on a third line and appearing in all but one of San Jose's 82 regular-season games.

With the NHL resumed in 2005–06 following an entire season lost to a labor dispute, Cheechoo got off to a slow start as did the team. His offensive production was seven goals and 15 points after 24 games as the favored Sharks slipped into last place in the Pacific Division. That all changed, however, with the arrival of Joe Thornton via trade from Boston on November 30, 2005.

Cheechoo was promoted alongside Thornton, regarded as one of the game's best passers, and the two clicked immediately.

"I remember one of our first shifts together in Buffalo," Cheechoo recalled of Thornton's first game in teal. "Joe sent me a perfect saucer pass from the corner over a couple of bodies, and it landed perfectly flat at my feet in front of the net and I scored. I thought to myself, *Wow! This must be how it feels to be in heaven.*"

Cheechoo scored 49 more goals in his third NHL season, connecting on an amazing 21.2 percent of his shots, and collected a franchise-high five hat tricks along the way. Thornton assisted on 38 of Cheechoo's goals. Cheechoo edged Jaromir Jagr of the Rangers by two goals to win the Rocket Richard Trophy and San Jose rallied to finish fifth in the West and grab a spot in the Stanley Cup playoffs.

"From Day 1, I just played real well with Cheech," said Thornton, who won the Hart Trophy as league MVP after scoring the scoring title with 125 points. "You don't plan for something like this. These two awards are definitely team-oriented, and we're just happy for each other."

Cheechoo shattered Owen Nolan's club-record 44 goals for one season in a late March game, taking a drop pass from Thornton, of course, and drilling a one-time shot for his 45th of the season. That was Cheechoo's customary way of scoring, get in position 10 to 15 feet from the goal, wait for Thornton to feed him and execute his quick release.

"It's neat to get that many goals, I never expected to," Cheechoo said. "I just wanted to contribute to the team's success and luckily I found the back of the net."

A marked man the following season, and armed with a five-year, $15 million contract extension, Cheechoo still managed 37 goals to lead the team, but fell short of expectations. Three more hat tricks meant eight over two seasons, the most produced by one NHLer since 1991. It became obvious in 2007–08 Cheechoo would not approach the 40-goal mark, let along 50 goals, again. He was third on the team with 23 goals in '07–08 and slipped to only 12 during 66 games in 2008-09, which would be his last full season with the Sharks.

Trace back to the lockout season, and the crackdown on hooking, clutching and grabbing to encourage more scoring, and Cheechoo's subpar skating abilities were more enhanced. He just wasn't able to get to the scoring areas where he'd one-time the Thornton feeds with such ease.

Cheechoo was packaged with Czech forward Milan Michalek and a second-round pick to Ottawa in exchange for goal-scoring forward Dany Heatley and a fifth-rounder a month before the start of the 2009–10 season. Cheechoo played only 61 more games in the NHL, all with Ottawa that season, and scored only five goals and 14 points.

Though Cheechoo was out of the league before his 30th birthday, it did nothing to diminish the great run he had in San Jose.

Not bad for a kid from Moose Factory.

Sharks Major Award-Winners

Hart Trophy: Joe Thornton (2005–06) led the NHL with 125 points on the strength of a league-high 96 assists in 81 games during a season in which he first played 23 games with Boston and the final 58 with San Jose.

Art Ross Trophy: Thornton's (2005–06) 125 points edged Jaromir Jagr (123) of the Rangers.

Maurice "Rocket" Richard Trophy: Jonathan Cheechoo (2005–06) benefitted from playing right wing alongside Thornton to score a career-high and league-leading 56 goals.

Calder Trophy: Evgeni Nabokov (2000–01) led rookie goaltenders in games (66), minutes (3,700), wins (32), shots against (1,582), and shutouts (6) while finishing third in goals-against average (2.19) and save percentage (915).

Masterton Trophy: Tony Granato (1996–97) rebounded from brain surgery the previous season while a member of the L.A. Kings to score 25 goals and 40 points, including two hat tricks and an All-Star Game selection, during the first of five seasons with the Sharks.

86 Playoff Reputation

The Sharks reached the Stanley Cup playoffs in 18 of their first 24 seasons. And it was hard to tell, at times, whether that was a blessing or a curse.

No NHL team heard and read more criticism for failing to reach a Stanley Cup Final before 2016, let alone winning the coveted chalice. Often the trendy preseason pick by prognosticators, the Sharks were reminded they had choked again by postseason's end.

Fair or not fair? It's one of those glass half-full, half-empty questions.

"I view it as missed opportunity," said Jamie Baker, who played in two of San Jose's postseasons. "They've had some great teams here."

The Sharks' consistently strong regular-season success set the team up over and over for postseason disappointment. San Jose finished first, second or third 14 times to string together 15 playoff appearances during a 16-year stretch from 1998–2014. And the Sharks won six Pacific Division titles during a nine-season stretch from 2001–02 through 2010–11.

The Sharks broke the century mark in points in eight of 10 full seasons from 2003–04 through 2013–14, and earned 99 and 96 points in the other two. San Jose finished first or second in their division eight straight years, and were Pacific champs four straight from 2007–11.

With numbers like those, it's not hard to imagine why the fan base was let down when things didn't go as well in the playoffs.

"The reality also is, I think by far of all major pro sports, it is the hardest championship to win," said Randy Hahn, the team's longtime television voice.

Thirteen different teams won the Stanley Cup between the time the Sharks entered the league in 1991–92 and 2015–16. Six teams won multiple Cups including four for Detroit, three each for Chicago, New Jersey, and Pittsburgh, and a pair for Colorado.

Particularly galling for Sharks fans is the fact their two Southern California rivals have combined to win three Cups. Anaheim, which entered the league after San Jose, won its Cup in 2007 and Los Angeles captured a pair—2012 and '14—with ex-Sharks general manager Dean Lombardi in charge and former Sharks coach Darryl Sutter behind the bench.

Coincidentally, the Kings' '14 Cup run was kick-started by rallying from a 3–0 deficit in games against San Jose to win in the first round. It marked only the fourth time in NHL history a team that won the first three games of a playoff series failed to advance.

"That's on the players," Hahn said. "Did they choke? What's choke? They just couldn't win one more game as hard as they tried. If you don't think those guys didn't empty their tanks those four games you're fooling yourself."

There was hardly a difference between the two teams during the regular season. The Sharks finished second in the division with 111 points and the Kings were in third one point back at 110. And it was a rematch from the previous spring when Los Angeles edged the Sharks in seven games in the second round.

If 2014 wasn't the team's biggest postseason disappointment, then 2009 was. San Jose earned its only Presidents' Trophy with 117 points only to fall in the first round in six games to eighth-place Anaheim, which finished with 26 less points.

The Sharks have been a No. 1 playoff seed in the West twice, a No. 2 seed four times and a No. 3 seed once. Of those seven playoff seasons, the Sharks were eliminated by a higher seeded team only twice.

Conversely, San Jose registered three huge upsets—in 1994 against Detroit, in '95 vs. Calgary and in 2000 against St. Louis (all seven games). The Sharks were No. 8 seeds twice (vs. Wings and Blues) and No. 7 against the Flames.

And they advanced to their first Stanley Cup Final in 2016, losing in six games to Pittsburgh.

"Do they deserve criticism? Is there a constant theme or trend over all of these seasons?" Hahn asked. "In '93–94 they went to Game 7 of the second round and lost to Toronto. You can't say they came up short. And then they lost to the L.A. Kings in 2014. To say that the same problems are still here—it's different coaches, different players, different everything."

"If they'd ever win a Stanley Cup they'd parade it around downtown, they'd take it around San Francisco, they'd take it everywhere," Baker added. "I think if this team won a Stanley Cup, we'd have the same fan base but you could multiply it. We'd have a lot more fans."

87 Yes, Belfour Was a Shark

Which Sharks goalie is in the Hockey Hall of Fame?

Ed Belfour, of course.

Ed Belfour?

The curious tale of Belfour's short time in San Jose started on January 25, 1997, when the Sharks and Chicago Blackhawks—two struggling teams—hooked up on a four-player trade. San Jose sent Ulf Dahlen, Michal Sykora, and Chris Terreri to Chicago in exchange for Belfour, who after eight seasons and two Vezina Trophies had fallen out of favor in the Windy City.

"I was sad at first," Belfour said at the time of his departure. "I had a lot of history there. I gave my heart and soul and things didn't work out....It slowly felt like I was getting pushed out."

Meanwhile, Sharks general manager Dean Lombardi, who engineered the deal with Chicago G.M. Bob Pulford, was fearful the deal was going to fall apart.

"To move into the upper echelon, you have to get a top goalie," said Lombardi, also Pulford's son-in-law. "When Belfour became available, it made sense."

Due to be an unrestricted free agent, Belfour's stated intentions were to make San Jose his long-term home. "I plan on doing that," he said. "I like Lombardi's attitude. He wants to win a Stanley Cup in San Jose. I want to help him do that."

Belfour was a welcome addition in San Jose, according to Bernie Nicholls.

"I was fortunate enough to play with him in Chicago, and I understood Eddie," Nicholls recalled. "Of all the goalies I played with he might have been as fierce a competitor as any of them. He may have been as loose in the head as any of them.

"Eddie was wound pretty tight. I saw Eddie fight one of our players, I've seen him take his goalie stick to a $5,000 projector in our dressing room. But when he put his pads on, he came to play. And Eddie was awesome."

Belfour made four straight starts upon his arrival. He didn't win until his third appearance. Then disaster struck during his home debut in start No. 4, just one game before Belfour was set for a visit from the Blackhawks. Belfour sustained a sprained medial collateral ligament that not only prevented him from facing his ex-mates but he was still out 10 nights later when San Jose played in Chicago.

It was untimely, too, because Belfour was bonding with his new teammates.

"I liked Ed a lot," recalled Kelly Hrudey, who shared the net with Belfour. "He and I got along extremely well, especially considering I'd heard that Ed didn't get along with a lot of his partners. I don't know if that was true.

"He clearly was a little bit quirky in his preparation, never bothersome. He just prepared different from other guys, and that was no biggie for me."

When the 31-year-old returned, Belfour managed to win only two of nine starts when the injury bug struck again before an April 1 game in Phoenix. And this was no April Fools' joke.

Belfour began season-ending therapy and rehabilitation to correct a slightly bulging lumbar disk, a back condition that had bothered him for two seasons.

"He's been playing hurt," Sharks assistant G.M. Wayne Thomas said of Belfour at the time. "But Chicago and San Jose have been trying to treat the symptoms. Eddie feels it's time to start treating the source."

Despite his age and questionable health, the Sharks were determined to extend Belfour. They offered a three-year, $10.5 million deal, but Belfour bolted San Jose on the second day of free agency for Dallas where he'd play in the tax-free state of

Texas for three years and $10 million. It turns out money wasn't the difference.

"My main goal is to win the Stanley Cup and be part of a team that is headed in that direction," Belfour told Dallas media after signing. "That's why I chose to make myself available to Dallas."

Without Belfour, the Sharks finished last in the Pacific Division for a second straight season, while an improving Dallas team won a Stanley Cup in two short years.

"I didn't know Eddie that well until we played together later in Toronto," Owen Nolan said. "He was a great competitor, and I learned why he was so coveted by the Stars."

"As a player you want to go where you're going to have the best opportunity to win," Nicholls added. "He leaves the Sharks and wins a Cup."

88 Colorful Coaches

Peter DeBoer became the eighth head coach of the Sharks before the start of the 2015–16 season. He holds two law degrees, was a Buffalo Sabres fan growing up in southern Ontario and visited California only once in his life on a non-related hockey venture before landing the job in San Jose.

When it comes to diverse backgrounds, DeBoer continues the trend of different personalities behind the San Jose bench.

George Kingston was the team's first head coach. With 16 years of collegiate head coaching experience and three years as an assistant with Calgary and Minnesota, the native of Biggar, Saskatchewan, stepped behind San Jose's bench at age 52 fresh off of two years as the Norwegian national team coach.

Classy, patient and educated best described the tall professorial, mustachioed figure who did his best with essentially a revolving door of players on the expansion team that called the archaic Cow Palace its home. The Sharks followed a 17–58–5 inaugural season with an abysmal 11–71–2 mark in Year 2. Kingston was fired as the team prepared to move into their new arena.

Kevin Constantine was 34 years old when he took the reins, having made his mark coaching the Kansas City Blades to the International Hockey League title in 1992 and guiding the 1991 U.S. National Junior team to its then best-ever record at the World Junior Championships.

Constantine was a sometimes brash, sometimes cocky first-year coach, who possessed a sarcastic wit and sported red spiked hair that gave him a distinctive look behind the bench. His team, playing in the newly opened San Jose Arena, got off to an 0–8–1 start in 1993–94, but rallied to a 33–35–16 record. The Sharks set an NHL mark with a 58-point improvement in the process to not only reach the Stanley Cup playoffs, but upset top-seed Detroit before losing to Toronto in a seven-game second-round series.

The Sharks had a losing record again in lockout-shortened 1994–95 under Constantine, but also squeaked into the playoffs where they upset Calgary in double overtime of Game 7 before getting swept by Detroit in Round 2. When San Jose limped out of the gate 3–18–4 the following year, Constantine was fired on December 2, 1995.

San Jose dipped into the minors again, promoting Kansas City Blades coach Jim Wiley as interim coach. Wiley was the first Sharks mentor with previous NHL playing experience (62 games between Pittsburgh and Vancouver). But he really never had a chance. The Sharks went 17–37–3 the rest of the way and missed the playoffs. Wiley wanted to continue in the role, but Dean Lombardi had other ideas.

The general manager went outside the organization for the first time and hired former NHL defenseman Al Sims, who was paired with Bobby Orr on Boston's blue line for two seasons. Sims was plucked from Anaheim's staff, having assisted original Mighty Ducks coach Ron Wilson for three seasons.

Things did not go well for Sims and the Sharks. San Jose went 27–47–8, finished far out of the playoffs for a second straight year and Sims was shown the door.

Lombardi got a second chance to get it right, and he sure did with the hiring of Darryl Sutter. Lombardi visited his next hire on the Sutter ranch in Viking, Alberta, and came away convinced Darryl Sutter was the perfect fit to give the Sharks a foundation, direction and an identity that would translate into a return to the postseason.

Sutter changed the culture immediately. He demanded his team adhere to a defensive system, they cut down on goals-against, improved on the penalty kill and thrived on a strong work ethic. Sutter's Sharks reached the playoffs during all of his five full seasons behind the bench. The team reflected the coach's gritty character even if it didn't have enough skill to climb all the way to the top of the mountain.

The first coach to log a winning record in San Jose (192–167–75), Sutter was a personable, thoughtful, family-first man who had a bottomless vat of entertaining stories to share once he'd drop his sometimes gruff exterior. However, when San Jose got off to a disappointing 9–12–2–1 start to the 2002–03 season, Sutter's sixth year in San Jose was abruptly cut short with a firing after just 24 games.

Lombardi, who would be relieved of his duties months later, hired Ron Wilson, the ex-Mighty Ducks coach who himself was fired from Washington only months before coming to San Jose. Wilson had a sharp wit and could be both supportive and critical of his players depending on his motives and mood.

Wilson couldn't change the Sharks' fortunes in 2002–03— they finished out of the playoffs after going 19–25–7 under their new coach—but after teaming up with new G.M. Doug Wilson (no relation), Ron Wilson led San Jose back to the playoffs during each of his four remaining seasons with the organization.

An ex-NHL defenseman, who enjoyed success coaching on the international stage as well, Wilson embraced the latest technology into his preparation. He teamed with Silicon Valley programmers to develop software that would help analyze players long before the term "analytics" entered hockey's mainstream.

A practical jokster, Wilson's time was up in San Jose despite appearing in nine playoff rounds over four springs. The Sharks lost three straight times in the second round, and G.M. Wilson termed it "a time when the classroom needed a new teacher." The Sharks went 206–134–45 under Ron Wilson.

That's when the Sharks turned to Todd McLellan, a three-year assistant with Detroit under the respected Mike Babcock. Despite never being a head coach in the league, McLellan had never missed the playoffs as an assistant or head coach in junior or minor hockey.

The Sharks won the Presidents' Trophy with a club-record 53 wins and 117 points in 2008–09, McLellan's first season behind the bench. The team's regular-season success continued for five more campaigns as two more 50-plus wins seasons and a pair of 40-plus seasons followed. San Jose appeared in 11 playoff rounds from 2009–14 under McLellan, including consecutive visits to the West Finals (2010 and '11), but the team never achieved an elusive Stanley Cup Final.

McLellan received a vote of confidence after the 2013–14 Sharks squandered a 3–0 first-round series lead to the eventual Cup champion Los Angeles Kings. However, San Jose failed to reach the postseason in 2014–15, snapping the franchise-long streak of 10 straight playoff appearances, and McLellan's personal mark of 20 straight visits to the playoffs. With one year remaining on his contract, McLellan and the Sharks had a mutual parting. With a 311–163–66 record over seven seasons, McLellan ranked as San Jose's all-time winningest coach.

Sharks Coaches

George Kingston (1991–93) 28–129–7

Kevin Constantine (1993–95) 55–78–24

Jim Wiley (1995–96) 17–37–3

Al Sims (1996–97) 27–47–8

Darryl Sutter (1997–02) 193–167–75

Ron Wilson (2002–08) 206–134–45

Todd McLellan (2008–15) 311–163–66

Peter DeBoer (2015–present) 46–30–6 (through 2016)

*Cap Raeder served as an interim head coach for the December 3, 2003, game at Phoenix—a 3-2 overtime win—between Sutter's firing and Wilson's hiring

89 Joe Pavelski

Joseph James Pavelski has had his share of nicknames.

To create a distinction from Joe Thornton, Pavelski was tagged "Little Joe" by Sharks television voice Randy Hahn after the rookie burst on the scene with seven goals and 10 points in his first 12 games. Pavelski was one of 11 Sharks through 2015 to score a goal in his debut, which came November 22 against Los Angeles.

Pavelski quickly found himself as a trusted and versatile player by only his second year in 2007–08. He took key faceoffs, played the final minute of tied or one-goal games and logged minutes on special teams. Coach Ron Wilson referred to Pavelski as hockey's version of a swiss army knife.

Then, by the 2010 postseason when Pavelski was well established after four seasons in the league, he was the first player since

Mario Lemieux in 1992 to post three straight multi-goal games in the playoffs—all resulting in wins—and picked up the moniker "The Big Pavelski."

By any name, Pavelski in known as one of San Jose's go-to performers.

"He's probably one of the few guys in the world where you say, 'Hey, we need a goal.' Who do you put on the ice? Joe fits the top five of that category," Thornton said.

"He puts in the work, he puts in the effort," ex-teammate Jeremy Roenick said of Pavelski. "He's one of the most underappreciated players in the league, but I think he's starting to get a little more attention, rightfully so."

Not drafted until the seventh round, Joe Pavelski made himself not only into a consistent NHL regular, but one of the best clutch performers in addition to becoming the club's ninth full-time captain.

A native of Plover, Wisconsin, Pavelski was not selected until the seventh round in 2003. Higher picks in that draft—Milan Michalek, Steve Bernier, and Matt Carle—played in San Jose, but didn't stick as long or make as much of an impact as Pavelski. In addition, Josh Hennessy, Patrick Ehelechner and Jonathan Tremblay were also chosen by the Sharks before Pavelski, and they had no impact.

Pavelski graduated from Waterloo of the United States Hickey League to play for two seasons at the University of Wisconsin where he led the Badgers to the 2006 Division I title. He added that trophy to those won at the Wisconsin State Hockey Championship in '02 and the Clark Cup with Waterloo in '04.

Just 16 games spent at Worcester, where he scored eight goals and 26 points in 16 games at the outset of 2006–07 campaign, suggested Pavelski was ready for the NHL at age 22.

"I don't think about being that seventh-round pick very often," Pavelski said. "You're young, and even too dumb to realize where you are. You're playing because you love it. The way development happened from USHL to college to the American League to here in San Jose, it goes fast."

Roenick's final two seasons of a glorious 20-year career coincided in San Jose with the second and third season for a young Pavelski. Roenick was a mentor to a number of the Sharks' young would-be stars, but he never saw the need to coax Pavelski along. He already saw a mature hockey player despite his relative time in the NHL.

"Joe was one of those guys you didn't really have to talk to," Roenick said. "It was bred in him. He instinctively knows how to win, how to play and how to compete. You don't have to sit there and tell Joe how important the game is, or where to go or where to be.

"He has uncanny abilities as an athlete to be one of the best students of the game, and to know the game as well," he added. "He makes decisions he doesn't even have to think about, it's just instinctive. That's why he's so good."

Pavelski always possessed the hockey smarts, but that didn't mean everything came easy. Standing at 5'11", Pavelski gave away height, especially down low where he likes to park in front of the net and work for the hard goals. He wasn't particularly big or fast on his feet. All of his skills were developed over time, with hours spent in a gym, with dedication and sweat in the offseason when it would otherwise have been easy to rest up.

"It's not like he's 6'5" and built," Thornton said. "He has to put in work in different areas—tipping pucks, things you don't even think of—the way his skates are when he shoots and faces the net. He has to work on things that gifted players who are tall or strong don't have to work on. But somehow he keeps improving."

A top third-line center who was effective on both ends of the ice early in his career, Pavelski changed his game when asked to slide alongside Thornton and become a goal scorer. Pavelski potted a career-high 41 goals in 2013–14, and followed that with 37 the following season and 38 more in 2015–16.

"As your career goes on, you play more games and you've got to keep trying to learn," said Pavelski, a U.S. Olympian in 2010 (silver) and '14. "You want to keep getting better."

And, by any name, he's done just that.

90 Doug Wilson: The Executive

Doug Wilson assumed the Sharks general manager seat on May 13, 2003, and went about the executive's role with much the same vigor and determination as during a 16-year NHL playing career.

Wilson also wasn't afraid to do things his way.

Doug Wilson was the team's first captain as he capped a 16-year NHL career with expansion San Jose. He returned in 1998 after working four years for the players' association, and has been back ever since—21 years and counting with the organization.

A first-year G.M. in 2003–04, and with his team struggling on the road after two periods, Wilson tried something different. He sat during the third period between the two newspaper beat writers who traveled. San Jose rallied, but ultimately lost.

From that point forward, the superstitious Wilson made it a habit to sit between the same two writers for each of the remaining road games all the way through Game 3 of the Western Conference finals against Calgary before discovering a press box was not a good place to display emotion in a hostile environment.

Nevertheless, Sharks scribes were never short a good quote.

"Doug does things his way and doesn't worry about what others say," said former hockey executive Wayne Thomas, who spent 22 years with the Sharks. "And it's hard to argue with his track record."

The team reached the playoffs during each of Wilson's first 10 seasons as G.M., won a Presidents' Trophy in 2009, captured five Pacific division titles and advanced to the Western Conference Final three times. Throw out the lockout-shortened campaign and Wilson's teams averaged 107 points in the standings from 2003–14 along with winning at least 50 games four times.

"As great a job Dean did, for whatever reason I think the franchise needed kind of an image change," Thomas said of Wilson, who replaced Lombardi. "And I think Doug was perfect for it."

Wilson will always be known for pulling the trigger on the franchise-altering three-for-Joe Thornton deal on November 30, 2005. Brad Stuart and Marco Sturm, former first-round picks of the Sharks, and Wayne Primeau were packaged to Boston in the early-season blockbuster.

"He had the nerve to use the assets that Dean built to make the Thornton trade," Thomas said. "It was a pretty gutsy move. Doug was a fresh face at the G.M. level, a different voice. He was able to do that and not destroy the franchise. He really turned things around."

"He doesn't make rash decisions," Hall of Fame defenseman Larry Robinson added. "In the end it's his butt that goes on the line, too."

Wilson retired following his second season with the Sharks in 1992–93 after spending the first 14 years of his career racking up enough points to rank as Chicago's all-time leading scorer from the blue line. Wilson spent several years in management with Coca-Cola. A past president of the NHL Players Association and a consultant for Team Canada's World Junior teams from 1994–97, Wilson returned to the Sharks for a six-year run as director of player development before ascending as G.M.

"He's one of the best G.M.s and hockey minds in the game," Jeremy Roenick said. "When you have a personality like his, and you have the knowledge, you team everything together and there's nothing he can't do."

Wilson saw first-hand how the dynasty Montreal Canadiens of the 1970s operated. His older brother, Murray, won four Stanley Cups during his seven years with the team. That's where Wilson began a now lifelong relationship with Robinson before embarking on his own playing career.

"We came through the right organizations," Robinson said. "Doug wasn't a 'me, myself, and I' kind of person. That's why he was a captain when he played. I certainly was a team-first guy. That's probably why we got along so well."

Wilson gleaned knowledge and good habits while playing junior hockey for legendary Ottawa 67's head coach Brian Kilrea. His first roommate in Chicago was Hall of Famer Stan Mikita, who Wilson calls "his second dad." Wilson was also a teammate with Bobby Orr.

"He's always tried to address certain areas where we had needs, and that's what you want as a player," Patrick Marleau said. "He's looked at our club and tried to make it better every day."

Exposure to so many greats in the game coupled with an easy-going exterior that belies his competitive underbelly, Wilson has learned to separate the emotion and pressure from the job to stay the course and keep the franchise as his No. 1 priority.

"It's not just as easy as everyone thinks," Robinson said. "He doesn't show a lot of his feelings, which can be a strong point. There are other G.M.s that try to get under your skin so maybe you make a rash decision. You have to be able to keep your cool, and he does."

91 Todd McLellan

The Sharks knew they were taking a calculated risk when they hired Todd McLellan as head coach on June 12, 2008. General manager Doug Wilson entrusted a talented roster that had qualified for the playoffs three straight seasons with a rookie NHL coach. McLellan had spent three years as Detroit coach Mike Babcock's right-hand man after building a resume of winning on all lower levels.

Still, there was no lifeline now.

"I wouldn't have been ready had I not spent some time in the NHL as an assistant coach," McLellan said reflecting back. "There probably wasn't a better place for me with the pressure on that team to win, Hall of Fame players who were on that run and the media scrutiny that comes with being an Original Six team. The failure, the success. Everything about it was perfect, even the amount of time spent there—the three years—was a perfect window."

McLellan followed two colorful, experienced, big-name NHL coaches—Darryl Sutter and Ron Wilson. It was Doug Wilson's first coaching hire. He inherited Ron Wilson (no relation) when he became G.M. in 2003. Doug Wilson interviewed 21 candidates before deciding on McLellan, a native of Melville, Saskatchewan, whose experience as a player included all of five games with the New York Islanders in 1987-88.

As it turned out, McLellan did everything asked, and then some, short of appearing in a Stanley Cup Final.

In terms of numbers and accomplishments, the Sharks posted five 40-plus win seasons, had four 100-point campaigns, captured a Presidents' Trophy in 2009, raised three Pacific Division banners and made back-to-back visits in the Western Conference Final (2010 and '11) under McLellan's leadership.

Dig deeper and you find a tireless planner who studied trends in the game, set his ego aside and adjusted to what worked. McLellan built the reputation as being able to take young players, fold them into the lineup and show patience as they made mistakes but continued to grow into NHL regulars. He remained even-keeled during good times and bad, accommodated all media demands and gladly volunteered his spare time away from the game to engage with a community that became a home for his wife and two sons.

In the end, no doubt McLellan was a great hire.

"I've told Todd I would have loved to play for him," said Mike Ricci, the team's development coach and former NHLer. "I think that's a compliment you want to give a coach."

McLellan made an immediate impact during his first season with the Sharks, who went 53–18–11 in 2008–09 to win the Pacific Division under the direction of their 41-year-old rookie coach. McLellan brought an aggressive, shoot-from-all angles philosophy to a good skating team that earned an instant identity and flourished under his beliefs.

"You come in on Day 1 with strong beliefs and try to instill them in the organization," McLellan said. "But you're still a first-year coach, a first-day coach."

McLellan was a finalist for the Jack Adams Award as top NHL coach. He became the first rookie coach since 1990, and the sixth overall, to lead his team to the Presidents' Trophy.

"He has bullet points in his mind, stresses those and just eliminates gray areas," Ricci said. "It's good for players. There's a right way and a wrong way. They know exactly what needs to be done. It's something small, but it was the first thing I noticed when he got here."

"The real measure of a coach is if he can maximize the abilities of all the players around him, and he has a gift for that," said Jay Woodcroft, an assistant under McLellan during his tenure in San Jose. "Probably at the forefront of his skill set is his ability to communicate and let people know in an upfront, personal kind of way what he expects. Once he does that, he makes sure to hold people accountable to those expectations."

Top seeds in the 2009 Stanley Cup playoffs, the Sharks suffered a six-game loss to Anaheim in the opening round. Regular-season success and early-round playoff exits followed except when San Jose advanced as far as Round 3 before getting swept by Chicago in 2010, and losing in five to Vancouver in 2011.

Finally, having reached the playoffs as head coach or assistant during all 20 years of McLellan working behind a team's bench, the streak ended in 2015 when the Sharks dropped to 12ᵗʰ in the West. McLellan's seven-year run with the team ended as well.

It was mutually agreed that he and San Jose would part ways. McLellan led Team Canada to the 2015 World Championship title and was hired by the Edmonton Oilers to coaching within a month after leaving the Sharks.

"I expected to be in the playoffs, it's as simple as that," McLellan said of his final year with the Sharks. "I thought we had a group that could get there. Obviously we didn't perform well enough in certain segments during the season and that effected the standings so we're forced to watch the playoffs.

"And for me, that's the biggest disappointment."

92 J.R. to the Rescue

Jeremy Roenick knew he'd crossed the line when, in a fit of anger, he flung a coveted Martin Brodeur hockey stick given to Ron Wilson across the coach's office. The incident capped a tense, expletive-filled exchange between player and coach during the second intermission of Game 5 between Calgary and San Jose in 2008.

Jeremy Roenick celebrated the final 18 goals of an illustrious if not controversial 20-year NHL career as a Shark, which included scoring his milestone 500th regular-season goal in a San Jose sweater.

Without a point in the first five games of the series, and fresh off the emotional run-in with his coach, J.R. found himself a healthy scratch for Game 6, won by Calgary to knot the series at three victories apiece.

"I totally got it, and totally expected it. We've chuckled about it many times since," Roenick said of Wilson's decision. "Ronnie did what he had to do, which I didn't like. I had a little spur up my, um, back. I wanted to show him I could come back, and I was going to make amends."

That set a stage for when Roenick was at his best—Game 7.

"He and Ronnie had a big feud," Joe Thornton recalled. "And J.R. was pissed he got scratched. I knew he was going to have a big game for us. We were all very, very confident going into that game."

Going into the first-round series' decider Roenick had no points in the series, was a minus-2 and had put only three shots on goal in the first five games while logging 10–12 minutes of ice time. There was no sign the 38-year-old might emerge a hero.

That is until Ron Wilson delved in the history books and called Roenick out in front of the team during the morning skate of Game 7.

"Ronnie brought everybody to center ice and explained these were the kind of games that make reputations," Roenick started. "And he said, 'But don't worry about that because J.R. has four goals in Game Sevens, and he's going to carry us. Right J.R.?'"

Wilson must have known something, or he knew which button to push.

"He put the pressure on me really big," Roenick said. "And I liked that he kind of called me out for some of the good things I've done."

Trailing early in the second period after ex-Sharks captain Owen Nolan, then with Calgary, gave the Flames a 2–1 lead, Roenick scored at even-strength with a pinpoint shot through a screen. Exactly three minutes later, and rewarded with power play time on a unit that was only 4-for-27 in the series, Roenick picked the top corner on Calgary goalie Miikka Kiprusoff, another ex-Shark, for a 3–2 lead the hosts would never relinquish.

"The experience J.R. brought, even though he was a little older in his career, he knew how to handle different situations," Nolan said. "He stepped his game up and found a way to score."

With an assist on the game's first goal, Roenick struck again with the only helper on Devin Setoguchi's back-breaking goal tally that made it 5–2 San Jose late in the second period of a game the Sharks won 5–3 to advance to Round 2.

"What can you say? It was an amazing performance," Thornton added. "With he and Ronnie battling, and him sitting out, you knew he was going to show up and accept the challenge. What a night."

Roenick's final line: two goals, two assists, four points, a plus-2, all during only 12:13 of ice time spread over 16 shifts.

"It was just one of those games where I felt great, I felt motivated and I was really fortunate to have that opportunity to play and play well," Roenick said. "I felt I always was going to succeed with whatever I put my mind to. I felt when I was playing I could have an effect on every single game. Maybe not every shift, but every single game."

"You couldn't have scripted it any better, especially at 38 years old, having a big night like that in a Game 7," Thornton added.

Coincidentally, Mike Keenan was behind Calgary's bench that April 22nd night in San Jose. It was Keenan's 19th and penultimate season as a coach in the NHL. Keenan was also a first-year coach in Chicago when he had a say in keeping a skinny, 19-year-old Roenick with the talented Blackhawks of 1988–89. Demanding and no-nonsense, Keenan rode Roenick hard in those early years, seeing the potential in the future star yet not allowing J.R. to settle to anything less.

"He's the guy who really made me who I was," Roenick said of Keenan. "To have that game 18–20 years later against the guy who picked me was pretty special.

"All in all, it is one of my more special favorite moments in my life."

Roenick's 500th Goal

Chalk it up to a woman's intuition.

With an inkling her husband was on the brink of history, Tracy Roenick insisted the couple's daughter accompany her brother to watch Dad play hockey that night.

And Jeremy Roenick didn't disappoint.

Roenick scored his 500th career goal midway through the second period against his most recent former team—Phoenix—on a dump-in that was misplayed by Coyotes goalie Alex Auld into the net. Regardless, Roenick became only the third American-born player to achieve 500 goals in the NHL.

"The fact it happened against Phoenix was a very cool thing, and something I thought about when I looked at the schedule, knowing something could happen against my old team," Roenick said. "I had that in my mind."

Following the Sharks' 4–1 win on that Saturday night of November 10 in 2007, Roenick put his son, Brett, on his shoulders and skated around the ice to the delight of a delirious sellout crowd. The historic goal, his fifth of the season, came 17 games into Roenick's first of two seasons with San Jose. And, had it not been for a longstanding relationship with Sharks general manager Doug Wilson, Roenick may have never had the chance to reach 500 goals. "Three months earlier I was pretty much retiring, and thought I'd be sitting on 495," Roenick admitted. "It made it even more special that a good friend of mine, and a smart man—Doug Wilson—gave me that opportunity and I took advantage of it."

After the game, Roenick presented the 500th-goal puck to Wilson, who was also J.R.'s first roommate with the Chicago Blackhawks 19 years earlier.

93 Commentators Add Color

When it comes to putting the color in commentator, the Sharks have had it covered whether on television or radio.

With Randy Hahn and Dan Rusanowsky standing as virtual broadcast pillars throughout franchise history, the two have worked with a number of strong voices that have kept Sharks viewers both informed and entertained. Hahn has been the television voice full-time since 1993 and Rusanowsky has been on the radio since Day 1.

Hahn worked alongside six different color analysts, five of whom were former players in the NHL. The one who wasn't— Drew Remenda—formed the longest and closest bond with Hahn and San Jose's fans.

The team of Hahn and Remenda, which enjoyed a 13-year run over two stints, resulted in four Northern California Emmy Awards in addition to many laughs and inside jokes shared with loyal viewers. The two Canadian natives—Hahn from Edmonton, Alberta, and Remenda from Saskatoon, Saskatchewan—forged a friendship and mutual respect in the booth and away from the ice that was a key for their remarkable chemistry.

Remenda, however, was probably lucky to get that chance to work with Hahn. There was one road block in the front office he had to overcome to move from radio—where he worked for three years beside Rusanowsky—to in front of the cameras on television starting in 1999.

"When I got the job as the TV guy, Dean Lombardi—and you've got to love him for this—brought me into his office and told me he didn't want me to have this job," Remenda said of the team's general manager at the time. "He said, 'I just wanted you to know from me, I think you're too much of a loose cannon, you've said some things that really pissed me off, that's why I didn't want you to have this job.'

"And I looked at him and thought, *What am I supposed to say to that?*" Remenda recalled.

An assistant coach with the Sharks from 1991–95, Remenda combined his hockey expertise and the trust he earned from players and coaches to deliver passionate commentary on a nightly basis, even if he ruffled the feathers of management with heartfelt criticism from time to time.

Remenda's first run with Hahn ended in 2006 when he signed off from San Jose's playoff ouster with a tearful goodbye. His time away—a year spent as analyst for *Hockey Night in Canada*—was short. Remenda was back again for 2007–08 to begin a seven-year run that ended in 2014.

Affectionately nicknamed the Suit Doctor, Remenda not only took pride in his fashionable appearance, but helped when asked by young players who had yet been introduced to the world of custom suits and trendy neckties.

"I was a little more conscious about money, and he helped me with a wardrobe that was a little cheaper," said Ray Whitney, who debuted with the Sharks at age 19.

The three television commentators who preceded Remenda— Dennis Hull, Pete Stemkowski, and Steve Konroyd—brought a combined total of 44 years of NHL playing experience to the booth. Marty McSorley (17 years as a player) served as Hahn's sidekick between Remenda's gigs. And it was Jamie Baker who followed Remenda's second go-around. A veteran of 10 NHL seasons, Baker spent four years over two stints with the Sharks.

On the radio side, Rusanowsky enjoyed what Hull and Stemkowski brought to the early broadcasts as both analysts were versatile moving from television to the radio.

"There's something the same about all of them from that era," Rusanowsky said. "These guys are just great, salt of the earth people, who were passionate about the game. They weren't as worried if their tie was on straight. They were just basic, blue-collar hockey guys. I loved 'em all."

Chris Collins, Remenda, Baker, and Bret Hedican also served as commentators alongside Rusanowsky over the years. Only Collins and Remenda lacked NHL playing experience.

"All of these guys are unique characters, terrific people, great to work with, fun to be on the road with," Rusanowsky said. "But, most importantly, all are passionate about the game, and all are passionate about the team."

94 Fabulous on Figueroa

The Sharks are no strangers to Stanley Cup playoff drama, and some of it has even gone their way despite having earned the reputation as postseason underachievers—never mind two early-franchise spring miracles.

Who can forget Jamie Baker's game- and series-winning goal late in Game 7 at Detroit when Red Wings goalie Chris Osgood's clearing pass went awry and the upstart Sharks stunned the top seeds in the 1994 West quarterfinals?

How's about Ray Whitney's goal 1:54 into double-OT a year later at Calgary in Game 7? Or Owen Nolan's blast from center ice past Roman Turek seconds before the end of period 1 in Game 7 that felled Presidents' Trophy-winning St. Louis in 2000? And Joonas Donskoi's turnaround roof job against Pittsburgh in OT of Game 3 of the Stanley Cup Final in 2016?

Yes, no shortage of San Jose playoff heroes as the Sharks have enjoyed 21 sudden death winners in the playoffs, three of which have dramatically ended a series once the puck settled in the back of the net.

None of those moments occurred during Game 3 of the 2011 Western Conference quarterfinal series between the Sharks and Kings, a wild overtime battle contested on April 19 at Staples Center in downtown Los Angeles.

The game didn't start out like it would be a classic. Forty-four seconds into the second period it was 4–0 for the hosts on strikes from unlikely goal-scorers Willie Mitchell, Kyle Clifford, Michal Handzus, and Brad Richardson. Backup goalie Antero Niittymaki was summoned for early-exiting starter Antti Niemi.

"The second you hang your head and feel sorry for yourself then it turns into six, seven, eight to nothing," Sharks forward Devin Setoguchi said.

It seemed fairly insignificant at the time, but when Patrick Marleau tipped a Dan Boyle point shot past Kings goalie Jonathan Quick the Sharks were finally on the board 3:08 into the middle period.

"It would have been easy to fold the tent, but we hadn't scored last game and we just wanted to get that (first) goal," rugged Sharks forward Ryane Clowe said. "Once we got one, momentum is a strong thing."

Momentum is one thing. A five-goal second period is another.

Clowe scored at 6:53 on the power play and Logan Couture followed during even-strength at 13:32 to cut it to 4–3.

"All of a sudden the light turned on that we can do it, we can get pucks past this guy," Sharks forward Devin Setoguchi said. "We got it deep, worked hard, we beat guys off the wall. We got the second and third opportunities that led to the goals."

A Ryan Smyth tally at 13:47—the only puck to slip past Niittymaki—did nothing to stop San Jose's wave of offense in the period. And it was the last time on what had been a festive night for the hungry home crowd that their classic locomotive train horn would echo through the sold-out building.

"We had nothing to lose, so we started to play loose," Sharks coach Todd McLellan said. "It started to go in our favor and you could feel it on the bench. The more we did it, the more we believed it could happen."

Clowe scored his second at 18:35 into an open net off of a great feed from Boyle. Joe Pavelski gained inside position on Kings defenseman Drew Doughty, drove the net and beat Quick to bring the visitors all the way back at 19:29.

It was 5–5.

"You see games like this every once in a while, when pucks are going in and for some reason you're scoring a bunch of goals," said Pavelski, who won the series opener in overtime.

The game stayed that way into overtime after a scoreless third period.

The winner would come quick—just 3:09 into sudden death. It came on San Jose's second shot of overtime. The Kings didn't have any.

Marleau broke across the Los Angeles blue line with speed and Joe Thornton to his right, a 2-on-3 rush that the Kings had covered until Setoguchi appeared as an unmarked trailer skating free in the slot. Marleau made a lightning-quick, cross-ice feed on the tape of Setoguchi's stick, and the 24-year-old native of Taber, Alberta, let a low wrister go that hit the net.

Game over, 6–5 Sharks.

"It's crazy, but before the game I was looking at the TV," Setoguchi said. "It was about the Kings coming back from 5–0, so it was kind of ironic that we came back from 4–0."

Setoguchi referred to the Miracle on Manchester, the street off of which the Kings' original home—the Fabulous Forum—was located, and which housed L.A.'s wild 6–5 playoff win over the Edmonton Oilers in 1982.

We now had the Sharks' version of Fabulous on Figueroa.

"This is a game that you don't expect to happen," said McLellan, whose Sharks would win the series in six games. "We were very fortunate to come back from that deficit. We're excited about it, but we also know the mulligan we used won't be available to us again."

95 Captains Stripped

Despite growing up more than 2,000 miles apart in Canada, it seems Joe Thornton and Patrick Marleau have been linked throughout their hockey careers.

Born just 75 days apart in 1979—Thornton in the bustling city of London, Ontario, and Marleau in the rural hamlet of Aneroid, Saskatchewan—the pair of natural centers ascended to the top of the 1997 National Hockey League entry draft. Thornton went No. 1 to Boston, and Marleau was selected second overall by San Jose.

Fate would unite the top picks on the same NHL roster when Thornton was dealt to the Sharks in a blockbuster 3-for-1 trade on November 30, 2005. Marleau was already well established in the league, having made the leap straight from junior hockey as an 18-year-old seven seasons earlier, the same year Thornton debuted with the Bruins.

Both outstanding offensive players and fitness freaks in the off-season, it's no surprise two players with so much in common each would become team captains, too.

Marleau wore the *C* from 2004–09, and Thornton wore it from 2010–14—a combined nine seasons that all ended with the Sharks reaching the Stanley Cup playoffs.

Here's where the commonality gets weird.

Marleau and Thornton, two of the most respected players in the locker room, both had the captain's designation stripped. It's not that either did anything egregiously wrong. Both paid the ultimate price in terms of lost leadership following playoff ousters. And neither got dealt before the next season started.

Odd.

"It's a big honor and it's a big responsibility so it's a little strange when they take it away from you," Thornton said.

Rewind to the start of the 2003–04 campaign, the first under the direction of Doug Wilson as general manager, and the first full season for head coach Ron Wilson. The Sharks were in need of a new designated leadership in the locker room since previous captain Owen Nolan was dealt to Toronto at the trade deadline late in 2003.

The team came up with the non-traditional approach of rotating the captaincy based on player input after each 10-game segment. Mike Ricci wore the *C* for the first 10 games; Vincent Damphousse held on to it for the next 20 games; Alyn McCauley was next for 10 games; then it fell to Marleau, who at age 24 was the youngest of the foursome to assume the role.

When Marleau's 10-game segment ended, it was suggested McCauley take another turn. But the 26-year-old forward, who was acquired as part of the Nolan deal with the Maple Leafs, said thanks but no thanks. McCauley saw enough leadership from Marleau that told him he should be the permanent captain, and the room agreed.

Only in 2007–08—when he scored 19 goals—did Marleau manage less than 32 goals and 71 points during his four full seasons as team captain. However, he became a lightning rod for public criticism when the Sharks disappointed in the postseason.

Todd McLellan replaced the fired Ron Wilson before Marleau's final year as captain. Marleau opened the door for change by saying, "We've discussed some things and I am waiting to see how that unfolds. I've told Doug (Wilson) that I'm willing to do whatever it takes to get this team to the next level."

Veteran defenseman Rob Blake, in his second and final season with the Sharks, was told he'd be captain. That lasted only one season, however, as Blake retired at age 40 with 20 years of NHL experience, and the Sharks lost to Chicago one round short of reaching their first Stanley Cup Final.

The logical next choice was Thornton, who after 4½ seasons in San Jose had clearly established himself as the offensive leader, the loudest voice in the room and a fan favorite. Thornton's tenure lasted four seasons, all ending in playoff losses that fell short of expectations. The killer was in 2014 when the Sharks watched a 3–0 lead turn into an epic seven-game series loss to Los Angeles, which served as a springboard to the Kings' second Cup title in three seasons.

"We're starting with a clean slate," said the G.M. Wilson, who coincidentally served as San Jose's first captain from 1991–93. "Coming into training camp, everyone is starting with no equity—from rookies through all the veterans."

Sharks Captains

San Jose has made it interesting when doling out the *C*. The Sharks have gone with experienced veterans and first-time captains; they've rotated the captaincy, stripped it twice, and awarded it to an enforcer; and went without one entirely for the 2014–15 season:

Doug Wilson (1991–93)

Bob Errey (1993–95)

Jeff Odgers (1995–96)

Todd Gill (1996–98)

Owen Nolan (1998–03)

Vincent Damphousse (2003)*

Mike Ricci (2003)*

Alyn McCauley (2003)*

Patrick Marleau (2003–09)

Rob Blake (2009–10)

Joe Thornton (2010–14)

Joe Pavelski (2015–present)

* Rotating captaincy every 10 games until landing with Marleau

96 Sutter the Nemesis

If a hitter in baseball gets knocked down, his preferred recourse is to get a hit—preferably a home run. Take that, pitcher.

The best revenge in hockey isn't an eye-for-an-eye, but rather converting on the power play to make it hurt on the scoreboard.

So how does a coach earn payback when he's been fired, especially if from the outside it feels rushed or unjust?

If you're Darryl Sutter, you don't say a word. Instead, you go about your business, get another job, and proceed to be a thorn in the side of the organization that rejected you. And you do it over, and over, and over again.

Sutter guided the Sharks to the playoffs all five of his full seasons behind the San Jose bench, no easy task early on. But with the team just 9–12–2–1 after 24 games in 2002–03, the axe surprisingly fell on December 1. No one is sure what really happened behind closed doors to arrive at this decision. Sutter certainly deserved more time to rally his team considering the equity he'd built with recent past success.

It's hard to imagine Dean Lombardi wanted to pull the trigger considering Sutter saved the general manager's hide following the disastrous hiring of Al Sims one year prior to Sutter taking over. Many G.M.s wouldn't have gotten a second chance to get it right. Maybe a new ownership group that purchased the team from original owners Gordon and George Gund III felt the need to flex its muscle.

Either way, Sutter was unemployed for all of four weeks. The Calgary Flames coincidentally fired Greg Gilbert two days after Sutter was dismissed in San Jose, and offered their head coaching job to the nearby Viking, Alberta, native on December 28. The Sharks were six points ahead of the Flames in the standings the day Sutter took over in Calgary. Fast forward to season's end, and after Calgary went 19–18–8–1 under Sutter, and the Flames finished two points ahead of San Jose (75–73).

It started to get real interesting the following season when Sutter took on the dual role as Calgary's coach and G.M. The Sharks had a new G.M., too, as Doug Wilson took over for the fired Dean Lombardi. San Jose had a logjam in goal—Evgeni Nabokov,

Vesa Toskala, and Miikka Kiprusoff were all on the NHL roster. Without a way to circumvent waivers and at risk of losing one of the three for nothing, the Sharks needed a trade partner—and fast.

Enter Calgary, where Sutter's injured No. 1 netminder—Roman Turek—and underperforming backups created a need. Dealing Kiprusoff to Calgary represented Wilson's first trade of a player off the Sharks' roster to another team. San Jose received a 2005 second-round draft pick, used to select defenseman Marc-Edouard Vlasic.

As fate would have it, both the Flames and Sharks rebounded nicely in 2003–04 to secure Western Conference playoff spots—San Jose at No. 2 and Calgary at No. 6. While the Sharks dispatched St. Louis and Colorado in the first two rounds, the Flames upset Vancouver and Detroit to set up the unlikely Calgary-San Jose West Final.

Sutter extracted his first measure of revenge when his lower-seeded Flames—with Kiprusoff dueling good friend Nabokov in each game—advanced to the Stanley Cup Final with a six-game series win.

"You've got to tip your hat to Calgary," said Sharks coach Ron Wilson, who had replaced Sutter the previous season. "They work hard, they're well coached, and they wear you down."

"I said to Darryl, 'You deserved to win,'" Sharks forward Todd Harvey said at the time. "Good luck to them."

The Flames lost in Game 7 to Tampa Bay in the Final, but broke a seven-year playoff drought and beat three straight division champs along the way under Sutter. After the 2004–05 NHL season was canceled due to a labor strife, Sutter stepped down as coach in July of 2005 to concentrate solely as Calgary's G.M., a position he held until resigning in December of 2010.

Sutter's next move, after nearly a year off, was to reunite with Lombardi in Los Angeles and become coach of the Kings. Los Angeles was looking for a spark after Terry Murray was fired as coach at mid-season. Sutter guided San Jose's division rival to an eighth-place finish in the West, just one point behind the Sharks.

While San Jose was ousted by St. Louis in Round 1, Los Angeles roared through the West and beat New Jersey in the Final to win the club's first Stanley Cup.

The following year, in 2012–13, the Sharks finished two points behind the Kings in the standings, and met Sutter's team in the second round of the playoffs. In a series that featured only wins by the home team, Sutter's Kings ousted the Sharks in seven games as five were decided by a single goal.

And, as for good measure, the two teams met again to open the 2013–14 postseason. This time Sutter's Kings rallied to become only the fourth team in NHL history to advance with four straight wins after dropping the first three.

"They fixed their problems; we didn't," Sharks coach Todd McLellan said of the Kings. "Our problems got progressively worse."

If that wasn't enough, Sutter's Kings came to Levi's Stadium in Santa Clara to spoil San Jose's outdoor game event with a 2–1 regular-season victory on February 21, 2015. The loss knocked the Sharks out of a playoff spot for good as San Jose went on to have a 10-year streak of reaching the postseason snapped by season's end.

San Jose extracted a measure of revenge with a five-game first-round win in 2016, but Sutter remains a nemesis in the big picture.

97 Larry Robinson

Doug Wilson was early in his teenage years when he first met Larry Robinson. Murray Wilson, the older brother of the Sharks' general manager, was a young defenseman trying to earn a roster spot in Montreal in 1971.

Doug was close to his older brother, who let him tag along. That opportunity provided Doug with the unique and privileged access into a Canadiens team embarking on a dynasty.

Like Murray Wilson, Robinson, too was a 20-year-old rookie on coach Scotty Bowman's 1971–72 team, the first of four eventual Stanley Cup winners during the decade. From those early days of magical team success and family-like camaraderie, Doug Wilson and Robinson forged a relationship built on respect that has lasted for more than 40 years.

Fast forward to the summer of 2012 when Robinson, at age 61, was leaning toward retirement. Having worn several hats for seven seasons during a second stint coaching the New Jersey Devils, Robinson had just finished a grueling campaign that ended with a disappointing exit from the Stanley Cup Final in Los Angeles. The Kings were crowned champions with a decisive victory in Game 5.

Wilson knew it was time to strike once July 1 hit and Robinson was no longer bound contractually to the Devils. Relocation would put Robinson and his wife closer to their West Coast-based grandchildren, and Wilson knew, too, his longtime friend would be re-energized with the challenge of working with a blue line corps eager to soak up his teaching and guidance.

"When you get to know somebody, it's not what they say to you, it's not what they do for you. It's how they make you feel," Wilson said. "When you're around Larry, he's got that sense about the right thing to say, and the right thing to do. Just how he carries himself, he can say a lot in a few words."

So the title of associate coach would fit just fine, and that's as much as Robinson would accept.

"That was the first thing I said when I came into the room," Robinson recalled. "I don't want to be a head coach."

Robinson's name appears nine times on the Stanley Cup—six as a player, twice as an assistant coach, and once as the Devils' head man. That came in 2000 when he took over late in the regular season and guided New Jersey over Dallas in the Final, denying the Stars a second straight Cup in the process.

Robinson was content to reunite with Wilson in what he perceived a challenging role and do something for his family at the same time.

"I just found it very difficult for my wife," Robinson said of remaining with the Devils on the East Coast. "She spent a lot of days by herself. I didn't want that burden on her again. She missed the kids and being around her grandkids. That's what made this move that much easier for us."

The Hall of Fame defenseman, who reached the playoffs for all 20 of his NHL seasons (17 with Montreal and 3 with Los Angeles), was back behind a bench for two seasons in San Jose. Robinson worked primarily with defensemen and improving the team's penalty killing unit. But he also felt the rigors of the demanding travel.

Wilson recognized the need to keep Robinson fresh, and struck a compromise that would benefit the organization and take advantage of the two-time Norris Trophy winner's versatility. Coming off of an epic first-round playoff loss, Wilson convinced Robinson to agree on a three-year deal that made him the team's director of player development.

Robinson continued his work alongside head coach Todd McLellan at home and for a select number of road games while working with the organization's prospects at Worcester of the American Hockey League.

"When he's smiling on the bench and acting a little loose, that's what we need at times, it's Larry Robinson," McLellan said. "He's earned the right to be that way."

Currently, Robinson works closely with player development.

"It's a great working environment," Robinson said of his continued role with Wilson in San Jose. "And through development,

I'm not only working with the defense, I'm trying to help everybody get better."

98 Burns from D to F to D

Late on an early third-period power play, Chicago penalty-killing forward Brendon Saad found himself one-on-one with backskating Sharks defenseman Brent Burns. Saad drove Burns wide, noticed he had a clear lane to shoot and fired a tie-breaking goal past San Jose netminder Antti Niemi that would stand up for a 2–1 Blackhawks win.

It was the second time during the late February road game in chilly Chicago that Sharks general manager Doug Wilson noticed Burns failed to pivot and angle an attacking Blackhawk away from a scoring chance. One night later in Dallas, Burns left a game in the first period. He could no longer skate on one leg.

A seven-game stay on injured reserve gave Burns time to rehab and get back on the ice, but not on defense. With the team struggling for offense and the physical demands of his old position placing Burns at risk for further injury, the Sharks chose to reach into the talented skater's past for a reasonable compromise.

Brent Burns moved to forward.

"He's an animal out there," was forward Logan Couture's initial reaction after watching Burns skate up front. "He's reckless, but in a good way. He really doesn't have to think. He just goes in there and plays his game. He's a big body, strong, skates well and shoots well."

Burns made an instant impact, playing on right wing with Joe Thornton as his center. Burns scored one of the Sharks' two goals during a 4–2 loss at St. Louis in his debut game at forward. A goal and an assist followed against Los Angeles two nights later. Then two more assists the next game. An assist in the next. And on it went.

Burns finished the 48-game 2012–13 season with nine goals and 20 points in 24 games at forward after failing to register even one point during the first six games of the lockout-shortened campaign while skating on defense. Burns was an imposing challenge on the wing standing 6'5" out of skates and weighing 230 pounds. His size and speed forced opposing defenders to give him space when they weren't feeling the wrath of a hard Burns forecheck.

And that shot. Oh, that shot. Burns possessed a howitzer. He might not always know where it's going, but it's hard to stop when it hits the four-by-six. And goalies had a lot less time to react when he was shooting from close range as a forward as opposed to from the blue line on defense.

Playing forward was nothing new for Burns, who entered the 2003 NHL entry draft as a right wing after scoring 15 goals for the Brampton Battalion as a 17-year-old skater in the Ontario Hockey League. The Minnesota Wild selected Burns 20th overall, and by 2004–05—with the NHL season canceled due to labor strife—he played for top affiliate Houston of the American Hockey League where Aeros head coach Todd McLellan was asked to turn Burns into a defenseman. Yes, the same Todd McLellan who would get caught in a role reversal years later in San Jose.

Burns played forward again in 2013–14, and continued to click with Thornton as the pair had during the successfully experimental season before. This time Burns scored 22 goals, 26 assists, and 48 points in 69 games while flashing an impressive plus-26 plus-minus.

Change was in the air again, however. Deciding to retool after an epic playoff loss to the Kings, Burns moved back to defense for 2014–15. A new career-high in points (60) followed on the strength of 17 goals and 60 points in addition to a second All-Star Game appearance on the blue line, which now is Burns' permanent spot.

"I always will be hard on myself and that's fine," Burns said when analyzing the challenges of moving back and forth. "I want to be a top guy and that's a part of it. I'm going to be and I'm there now. Along with that you don't want to make mistakes. It's part of my personality and I'm not going to change it."

Burns prefers defense, but admitted the fun he had at forward. All that really matters is he is playing hockey, something he identified as a goal early on that otherwise drove his elementary school teachers nuts.

"I remember my teachers giving me grief. I'd say, 'Hey, I already know what I'm going to do. I don't really need algebra,'" Burns said. "I'm either going to play hockey or be in the military.'"

99 Gretzky Was Almost a Shark

How close was Wayne Gretzky to being a Shark? Depends who you ask.

"I remember there being very serious discussion about Wayne Gretzky becoming a member of the San Jose Sharks," recalled radio voice Dan Rusanowsky.

"Hmm," Tony Granato wondered. "I don't know if that was people just wishing."

And from Gretzky himself?

"Each and every time I met with the Sharks I became more and more impressed with their organization," the Great One said in the summer of 1996 shortly after signing instead with the New York Rangers. "I met their new coaching staff. And that's what made my decision so difficult."

Well then, there was validity to all of this.

Backing up, a 35-year-old Gretzky had an expiring contract in Los Angeles when dealt by the fading Kings to St. Louis three weeks before the '96 trade deadline. This move didn't create near the shock waves felt by the hockey world as eight years prior when Gretzky was first traded from Edmonton to L.A.

The Blues made a bold push by adding seven veterans in addition to Gretzky before the deadline. Welcomed with open arms, Gretzky scored eight goals and 21 points in St. Louis' final 18 regular-season games.

After beating Toronto in the first round, St. Louis rallied from an 0–2 deficit to take a 3–2 series lead on a Detroit team that finished the regular season with 131 points (50 more than the Blues). But when Steve Yzerman gathered a puck that deflected off of Gretzky's stick at center and scored on a long slap after 81 minutes of scoreless hockey, the Blues were eliminated in double overtime of Game 7.

As much as Blues executives wanted him signed for the long term, Gretzky did not want to play for Mike Keenan, St. Louis' general manager and head coach. So it was open bidding starting on July 1.

"I had serious conversations with them," Gretzky said of the Sharks. "I met numerous times with (G.M. Dean) Lombardi."

The Sharks were in transition, looking to rebound from a last-place finish in 1995–96 and upgrade the roster by adding character-type veterans to surround a group of NHL-ready draftees. And San Jose was thin down the middle of the ice. Aside from the potential price tag, Gretzky and the Sharks made sense on the ice and at the box office.

"I always remember talking to (PR director) Kenny Arnold about it," Rusanowsky said of what heightened attention Gretzky could provide. "They talked about hiring someone just to take care of Gretzky the way the Kings had. They'd have to because of the sheer amount of attention he got everywhere."

Gretzky was getting plenty of attention on the open market. Besides St. Louis' continued pursuits, Arizona, Vancouver, and the Rangers were also in the running.

"From the standpoint from where our game was going and growing, you probably started thinking, *OK, well he did it in L.A., let's keep expanding the game and go to Northern California,*" said Granato, one of five free-agent vets to sign with San Jose that summer. "I don't really know how much truth there really was to it."

Vancouver dropped out; Arizona ultimately wasn't a viable option; Keenan was not leaving St. Louis; and Gretzky finally made his choice by signing a two-year deal worth approximately $10 million to play with the Rangers and an ex-teammate from his Stanley Cup winning days in Edmonton.

"The direction of this organization seemed to be very positive, so I had to make a decision," Gretzky said of San Jose. "Do I want to get on that train, kind of rebuild an organization, or do I go to a team that is more established and get a chance to play with Mark Messier again? It made it more difficult."

With money now to spend, and in addition to Granato, Lombardi signed Bernie Nicholls, Kelly Hrudey, Todd Ewen, and Tim Hunter. He traded for Todd Gill, Al Iafrate, and Marty McSorley.

"It would have been fascinating to see Gretzky come here, but as it turned out that was just never meant to be," Rusanowsky said.

100 Presidents' Trophy Winners

The Sharks had a regular season in 2008–09 like none other in franchise history. Unfortunately for San Jose, what happened in the seven playoff games that followed overshadowed what had been their first Presidents' Trophy campaign.

A crushing first-round exit from the Stanley Cup playoffs against a fierce division rival tends to ruin a great regular season.

But back to those special 82 games.

The Sharks were coming off a second-round ouster to Dallas in 2008 after San Jose won the Pacific Division, were the West's No. 2 seed, and had knocked off Calgary in the opening round. The Sharks rallied after losing the first three games to force a Game 6 in Dallas in what would turn out to be San Jose's longest game in franchise history and the eighth longest in NHL annals. Dallas' Brenden Morrow scored to eliminate the Sharks with a power-play goal in the fourth overtime session as it took more than 69 minutes of sudden death to decide it.

Fallout was swift and decisive. Coach Ron Wilson was fired and the Sharks looked to Detroit assistant coach Todd McLellan to take over. McLellan had never been the head coach of an NHL team, but had reached the playoffs every year as a head coach or assistant in the minor or junior ranks. The roster underwent a makeover, too, primarily on defense where veterans Dan Boyle, Rob Blake, and Brad Lukowich were added to bolster the blue line.

The Sharks came out of the gate fast in October, winning their first four games, then finishing the month with three in a row as part of a seven-game winning streak. McLellan's system that called for utilizing team speed and directing as many shots on goal as possible was working. San Jose eclipsed the 40-shot mark five times during a 9–2 October.

The results were even better in November as the Sharks went 11–1–1. An 8–1–4 showing in December served notice that San Jose not only had every intention of running away in the Pacific, but leading the league in points was coming into focus.

Until the Sharks lost on New Year's Eve to Minnesota, they were 36–6–5. San Jose went 8–3 in January before managing a respectable, yet far less impressive, final three months—6–3–4 in February, 8–5–2 in March, and 3–3 in April.

All told, the Sharks went 53–18–11 for 117 points, five more than Central Division champ Detroit's 112 and 26 more than their next closest pursuer in the Pacific, Anaheim at 91. San Jose scored 257 goals and allowed only 204, the fewest among the West's eight playoff qualifiers. The Sharks were also dominant at home, going 32–5–4.

Besides setting new club highs for wins, points, and home wins, San Jose established team records for best power-play percentage overall (24.2 percent) and for the road (28.2 percent), most road power-play goals (46), most shots (2,720), most 40-plus shot games (19), and most 45-plus shot outings (nine).

Individually, alternate captain Joe Thornton led the team in scoring with 86 points on 25 goals and 61 assists. He was one of three skaters with a team-high plus-16 plus-minus. Captain Patrick Marleau led with 38 goals while Devin Setoguchi had a career year with 31 goals and 65 points. The Sharks boasted 10 double-figure goal-scorers as Joe Pavelski (25), Milan Michalek (23), Ryane Clowe (22), Boyle (16), Jonathan Cheechoo (12), Mike Grier, and Blake (10 each) all joined in.

Goalie Evgeni Nabokov went 41–12–8 with a 2.44 goals-against average and a .910 save percentage while Brian Boucher provided more than adequate backup (12–6–3/2.18/.917).

"Nobody can take it away from us, but that's not the trophy we're playing for," McLellan said after the regular-season finale. "They don't hand out rings and they don't have parades for winning the Presidents' Trophy. We're proud of it, and we'll move forward."

Moving forward meant facing a rival from the south—the Anaheim Ducks, who finished the regular season on a 10–2–1 run, were just two years removed from winning a Stanley Cup and representing an all-California playoff match-up in the NHL for the first time in 40 years.

The Sharks lost the first two games in San Jose 2–0 and 3–2. A 4–3 win in Game 3 at Anaheim was followed by a 4–0 setback in Game 4. Backs against the wall, the Sharks won Game 5 at home in overtime 3–2, but were eliminated two nights later in a 4–1 result, despite Thornton picking a fight with Ryan Getzlaf on the opening faceoff hoping to inspire his mates.

"To a man, they were better," Boyle said. "Their goalie was better than ours. Their defense was better, and their forwards were better. We had a great regular season and a disappointing playoff, and for that you have to give them credit."

In the end, the six-game series loss equaled San Jose's fastest exit from the postseason—hardly the way the Sharks envisioned this otherwise great season ending.

Sharks' Best Regular Seasons

Season	W–L–T	Pts.	Finish
2008–09	53–18–11	117	1st
2009–10	51–20–11	113	1st
2013–14	51–22–9	111	2nd
2007–08	49–23–10	108	1st
2006–07	51–26–5	107	2nd

Acknowledgments

I had the dream job for any 13-year-old baseball nut. I cleaned the family home of Joe Rudi. My childhood hero played left field for the Oakland A's, who were fresh off the first of three straight World Series titles in 1972.

Once a week I'd dust, scrub, and vacuum the Rudis' four-bedroom ranch-style home off Westridge Avenue in Danville, California.

I might have slipped his World Series ring over two of my fingers from time to time. I know that shiny replica World Series trophy given by team owner Charles O. Finley didn't have a smudge on it when I was done. And I sure as heck didn't need to ask for a last name while taking a message when "Reggie" called.

After the A's won the second of their three crowns, Joe's wife, Sharon, broke the bad news to me. The Rudis could now afford a professional cleaner.

I firmly believe the experience provided a springboard for my eventual career in journalism. I knew I loved sports. Working at the Rudi home for a year—rubbing shoulders with Sal Bando, Gene Tenace, and that Reggie guy—taught me my childhood heroes were mere mortals and people who I could talk to.

Now I wanted a career in professional sports even more.

Forward to 1991, my first exposure to newspaper beat coverage of a professional team. Early in the San Jose Sharks' inaugural season, a colleague lost a contact lens in the team's crowded locker room following practice. Before I knew it, two players were on their hands and knees looking for the lens. One of them found it.

Reflecting on the care and concern the hockey players displayed, us beat writers wondered how that scene might have played out in a Major League Baseball locker room. We guessed players would have been climbing over each other to playfully step on the missing lens with their spikes.

That's when I decided covering hockey on a daily basis was the way to go.

Twenty-five years later that feeling has not changed. This book gave me the opportunity to not only relive what I covered first-hand throughout the Sharks' first quarter century, but it also allowed me to hear untold stories and recollections from the incredibly cooperative and selfless ex-players, managers, and people associated with the franchise.

How cooperative? Brian Lawton took time out from his 50th birthday in Italy to respond. Igor Larionov emailed while vacationing in the Bahamas. And Jeff Odgers talked on his cell as he walked the pastures of his cattle ranch in Saskatchewan.

For that I will be forever grateful.

My list of thanks is long so get ready for an extended stick tap. Thanks to the 50 or so people you read quoted in the book for taking the time to be interviewed and to share their recollections. Thanks to former NHL great and Sharks general manager Doug Wilson for providing the Foreword.

Thanks Adam Motin, Bill Ames, and all the editors at Triumph Books for giving me this opportunity. Writing a book wasn't on my bucket list. Now, as strange as it sounds, I think I'd welcome writing another.

Thanks to Victor Chi for providing a bridge between myself and Triumph Books. Thanks to Dan Wood, former Sharks beat writer, current radio analyst for the Anaheim Ducks, and good friend, for filling in the blanks. Thanks for the cooperation received from the San Jose Sharks' public relations staff and the entire organization.

A special thanks to Scott Emmert, who was in the trenches for many years on the road as a member of the Sharks' media relations staff before well-deserved promotion as team vice president, media relations and broadcast.

And, finally, thanks to my wonderful family—pets included—for putting up with me locked in my office at all hours of the day and night while I interviewed, researched, and wrote this book.

Thank you all.

Sources

Newspapers

San Jose Mercury News
San Francisco Chronicle
San Francisco Examiner

Magazines

The Hockey News
Sports Illustrated

Websites

SFGate. com
mercurynews.com
Hockeyreference.com
NHL.com
Hockeydb.com
Hockeyfights.com
espn.go.com
tsn.ca
cbcsports.ca
YouTube.com
HHOF.com
Sports.Yahoo.com
mattlevine.us
wikipedia.org

dallasnews.com
ocregister.com
stltoday.com
latimes.com
theglobeandmail.com
calgarysun.com
calgaryherald.com
edmontonjournal.com
torontosun.com
hockeydraftcentral.com
theprovince.com
denverpost.com
freep.com
startribune.com

Publications

NHL Guide & Record Book
San Jose Sharks Media Guides
Roenick, Jeremy, and Kevin Allen. *J.R.: My Life as the Most Outspoken, Fearless, and Hard-Hitting Man in Hockey*. Triumph Books: Chicago, 2015.